A sudden eruption of smoke and a deafening staccato of explosions shattered the morning silence with abrupt tremors along the 85 mile front. Mortars thrumped, rockets whished, and 88-cannon barrels boomed. The German operation had begun.

"What the hell's going on?" an American soldier asked.

"Ah, nothing," a sergeant grumbled. "Those goddamn artillerymen are lobbing shells. Why do they have to exercise those cannons at six in the morning?"

Suddenly, two mortar explosions threw up a mixture of earth and snow a short distance away from the two soldiers.

"Holy Christ!" the sergeant hissed. "It's the Krauts! They're pounding the shit out of us!"

The two men scurried to foxholes, now joined by hundreds of other GIs who had also sought shelter. The men who had not secured cover stood in horror as the area suddenly brightened in flash fires. Others half-dressed rushed out of their sleeping quarters in stunned confusion. They winced and flinched with each explosion, not believing their eyes.

In less than ten minutes the army camp lay in shambles with half the men dead or wounded. Almost a full company of men had become casualties. No one thoug
matter of survival now

HITLER'S FINAL SEIGE

BY LAWRENCE CORTESI

(PREVIOUSLY PUBLISHED AS OPERATION BODENPLATTE)

ZEBRA BOOKS
KENSINGTON PUBLISHING CORP.

ZEBRA BOOKS

are published by

KENSINGTON PUBLISHING CORP.
21 East 40th Street
New York, N.Y. 10016

Photographs courtesy of the Imperial War Museum, London, England; the U.S. Air Force, Washington, D.C.

Printed in the United States of America

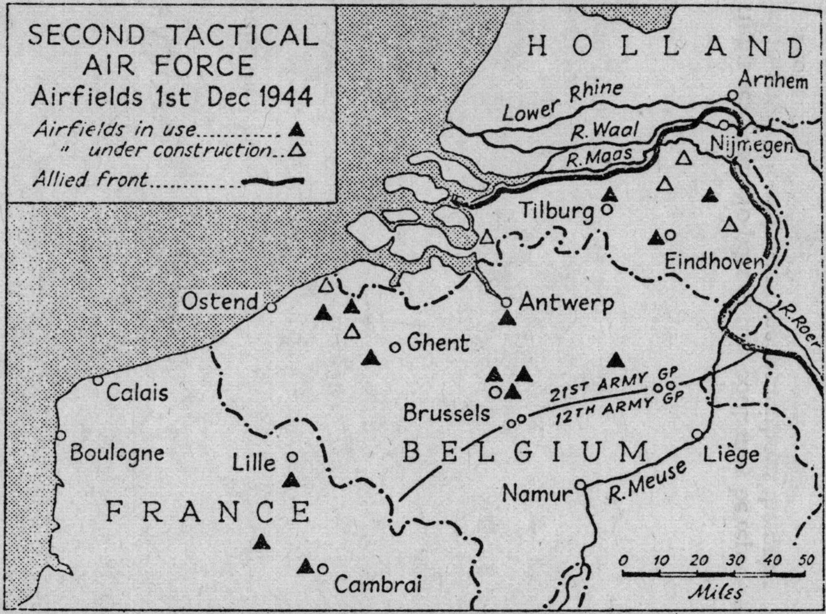
SECOND TACTICAL
AIR FORCE
Airfields 1st Dec 1944
Airfields in use
" under construction
Allied front
HOLLAND
Arnhem
Lower Rhine
R. Waal
R. Maas
Nijmegen
Tilburg
Eindhoven
Antwerp
R. Roer
Ostend
Ghent
Calais
21ST ARMY GP
12TH ARMY GP
Brussels
Boulogne
Lille
BELGIUM
Liège
Namur
R. Meuse
FRANCE
Cambrai
0 10 20 30 40 50
Miles

1. General Hoyt Vandenberg, commander of 9th Tactical Air Force, France

Chapter One

On November 3, 1944, General Alfred Jodl, head of the OKW (Oberkommando der Wehrmacht—German Armed Forces High Command) called a meeting of the army commanders in Field Marshal Gerd von Rundstedt's headquarters in Osnabruck. The battered town, von Rundstedt's German Armies of the West headquarters, lay some thirty miles east of Aachen, which had fallen to the American 7th Army in October.

Among the commanders besides von Rundstedt were Field Marshal Walter Model, commander of the German Army Group B, General Sepp Dietrich of the 6th SS Panzer Army, General Hasso van Manteuffel of the 5th Panzer Army, and General Ernst Brandenberg of the 7th German Army.

"Gentlemen," Jodl began before he opened the conference, "I must ask all of you to read this document carefully and sign it with your full name to promise total secrecy." General Jodl then warned the German commanders that if any of them should break the pledge of secrecy after reading the document, the offender could be put to death.

When the commanders read the document, they

gaped in astonishment. The Führer himself had ordered a grand offensive in the West, Operation Herbstnebel (Autumn Fog). Army Group B would make a lightning thrust through the Ardenne Forest, with German Panzer and infantry divisions rolling through Belgium, crossing the Muese River capturing Liege, and racing on to the seaport of Antwerp. A successful campaign, Hitler said, would force the Americans and British to seek armistice terms and allow Germany to concentrate her war efforts against Russia in the East.

"The Führer drew up the plan Watch on the Rhine," General Jodl said, "and I have convinced him to alter the plans to the one now called Operation Herbstnebel. He insists that we carry out this plan and that we begin in two weeks. The Führer believes we can begin by November 25. The moon will be new and the dark nights will provide cover for the movement of troops and armor."

Von Rundstedt shook his head. "This plan is madness," he told Jodl. "The Army of the West simply does not have the means for such an operation, much less launch this plan in two weeks."

But General Alfred Jodl insisted. He told the commander of the Armies of the West that Hitler would not agree to a postponement. "At the moment, a lull prevails on the Western front. The American 7th Army is spent after the Aachen campaign. Their 2nd, 4th, and 28th Divisions are badly depleted. Now, these divisions are spread in a thin line along the Ardenne front. They could not possibly muster the strength to stop a blitzkrieg out of the Ardenne forest. We believe that Field Marshal Model's Army Group B can successfully carry out this plan."

Model agreed with the OKW chief on the first point: the current lull did offer a good opportunity. But, he also supported von Rundstedt. Did they have the means to carry out such a plan? Would they have men and equipment? Jodl told Model that Army Group B would get whatever was necessary. But then, Model had another question.

"What about the Luftwaffe? We have barely seen them since the Allied invasion of Normandy. Without Luftwaffe support, how could we possibly carry out this proposed offensive?"

General Jodl grinned. "I can assure you, Field Marshal, you will see more Luftwaffe aircraft in the skies than you have seen since the offensive in the east began more than three years ago. Even now, the Führer is meeting with Reichmarshal Goring and the Luftwaffe commanders of Luftwaffe West.

True enough. On this same day in November of 1944, Adolph Hitler himself was meeting with four high ranking Luftwaffe officers at the Reich Chancellory in Berlin: Reichmarshal Herman Goring, OKL (Obercommando der Luftwaffe); General Dietrich Peltz, commander of Luftwaffe West; General Adolph Galland, commander of the 1st Fighter Corps; and General Josef "Beppo" Schmidt of Fliegerkorps IX. The German air officers had also signed the pledge of secrecy before Hitler outlined Operation Herbstnebel, the revised Watch on the Rhine plan.

All in the conference room faced Hitler, the supreme commander, a stooped figure with a pale and pulpy face. He hunched in a chair, his hands trembling, and his arms subject to a violent twitching which he did his best to hide. Hitler was obviously a sick man. His health had deteriorated rapidly over the past several months because of his burdensome responsibility. When he moved, he dragged one leg behind him.

As usual, Hitler held center stage and he rambled on in a self-righteous monologue. He harped on the necessity to succeed with Operation Herbstnebel and he urged the Luftwaffe commanders to do their utmost to lead and inspire the fliegers under them.

"I am determined to carry out this offensive, despite any risks," Hitler told the assembled Luftwaffe West brass. "The operation will demand the use of every soldier, tank, gun, and aircraft that we can muster. The Luftwaffe must provide ground support. The Reichmarshal," Hitler nodded toward Goring, "has assured me that he will have 3,000 aircraft available for this operation." Then Hitler grinned. "You may discount perhaps a third of the Reichmarshal's claims, but that should leave a thousand aircraft to support Field Marshal Model's Army Group B and another thousand to attack the enemy's communications, support units, and airfields. The Luftwaffe will conduct a *Gros Schlag* [Great Blow] such as it has not done since the war began."

General Adolph Galland was stunned when he heard the Führer's proposal. How could Hitler commit the entire Luftwaffe strength in a ground war? Galland had not been included in the original Hitler meetings to draw up the proposed Operation Herbstnebel offensive in Belgium, and he had shared no part in formulating the Luftwaffe phase of the operation. The lst Fighter Corps commander had been busy training new fighter pilots to mass up to four or five hundred planes at once against the hordes of Allied four engine bombers that had continually made strategic strikes over Germany's heartland.

Months ago, Galland had assembled his fighter unit commanders in his headquarters in Treuenbritzen to rehearse and carry out his plan for stopping the heavy strategic bombing raids over Germany. Now, the Führer would take away three months of hard effort.

"Mein Führer," Galland protested, "what you propose is out of the question. Four months ago we began training interceptor pilots to attack the hordes of heavy bombers and their escorting fighter planes. These pilots have little knowledge or experience in tactical operations. They could not possibly be used in the manner you propose."

Adolph Hitler threw a sneer at the commander of the 1st Fighter Corps. Galland has been a thorn in Hitler's side since the 1930s when Galland first led a staffel of planes in Spain during the Spanish Civil War. Over the years, Galland had consistently complained about the Führer's decisions to intervene in Luftwaffe operations, always hinting that Hitler should leave air tactics to air specialists.

Galland had entered the German Air Pilots Training School in 1934 at the age of twenty-two, and he had shown enough ability and leadership qualities to command one of the Condor Legion staffels two years later. He had then faced his first disagreement with Goring, when he refused to bomb helpless civilians in a Spanish town. During the Polish campaign, Galland had commanded JG 27, a fighter unit that had done a remarkable job in keeping away interceptors while Stuka dive bombers did their work unmolested.

By 1940, Galland commanded the famed Green Heart JG 54, the Abbeville Boys, on the Western front. By December of 1941 he had risen to the rank of colonel and became Inspector of Fighters at the air ministry in Berlin. However, by mid-1942 he was back as a geschwader commander on the Western front and by 1943 he had increased his kill score to nearly a hundred planes. He had then risen to general and placed in command of the 1st Fighter Corps.

When, in late 1943, Reichmarshal Herman Goring blamed the fighter pilots for the heavy Allied bombing raids over Germany, calling them cowards, Galland was enraged. He had ripped his Iron Cross from his neck and had thrown the cherished award in Goring's face. Hitler had been infuriated by the action, but he had not taken any action against the popular Galland.

Galland had incensed Hitler further when he berated the Führer for insisting that the new ME 262 jet plane should be used as a bomber instead of a fighter. Galland had maintained that Germany needed fighter planes to intercept Allied bombers now destroying Germany, and not bombers for an unrealistic plan to conduct another Battle of Britain. Such a plan would have been insane against the now overwhelming Allied air superiority.

Now, once more, Galland had brazenly disagreed with Hitler. He had protested the demand to use his newly trained airmen in tactical support strikes, since they had been trained as fighter interceptor pilots against four engine bombers. This latest protest had only added insult to injury so far as Hitler was concerned. The incorrigible Galland had again embarrassed the Führer in front of high ranking Luftwaffe staff officers. Still, Hitler remained calm, a rare response for a man with an irascible temper. The Führer merely glared at Galland.

"Herr Galland," Hitler said, "we will use our forces in whatever means we find necessary, and we will carry out Operation Herbstnebel." Then, Hitler turned to Goring. "The enemy sleeps for he is convinced that we cannot strike back. They have maintained a minimal defense along the Ardenne front. Therefore, if we strike hard and swiftly, the enemy will crumble. I stress one point to all of you," he gestured. "The Luftwaffe must do its utmost to support the Wehrmacht and panzer units if we are to succeed with Operation Herbstnebel."

"Be assured, Mein Führer, the Luftwaffe will not fail," Goring answered, clicking his heels and raising his hands in a stiff Nazi salute.

Adolph Hitler nodded, gave Galland a parting scowl, and left the room.

A solemn silence reigned for a full minute after the Führer left, with the three high ranking officers occasionally glancing at Goring. The Reichmarshal himself felt uneasy and uncertain. As leader of the Luftwaffe, he had rarely drawn up plans himself, preferring to indulge in pilfering paintings, sculptures, and other art works throughout Europe. Or, he spent his time riding about in his ornate railroad car, or indulging himself in parties and gourmet meals with friends.

Goring had no real ability to create Luftwaffe strategy. Yet, he constantly accepted any Hitler suggestion over the objections of experienced Luftwaffe commanders. This habit was one of the principal reasons for the failure of the German Air Force. Had Goring listened to General Schmidt in 1940 on the need for a heavy bomber in the Battle of Britain, perhaps Germany might have won that campaign. Had he listened to Air Marshal von Richthofen in the Battle of Stalingrad, perhaps Germany might have saved 300,000 men lost in that campaign. Had he listened to Galland on the need to make the ME 262 jet a fighter plane for defense, perhaps Allied heavy bombers might not have destroyed half of Germany's industry, communications, and oil refineries.

Goring always had a stock answer for protests from the Luftwaffe Commandos: "The Führer has decided, and we shall do it."

Logic dictated, of course, that the experienced Dietrich Peltz, with the aid of the equally experienced Galland and Schmidt, should draw up the Luftwaffe strategy for Operation Herbstnebel. Peltz had an excellent record for organization, Galland had a knack for training and inspiring pilots, and Schmidt had a unique instinct to learn of enemy operations.

Goring now looked at Peltz. "You will draw up the Luftwaffe strategy for this grand offensive and bring it to me within a week." Goring knew well enough that his three subordinates would comply for they were first and foremost German patriots. "You will consult with General Galland and General Schmidt and have the plan ready for me in detail."

Neither Peltz nor the others answered Herman Goring as they watched the Reichmarshal waddle out of the room. When he was gone, Peltz scowled. Goring was up to his old habits: throwing responsibility on subordinates and expecting them to come up with plans that satisfied the Führer. If the subordinates failed, Goring could blame them for incompetency. If the underlings succeeded, Goring would take the credit to enhance his standing with Adolph Hitler.

General Dietrich Peltz, like Galland, had also enjoyed a meteroric rise in the Luftwaffe, and he was now the youngest chief of staff general in the German Air Force. He had shown uncanny ability and leadership in the bomber arm of the Luftwaffe, and he had also joined the German Air Force when the Luftwaffe still operated secretly in defiance of the Versailles Treaty. Peltz had joined the German Air Force in 1934 when a youngster of 17. By age 20 he was commanding a staffel. By the outbreak of war in 1939 he was commanding the KG 60 divebomber unit in Poland. By the end of 1942, Peltz had become acting inspector for bombers, and in 1943, he had risen to general to command Luftwaffe West in France.

"Can we meet in two days?" General Peltz asked Beppo Schmidt and Adolph Galland. "By then you will have thoroughly familiarized yourselves with this grand offensive plan."

"Of course," Schmidt said.

The soft faced Josef "Beppo" Schmidt was a far cry from the stern faced soldier of the old Prussian school. Still, his soft countenance was deceiving, for Schmidt had been one of Hitler's staunchest supporters in the new order and he had thus won Hitler's favor. Schmidt had also begun his career as a pilot in the German Condor Legion during the Spanish Civil War, and he had risen steadily in rank. But, where Galland had always tried to conduct strictly military air sorties, Schmidt had never felt such compassion. He had agreed with the Hitler adage that displaced civilians were as important as displaced enemy soldiers.

In 1941, Josef Schmidt had won the position of chief intelligence officer at the Luftwaffe Reichstaff and had done a remarkable job. He had learned of the inferior capacity of Russian aircraft that would lessen resistance to the invasion of Russia. Luftwaffe generals had doubted his reports, but Beppo's assessments had been correct. The German Luftwaffe had met little or no opposition when the Germans invaded Russia in mid-1941.

By 1943, when the RAF began heavy night raids over Germany, Schmidt had devised the Zwahme Sau (Tame Bear) night fighter tactics to home in on English bombers through radio signals.

Thus, Reichmarshal Goring could not have selected a better trio of men to draw up the Luftwaffe plan for Operation Herbstnebel: the sedate Dietrich Peltz, the recalcitrant Adolph Galland, and the accommodating Josef Schmidt.

On November 10, 1944, while American troops still recuperated from the vicious battle at Aachen, the Allied commanders were already preparing for another offensive. General Dwight Eisenhower, Allied commander-in-chief, met at his SHEAF headquarters in Versailles with General Omar Bradley, 12th American Army Group commander, General Jacob Devens of the American 6th Army, General George Patton of the American 3rd Army, General Alex Patch of the 7th Army, General Courtney Hodges of the 1st Army, and General Hoyt Vandenberg of the 9th U.S. Tactical Air Force.

Among the British present were General Sir Bernard Montgomery of the British 21st Army, General Sir Francis de Guingard, the 21st Army deputy commander, the Air Marshal Sir Trafford Leigh-Mallory, commander of the RAF 2nd Tactical Air Force.

The Allies had successfully completed Operation Madison, the first thrust toward the German border in the north. General Montgomery's 21st Army had cleared the last pocket of resistance in eastern Holland; he now stood poised to cross the Mass River and drive deeper into Holland. In the center, the American 7th Army had successfully broken across the Alsation Plains and reached the German border between Wissembourg and Lauterbourg. The 7th Army had advanced across muddy, slippery terrain, and against heavy German opposition, but the Allied troops had forced the Germans to withdraw from the Strousberg defense positions west of the Rhine River. The 3rd Army had crossed the German border in several places and had seized the entire Saar area. Meanwhile, Simpson's 9th Army had sliced through portions of the Siegfried Line and was now knocking at the door of Dusseldorf.

In the south, General George Patton had made the most spectacular gains. His armored units had overrun the series of German forts southeast and east of Metz and the Americans had crossed the Moselle River. And, in spite of foul weather and slippery, soggy terrain, Patton's units had continued east, finally encircling and capturing Metz.

Now, General Eisenhower met with his army commanders and air force chiefs to propose Operation Varsity, a thrust across the Rhine River for an advance deep into Germany.

"We've now opened the port of Antwerp," Eisenhower told his commanders, "and we can bring in supplies with more speed than ever before. During recent operations, the enemy could not put up significant resistance or mount organized counterattacks, because their Luftwaffe could only offer negligible support. Meanwhile, our own units of the 9th and 2nd Tactical Air Forces have consistently struck the enemy's supply lines, communications, defenses, and ground forces with near immunity. I believe the opportunity is right to force a crossing of the Rhine."

General Hodges shook his head. "The Germans have stiffened with every advance toward the Rhine. Normally, we could break through anyway, but the fall weather has been absolutely terrible. Right now, the roads eastward are muddy tracks from the consistent bombings by our air units and the autumn rains. Vehicles and tanks too often get themselves mired in muck."

"With the full air power support and the unlikely possibility of German air interdiction, we should have few problems," Eisenhower said.

"We can't be sure of that, General," Hoyt Vandenberg suddenly spoke. "For the last few weeks, our tactical air units haven't seen as much as token opposition from the German Air Force. We know the Germans have increased aircraft production, so where the hell are these planes? I'd guess they're holding them back to strike out with all they've got if we try a new offensive."

"They don't have anything in the west," Eisenhower insisted. "That's why your flyers haven't seen any enemy aircraft. They're using whatever fighter planes they do have for interception against the heavy strategic bombers making raids over Germany from England."

"General, Sir," Vandenberg said, "I'd suggest you hold off until we're sure they can't catch our troops and armor in the mud."

"Hold off! That'd be foolish," Eisenhower said.

But Vandenberg did not flinch from Eisenhower's obvious anger. Vandy, a twenty-year veteran in the air force, had often disagreed with superiors. As a young colonel he had defénded Mitchell in urging the army to give the air force a bigger role. He had survived army disfavor, the Mitchell court martial, and possible persecution to himself.

Hoyt Vandenberg had been a fighter-bomber pilot when war broke out in 1941. He then became chief of staff for the new MTO Air Force. When General Carl Spaatz created the new 9th Tactical Air Force, he had appointed Vandenberg as commander and Vandy had immediately designated all fighter units as fighter-bomber units, that would conduct ground support missions as well as escort missions. Some of the fighter group commanders balked, but Vandenberg's orders held since the primary function would be to support a ground war.

General Hoyt Vandenberg was a quiet man, but he spoke up when necessary. The men under the 9th Air Force commander respected Vandy for his fairness to his pilots and as a defender of the air forces. American airmen had been particularly impressed when Vandenberg threatened to resign after someone had suggested that the 9th Air Force come under Air Marshal Trafford Leigh-Mallory and the 2nd RAF Tactical Air Force. The Americans were supplying most of the muscle in Europe. Why should they come under the RAF? So, the reverse occured. The 2nd Tactical Air Force came under the command of the 9th American Tactical Air Force, and under General Vandenberg, who directed all the air units in Western Europe. Thus, Leigh-Mallory did not exactly look with high favor on General Vandenberg.

When Eisenhower told Vandenberg that holding off on Operation Varsity would be foolish, the 9th Air Force commander looked his commander-in-chief squarely in the eye. "General, if the Germans use heavy air opposition against your proposed Operation Varsity while the ground forces are moving through November mud or December snow, there'll be hell to pay."

Eisenhower did not answer Vandenberg. He looked at Leigh-Mallory. "Do you agree, Trafford?"

Leigh-Mallory jumped at the opportunity to disagree with Vandenberg. "No," the 2nd Tactical commander said. "I believe the Luftwaffe *is* finished. RAF reconnaisance planes have seen no sign of Luftwaffe activity in the west. I don't believe the Germans can mount any air opposition if you decide to launch a new offensive."

Eisenhower nodded, satisfied. He saw no reason to postpone a drive to the Rhine, despite the current muddy terrain and impending winter. After all, the RAF and 8th Air Force in England possessed countless heavy bombers and fighter planes to bomb anywhere in Germany. In Europe, the Allies now had twenty-eight tactical air bases, stretching from Tillburg in Holland to Ciastres in France. The Allies possessed some 2,000 tactical bombers, fighters, and attack bombers between the 9th and 2nd Tactical Air Forces. They could easily handle any meager resources the German Air Force might throw against them.

The British and American air units in Europe had done very well in the recent Operation Madison, except when poor weather had grounded aircraft. The Allied air units had flown daily sorties throughout the operation, averaging more than 400 sorties per day. In one three-day period alone, along the Schnee Eifel sector in the Ardennes that separated Belgium from Germany, Allied tactical planes had destroyed 840 motor vehicles, 60 armored vehicles, 162 locomotives, 1,096 pieces of rolling stock, and 113 gun positions.

On a single day in late October, 12 American air groups had flown 537 sorties. In another instance, 9th Air Force tactical groups had destroyed every piece of rolling stock in the marshaling yards at Zweibruchen. In support of Patton's 3rd Army, 9th Air Force air groups had destroyed every German defense between Nerzig and Metz to enable Patton to seize the Saar region.

The 9th Tactical air units had also opened huge gaps in the forward defense of the Siegfried Line to allow the 5th, 90th, and 96th American Infantry Divisions to capture the rail junction towns of Fralsurten and Ensdorf.

During the entire phase of Operation Madison, the 9th Air Force had conducted over 5,200 sorties, with half of these from the 9th Bombardment Division, the arm that would support ground troops for the proposed Operation Varsity.

The 2nd Tactical Air Force, averaging more than 200 sorties a day, had also done well during Operation Madison. Besides supporting ground troops with strafing, 37mm cannon, and rocket fire, RAF pilots had knocked 157 German planes out of the air, including 116 Luftwaffe bombers.

Conversely, the Luftwaffe had mounted an average of only 25 to 30 sorties a day during the 26 day campaign. They had only knocked out 116 tanks, less than 500 motor vehicles, and less than a hundred aircraft. In not a single instance had the German Air Force stalled any Allied infantry unit or armor column for more than a few hours.

These statistics convinced General Dwight Eisenhower that his Allied Air Forces in Europe enjoyed a total superiority over the German Air Force. He thus dismissed Hoyt Vandenberg's objections to this new operation as merely an overcautious concern.

"After Operation Madison," Eisenhower told Vandenberg, "I cannot imagine the German Air Force mounting anything that your air units cannot handle."

"Perhaps you're right, General," Vandenberg conceded.

"Then we can expect maximum support from the 9th and 2nd Air Forces?" Eisenhower asked.

"Yes, sir," the 9th Air Force commander said.

General Eisenhower nodded and outlined his plan for Operation Varsity. Quite simply, the various Allied army groups would strike across the borders from Holland, Belgium, and Luxembourg to push swiftly into the Ruhr area, taking key cities along the way, and crossing the Rhine River at several points. The British Tactical Air Force would support infantry and armored units in the north, while the 9th Tactical Air Force would support advancing Allied ground units in the center and in the south.

Eisenhower wanted Operation Varsity to begin at once, but the SHAEF commander met some serious opposition. Both General Omar Bradley and General Bernard Montgomery said they would need at least several weeks to prepare for this new operation, perhaps even into January. Besides, Bradley said, tanks and vehicles could move much easier over the harder December or January terrain than they could over the soft, muddy terrain of November. General Montgomery agreed, one of the few times Montgomery had agreed with Bradley on anything.

By the time the conference ended, Eisenhower and his commanders agreed to launch Operation Varsity right after Christmas.

On December 12, Hitler met in his snug Eagle Nest near the town of Zeigenbed on the Hesse to complete plans for Herbstnebel with his Armies of the West commanders. Simply, the 6th German Panzer army would advance along a northern track out of the Ardennes toward Antwerp. In the center, the 5th Panzer Army would cross the Muese after its drive out of the Ardennes to provide flank coverage for the 6th Panzer. Thc 7th Army would roll westward from the south along the Moselle River, repelling any Allied forces that tried to interfere with the 5th and 6th Panzer Armies. The three armies would have a total strength of eleven panzer divisions and eighteen infantry divisions, more than 300,000 men.

Three separate air divisions of Luftwaffe West, numbering about 1,600 planes, would support the three ground armies of Army Group B for the offensive.

Thus, none of the Allied generals had guessed that the Germans would move first, striking with such force that Operation Varsity would give way to a desperate defensive effort to stem the unexpected German onslaught. And, if anyone wondered what happened to the Luftwaffe, the Allies would soon find out.

Chapter Two

Throughout late November and early December, when weather permitted, Allied air units flew out to conduct combat sorties. However, they found little or no vehicular traffic, no troop concentrations, and almost no air opposition. The almost total absence of the German air and ground units only heightened General Vandenberg's suspicions that the Germans were holding back their resources to strike back hard against any Allied attempt to make a crossing of the Rhine. General Eisenhower, however, viewed the lack of opposition as proof that the Germans simply lacked the means to oppose the Allies.

While the air war had come to a near standstill, the GIs on the ground in their Ardenne defenses remained bored. Below the Schnee Eifel (The Snow Mountain of the Ardennes), the American soldiers of the 9th, 28th, 106th, 99th, and 4th Divisions sat dormant within their extended lines, waiting for the next action after Operation Madison. Most of the American soldiers had merely pulled sentinel duty, sitting monotonously in trenches that faced east. They rarely saw German troops, armor, or aircraft. In fact, aside from regular patrols and an occasional skirmish, life on the line had settled to a humdrum routine.

Since the fall of Aachen, the entire north-south perimeter, from Monschau, Belgium, in the north to Echternach, Luxembourg, in the south, a snaking front of 85 miles, had become quiet and gloomy by this late autumn. Only a damp, cold, pre-winter mist floated out of the Ardenne forests before them, so eerie and silent that the GIs now called their long, thin perimeter the Ghost Front.

The GIs had observed nothing in the dense trees for weeks and they wondered why they sat here, while each day became damper, colder, and foggier. Soon, the snows would come and they would still be sitting here, perhaps until spring. If any German Wehrmacht or Panzer or Luftwaffe commanders had reservations about Operation Herbstnebel, these German commanders need not have worried about surprising the Allies. Except for a few men like Vandenberg, no British or American from Eisenhower on down, and British Tommy or American GI on the line, expected the Germans to do anything but sit out the winter along the Western Front beyond Holland, Belgium, and Luxembourg.

On the afternoon of December 15, the same monotonous quiet prevailed over the Western Front that had prevailed since the fall of Aachen at the end of October. At his Versailles headquarters, Omar Bradley had completed a briefing for Operation Varsity with his ground commanders and with the 9th Air Force commander, General Hoyt Vandenberg. The offensive would begin right after Christmas as planned and the ground commanders could expect full air support from the 9th and 2nd Tactical Air Forces.

However, General Dietrich Peltz was ready to strike with Luftwaffe West. Peltz had prepared his three air divisions for Operation Herbstnebel: Jagdivision 3, with six geschwaders of 109s and 190 fighter-bombers; Jagbabschnitt Mittelrheim under General Galland with five geschwaders of 109 and 190 fighter-bombers; and Jagdivision IX under General Josef Schmidt with two geschwaders of ME 110 twin engine bombers, a staffel of AR 235 jet bombers, and a geschwader of ME 262 jet fighter bombers.

Jagdivision 3 would support Sepp Dietrich's 6th Panzer Army in the north. Galland's Jagbabschnitt Mittelrheim would support Hasso von Manteuffel's 5th Panzer Army in the center, and Beppo Schmidt's Jagdivision IX would support General Brandenberg's flanking 7th Army in the south. Each air division would keep at least one geschwader in reserve to hit Allied communications, airfields, and supply dumps.

At 0500 hours, December 16, 1944, 300,000 Wehrmacht and Panzer troops fully armed and clad in white snowsuits, stood poised in the foggy morning darkness. Overhead, droning HE 111s whined loudly to deafen the growl of trucks, tanks, armored cars, and mobile guns. Every command officer read the same message from Field Marshal von Rundstedt to his troops:

> Soldiers of the Western Front! Your great hour has come! Large attacking armies will strike against the Anglo-Saxon, and I need not tell you more. We gamble everything, and you carry with you the holy obligation to give all to achieve our objectives for the Fatherland.

The field marshal, although quite vehemently opposed to Operation Herbstnebel, did not hesitate to carry out this plan with determination once the plan got underway. The message from the esteemed von Rundstedt brought an excitement to the Wehrmacht troops. Once more they would be on the attack.

For the next hour, a quiet prevailed on the eighty-five-mile Ghost Front that stretched from Monschau to Echternach. The thick fog still hung over the Ardennes as the first light of dawn outlined the peak of the Schnee Eifel against a dark sky. Then, a German artillery officer of the 1st SS Panzer Division, Hitler's own, squinted carefully at his watch, waiting for the second hand to reach twelve. German cannoneers with shells in their arms or loaders at the open breeches stood rigidly, while range finders zeroed in on targets to the west. Then, at 0600, the artillery officer dropped his arm in a quick motion.

"Fire!"

Operation Herbstnebel had begun.

A sudden eruption of smoke and a deafening staccato of explosions shattered the morning silence with abrupt tremors along the eighty-five-mile front. Mortars thrumped, rockets whished, and eighty-eight cannon barrels boomed. The snow covered fir trees quivered in the Ardennes Forest as though frightened by the maddening tremors. Loose snow flew like exploding specks of flour, and the snow-covered ground shook violently. German gunners winced from the deafening din of their own making.

As the barrage began, the heavy rumble of tanks and the squishing boots of infantrymen heralded the movement forward for the German Army

Group B. Then, the sounds were smothered by the booming 255mm railroad guns, "Screaming Meanies," that sent two-ton shells whistling into the American positions on the Ghost Front.

Near Krinklet at the north end of the front, GIs of the 99th Division had just awakened for the morning watch and they froze in surprise at the thundering sound of guns.

"What the hell's going on?"

"Ah, nothing," a sergeant grumbled. "Those goddam artillerymen are lobbing shells. The bastards! Why do they have to exercise those cannons at six in the morning?"

But suddenly, two mortar explosions threw up a mixture of earth and snow a short distance away from the two 99th Division soldiers. Then, a Screaming Meanie, a 255mm shell from a German railroad gun, landed a hundred yards away, exploding with a devastating impact that flattened four tents and bounced the sergeant and the private off their feet.

"Holy Christ!" the sergeant hissed. "It's the fuckin' Krauts! They're poundin' the shit out of us."

The two men scurried to foxholes, now joined by hundreds of other 99th GIs who had also sought shelter.

To the south, near the Losheim Gap, an American watch sergeant of the 14th Cavalry Regiment was making his last check of the guards on the graveyard shift when a thundering shell landed around his perimeter. He stared again for a moment and then ordered his men to seek shelter. Then, the sergeant rushed to a house in the village of Krewinkel to report the shelling to the night OD officer. The noncom had barely come inside the building when a Screaming Meanie exploded outside and threw both the sergeant and the officer to the floor. The blast had shattered windows and doors of the house and sent powdery plaster from the ceiling on the prone bodies of the two American soldiers.

"The Krauts have opened up, Lieutenant, opened up bad," the sergeant cried.

The lieutenant crawled to a dangling field telephone. "Get me command! Get me command!" he screamed into the mouthpiece.

South of the gap, along Skyline Drive, the road that skirted the Ghost Front, all had been quiet in the command post of the 28th American Division. The two night duty sergeants had been staring into the now brightening cobblestone streets of the small village of Rocht. The town was an important highway junction on Skyline Drive, since roads branched off here to Berne and into St. Vith. At 0605, a sudden staccato of explosions stiffened the two noncoms in the command post.

"What the hell was that?" one of them cried.

"The artillery boys getting in some early morning practice," the companion said. His words would be the last he ever spoke. The next whistling shell landed squarely on the command post, disintegrating the small hut and the two sergeants inside. Other shells also landed in Rocht, knocking apart buildings and chopping holes into the crooked, narrow streets. GIs and civilians alike darted madly about the village like ants caught under trampling feet.

South of the 28th Division, along the Saur River, the tanks and armor of the 9th American Armored Division sat quiet and deserted in neat rows on this early morning. Most of the tank men still slept, with only the clank of dishes and pans in the mess hall interrupting the silence. Cooks and KP personnel were preparing breakfast, working calmly and leisurely.

But, at 0608, the first screaming shells landed on the campsite. The men in the mess hall gaped and then stood in horror as clods of earth and chunks of packed snow descended on the tin roof of the mess hall like a rain of cascading rocks. Then, the area suddenly brightened in flash fires as shells struck tanks and vehicles that ignited when shells hit their gas tanks. The 28th Division men in the mess hall scurried outside to seek shelter. Other GIs, half asleep and half dressed, rushed out of sleeping quarters and staggered about the campsite in stunned confusion, as though experiencing a half-real, half-dream nightmare. They scurried like dazed drunkards as they sought shelter.

Near Clervaux, in the center of the Ghost Front, the 110th Regiment of the American 106th Division sat in positions that stretched for several miles. A quiet had prevailed in the area throughout the night. The men in their bunkers, machine gun nests, and mortar posts waited for relief at 0600. They shivered in the cold, but looked forward to a hot breakfast and warm quarters. One of the men cursed. His watch showed 0610 and relief had not yet arrived.

But suddenly, a line of shattering explosions from artillery shells struck the length of the 110th positions, tearing apart men and guns, leaving a mixture of earth, snow, blood, and flesh in its wake. Survivors on the line stumbled about in dazed terror, wincing and flinching from each new explosion and repeating the same urgent cry: "Medic! Medic!"

In less than ten minutes the perimeter lay in shambles with half the men dead or wounded. To the rear, sleeping quarter tents, headquarter huts, and mess halls disintegrated in shattering fragments of fire and smoke. All telephone communications went out and almost a full company of men on the line became casualties. Remnants of the 106th's 110th Regiment scrambled to the rear, carrying wounded and whatever weapons they could; or they drove off in whatever vehicles had escaped devastation.

Of all the artillery barrages up and down the line, the German gunners near Echternach had zeroed in the best. All along the eighty-five-mile front, the German cannoneers had struck American positions with surprise and accuracy. But, no U.S. unit had been hit as hard as the 4th Division. Half of the sleeping quarter tents of three battalion campsites in the division had been leveled. Nearly sixty percent of the GIs in the three battalions had suffered death or injury.

The tremendous German barrage finally ceased at 0700, an hour later, and the American GIs, reeling in utter astonishment, welcomed the respite. They moved about their battered front line positions to assess casualties and damage. However, the pause was quite brief. German searchlights, artificial moonlight, cut through the fog and lit up the surprised faces of loitering American combat troops at the 4th Divisions near Echternach.

"What the hell are those lights?" somebody in the rattled 4th Division positions stammered.

"Beats me," a fellow GI answered.

The lights were aiming beams for the countless white sheeted forms, German infantrymen of

Ernst Brandenberg's 7th Army, who now emerged from the fog. The Wehrmacht hordes advanced in a slow, ominous battle line toward the shattered American positions. Within an hour, the Germans would overrun the Americans and send GI survivors scampering westward.

Far to the north, near Krinklet, infantrymen of Sepp Dietrich's 6th Panzer Army had also pierced the Americans with artificial moonlight before German infantrymen burst into the ripped positions of the 9th Division. The Germans unleashed heavy, accurate fire that scattered the GIs and forced the Americans to retreat. Some company commanders rallied their men to resist, but the overwhelming Wehrmacht numbers broke through the line between Monschau and the Losheim Gap and ripped the defenders to shreds. Further south, soldiers of the American 14th Cavalry also buckled and retreated before the German infantry hordes who soon overran the village of Krewinkel. The village population, mostly German sympathizers, welcomed the invaders with open arms.

At Versailles, General Dwight Eisenhower was shocked by the sudden German thrust with overwhelming numbers of men and tanks by the German Army Group B. The Allied commander-in-chief immediately called General Omar Bradley, commander of the American 12th Army Group. "What the hell's going on?" Eisenhower screamed.

"All I know is that Germans are cutting Hodges' 1st Army to pieces," Bradley answered. "I've asked Patton to release the 10th Armored Division and to hurry them north. Patton doesn't like it, but he has no choice."

"Where's the goddamn air force?" Eisenhower screamed again. "How the hell could our reconn people miss this kind of German build-up?"

"The poor weather, sir," Bradley said.

The 12th Army commander was lying. He dared not tell Eisenhower that pilots of the 67th Reconn Group had reported the German build-up in the Ardennes. However, 12th Army staff had shrugged off the reports as nonsense.

"Get a hold of Vandenberg," Eisenhower raved, "and tell him to get his goddamn planes in the air. And call Leigh-Mallory for some RAF support in the northern sector of this German breakthrough. The British are in this war, too."

"Yes, sir," Hodges answered.

However, the Germans also moved first with their aircraft. At 0640 hours, German ME 262 fighter-bombers and 30 jet Snowbirds took off from their base at Aschner. The jets whined westward under low hanging clouds, hugging the tree tops. Each ME 262 carried 24 R4M rockets along with two SC spitterbombs, high explosive fragmentation bombs. Allied airmen and ground troops had seen the jets around for the past several weeks, and they had been awed by their speed and quickness. The American P-51, the Allies' best fighter plane, was no match for the speedy jets, and neither American nor British flyers liked to see these respected new aircraft.

General Adolph Galland, continually apprised of the action on the Western Front since Herbstnebel began at 0600, had learned that American ground troop resistance had developed along the roads to St. Vith. The Americans maintained a huge supply and fuel dump here. Galland selected his jet planes to support German ground troops here, for the 1st Fighter Corps commander knew the fear that jets left in the hearts of Allied soldiers and airmen.

By 0700 hours, the whine of jet aircraft echoed under the dark clouds east of St. Vith, where the jet pilots of KG 7 found American units of the 14th Cavalry offering stiff resistance. The thirty ME 262's swept in low over the American positions.

One by one, the 600 MPH ME 262s zoomed across the target, unleashing rockets and then spitterbombs. American AA gunners could not even get a bead on the swift flying Snowbirds, much less hit them, even at low altitude. The jet attack awed both the GI defenders and the Wehrmacht attackers as the mere five-minute air assault shattered the American positions. The jets burned dozens of vehicles, pulverized stacks of supplies, and left dozens of dead and injured GIs. The attack had not only caused extensive damage, but the attack had shaken the morale of the 14th Cavalry resisters.

Before the Americans recovered from this first terrifying jet attack, a new wave of jets loomed from the east. Twenty-five AR 234 bombers of KG 51 had left Aschner only a half hour after the ME 262s of KG 7. The KG 51 bombers now arrived to finish the job. The terrifying Aredos zoomed like meteors across the area to unleash fragmentation bombs and R4M rockets.

Once more American defense positions disintegrated: vehicles caught fire, more American GIs died, gun positions erupted. After the attack, the 14th Cavalry survivors emerged from shelters with somber looks on their faces. Their positions had been shattered and they could never reorganize in time to resist the next German onslaught by elements of von Manteuffel's 5th Panzer Army. The Americans could only retreat to St. Vith.

Within two days, thanks to jet aircraft support, the 26th Panzer Division would force the Americans out of this vital supply base. By the morning of December 18, the GIs would abandon St. Vith and give the Germans a vital road junction through which passed five highways. The 26th Panzer would also win considerable booty: gasoline, food, and ammunition along with other supplies abandoned by the Americans.

On the same morning of December 16, other German air units also struck the bewildered Americans after the initial thrust of Wehrmacht and Panzer divisions. More than a hundred ME 110 twin engine attack bombers of Jagdivision 3, with escorting ME 109s and FW 190s, made sweeps north of the Schnee Eifel. The German planes struck communications, roads, and rail junctions at the American bases in Malmedy, Monschau, Krinklet, and the Losheim Gap. Whistling spitter-bombs and zooming rockets tore up highways, ripped up sections of railway pikes, and knocked out two bridges.

By 0730 on this same mid-December day, another wave of white sheeted Wehrmacht troops crossed the Our River in boats and surrounded the 106th American Division near Shonberg on Skyline Drive, at the foot of the Schnee Eifel. Forty-three Luftwaffe FW 190 fighter-bombers raked American 106th Division troop concentrations and motor vehicle columns west of the Our River. Within several minutes, the 190s, in low level sweeps, had expended its rockets and bombs and left a square mile of destruction in the Losheim Gap. The torn ranks of the 106th GIs collapsed before the onslaught of German troops who had crossed the Our.

Other Luftwaffe West aircraft swooped over American columns retreating southwest of the Schnee Eifel. German 190s and 109s struck along the Saur River to batter the retiring American GIs of the 9th Armored and 28th Infantry Divisions. Rockets and spitterbombs and strafing fire tore up more roads, more rail pikes, and long lines of trucks and armor.

To the south, General Beppo Schmidt sent out the geschwaders of Jagdivision IX, all the ME 110 attack bombers of his SG 4 and SG 20 from Ostheim—over 150 of them. They came fully loaded to hit the roads and American columns between Echternach and Clervaux, causing widespread destruction to American motorized and tank units, and bringing death and injury to hundreds of GIs.

By noon of this December 16 day, through the aid of the Luftwaffe strikes, Hasso von Manteuffel's 5th Panzer Army had opened a gap in the American lines as far west as Houffalize and Marche. To the south the American 4th Division was falling back to the defended towns of Clervaux and Wiltz, with German infantry marching after them in their snowsuits like columns of white ants.

No one any longer asked "Where is the Luftwaffe?" The German air units had conducted nearly 800 sorties on this one morning, more than they had in a year. Galland had frowned on Operation Herbstnebel, but he now admitted that Hitler had once again guessed correctly.

Of course, circumstances had played a role in the Luftwaffe West success. First, no Allied commander nor any GI, not even Vandenberg, expected this sudden, surprising, massive German offensive. Perhaps only the pilots of the 67th American Reconn Group could have had such a suspicion. But their reports had been ignored. Secondly, a misty fog and low clouds hung in the chilly air over eastern Belgium on this December morning. So, Allied planes had been sitting idly at their bases. If the Germans did have a considerable number of planes, as Vandenberg suspected, the Allied air commanders expected such planes to be grounded as were their own on this misty day.

By noon, General Vandenberg and Air Marshal Leigh-Mallory finally reacted to the surprising German aerial assaults. Hundreds of American and British planes took off to make counterstrikes. Blocks of American P-47 and P-51 fighter-bombers zoomed over eastern Belgium as did hordes of British Spitfires and Typhoons.

But, the weather had worsened even more by early afternoon, with the fog thickening as the day grew warmer and the humidity deepened. They could not find a single German aircraft under the dense, low clouds. Some of the American and British air units even flew deep into Western Germany, a few crossing the Rhine River. But they did not find one active German airfield, thanks to the bad weather and unique German camouflage. Other Allied air units failed to find any German armored or infantry columns in the thick fog.

By late afternoon, German ground troops had driven further into Belgium. All along the front, the three armies of Model's Army Group B had made substantial penetrations of five to ten miles beyond the Ghost Front. The German army units stopped only for respites and supplies, but by dawn of the 17th they expected to be off again.

General Hoyt Vandenberg had issued frantic orders to every fighter and bomber unit in the 9th Air Force: "Load up for sorties at dawn." To the north, Air Marshal Sir Trafford Leigh-Mallory issued the same pressing order to all RAF wings of the 2nd Tactical Air Force: "Prepare for tactical air strikes at first light."

But, the German Luftwaffe West was not finished. During the dark hours of December 16–17, a few minutes past midnight, the Germans prepared 15 Junker 88s and ninety Junker 52 transport planes at their bases in Paderhorn and at Lippspringe. Five thousand paratroopers in full gear, combat troops of the 5th German Paratrooper Division, boarded the planes. A dozen ME 110 night fighter pathfinders of NJG 4 were already airborne by 0100 hours, December 17.

The loaded transport planes soon followed the pathfinders, the Junkers droning through the dark sky above the even darker clouds. By 0315, the German transport planes had reached their designated areas west of Clervaux, thanks to the excellent work of the ME 110 pathfinders. Some of the Junkers were shot down or forced back by furious American anti-aircraft fire. But more than 3,000 of the German paratroopers jumped successfully to their drop positions near the roads west of Clervaux to cut off any reinforcements to this major American base in Belgium. Clervaux, within the next twenty-four hours, would fall to advancing German infantry and tank units of the 5th Panzer Army.

And finally, staffels of ME 110 night fighter-bombers gave the GIs no respite. The twin engine attackers made sweeps over Belgium during the dark hours of December 17 to hit an already rattled retreating American army.

At his headquarters in Treuenbritzen, General Adolph Galland was still awake at 0400, December 17, as he had been awake for almost the past twenty-four hours. He read the reports of the Operation Herbstnebel success with disbelief. Not only was he surprised by the swift advance of the ground forces, but also at the air units who had suffered very minimal losses. And at the Armies of the West headquarters in Osnabruck, Field Marshal Gerd von Rundstedt, also awake, was equally amazed when he, too, read the reports of the combined ground-air operation out of the Ardennes.

Both Galland and von Rundstedt had been quite pessimistic about Operation Herbstnebel. But perhaps this Ardenne offensive would succeed after all.

Chapter Three

By the morning of December 17, elation reigned throughout the German airbases in Western Germany. The morning dawned with thick fog and Luftwaffe airmen could not even find their aircraft revetment areas, much less fly. The day would be one of rest, a time to relax, rejoice, and recount their deeds of yesterday.

At the Badenheisen airbase, excitement had whetted the appetites of JG 54 pilots and they relished their breakfasts of coarse rye bread, ground pork patties, sauerkraut, and coffee.

"An entire motor column; a fat target," one pilot said. "I myself knocked out at least three or four trucks."

"Yah, yah, Karl," another young pilot nodded vigorously, "and I came in right behind you and saw the trucks burning. But I too got three trucks in the column."

"We had fine sorties," a third pilot grinned, leaning over the breakfast table. "There were so many targets that I almost flew past them before I remembered to strafe and release my rockets."

"Too bad the weather has grounded us," the first pilot gestured with his fork. "Every geschwader on the Western Front was out yesterday, and they all made successful strikes. Can there be any targets left?"

"There are plenty left," the first pilot nodded. "The Anglo-Saxons have thousands of tanks and trucks, men and guns. If we flew again today, we would find plenty of targets."

A mess flieger came into the pilot's dining room and placed more slabs of rye bread and bowls of sauerkraut on the table. The first pilot gripped his arm. "Flieger, have you heard anything on the radio?"

"Yes, Leutnant," the man nodded. "The Wehrmacht and the tank troops continue to advance in Belgium. The indomitable Oberst Jochen Peiper and the 1st SS Panzer has already penetrated ten miles with his spearhead of Tigers. We are told he is within sight of Clerveaux."

"Amazing," the pilot said.

"Why should not Peiper move so easily?" a second pilot grinned. "We have made it easy for him."

"Ah, but it was the ME 110s from Ostheim who opened the road to Clerveaux," another pilot said.

"But we did our part," the first young pilot said. He looked at the steward putting bread and sauerkraut on the table. "Flieger, what about the center of the front? Southwest of the Schnee Eifel? Have the Panzers advanced there?"

"Walter?" the steward shouted to the kitchen. When another man poked his head into the room, the steward continued. "You are listening to the radio. Have you heard anything about the front southwest of the Schnee Eifel? The leutnant would like to know."

Walter came over to the dining table and grinned at the young JG 54 pilot. "You did well yesterday, Herr Leutnant. I heard a report only a few minutes ago. The Panzer Lehr Division has crossed the Dasburg Bridge and they are advancing toward Houffalize."

"Houffalize?" the lieutenant asked quizzically.

The messman grinned. "Herr Leutnant, Houffalize is a most important Allied base in Belgium. If the Panzer Lehr captures this town, the Americans will be kuput."

"See, see," the first young officer grinned elatedly at his fellow pilots. "We have done our job. We have opened the way for the Panzer Lehr Division. What more could they ask for us?" He raised his cup of coffee. "Victor! Victor! Hail the Green Hearts!"

Those at the table responded with a cheering chorus. "Hail the Green Hearts!" Then they drank coffee to toast themselves.

Without doubt, these young pilots had joined a famed geschwader when training authorities assigned them to the JG 54 Green Hearts. The unit, one of the oldest in the Luftwaffe, had first served in Spain where Green Heart pilots knocked down over a hundred enemy planes in a few months, while they also conducted almost daily ground support sorties for the Fascist troops. Colonel Hannes Trautlot, who had won fame in the Condor Legion, had also done well in the Battle of Britain with 40 RAF kills. By July of 1943, Trautlot had scored 57 kills and won the Knights Cross.

In fact, while Trautlot commanded JG 54, a score of aces developed under his leadership: Otto Kittel, Hans Phillips, Walter Nowotny, Emit Lent, and the current JG 54 Commodore, Erich Rudorffer. After World War II, Trautlot became an officer in the new West German Air Force.

Colonel Erich Rudorffer was a man whose very presence drew awed looks from the faces of young pilots. Rudorffer was a tall, slender man, with a soft thin face, but piercing blue eyes. The lieutenant colonel had fought a long, grim war, beginning with the Condor Legion in Spain in 1937. During his career, Rudorffer had flown close to a thousand missions. In fact, when he led JG 54 yesterday, he had flown his 976th mission. On more than 300 of these missions, he had engaged enemy fighter planes in combat. For two years, Rudorffer had served with JG 54's I Gruppe on the Russian front where he had scored more than 150 kills. The slender flyer had accomplished the biggest aerial feat in history on that front when, on a single mission, he had shot down 13 Russian fighter planes during a two-hour dogfight.

While serving in Africa, Rudorffer had been just as deadly. On February 9, 1943, he had shot down, in a single engagement, eight P-40s and P-38s of the RAF. A week later, in back-to-back sorties, he had shot down seven P-38s of the 31st American Fighter Group, an event the pilots of the 31st still talked about.

Rudorffer, who had won three Knights Crosses, was only one of a dozen Luftwaffe pilots so honored. In his long career, he had been shot down sixteen times. He had parachuted to safety nine times and simply crash-landed seven times. Amazingly, he had never suffered more than minor injuries. By early November of 1944, when he assumed command of JG 54, he had downed 210 enemy planes to become the seventh highest scoring ace in Luftwaffe history.

Now, on this December 17 morning, Colonel

Erich Rudorffer sat at a small commodore's table in the Badenheisen dining room. Across from him sat Major Robert "Bazi" Weise of III Gruppe and Major Alfred Keller of IV Gruppe. When Weise saw his commodore frowning at the young pilots, the major leaned over the table and grinned.

"Erich, do not deny them their pleasure this morning. They have earned it."

"I do not want overconfidence," Rudorffer said. "We were victorious yesterday, the first time in months, perhaps years. We should be elated, but we cannot become overconfident."

"Still, they deserve to celebrate," Major Keller now spoke.

"Most of these young pilots have never met the enemy in the sky," Rudorffer said. "Those experienced American fighter pilots in their P-51s that are far superior to our Messerschmits and Folk-Wulfes. Nor have these young pilots seen the experienced British pilots who do wonders with their new model Spitfires. If our pilots become reckless, they will become fodder for Allied airmen." He shifted his glance between the two majors. "Do you think for a minute that the Spitfires and Mustangs will stay away as they did yesterday?"

"No," Major Alfred Keller answered softly.

"Will our pilots be prepared?"

"I don't know, Erich," Keller said.

"They are your pilots as well as mine; your responsibility," Rudorffer told his two subordinates. "Speak to them as though you were their fathers who are concerned for their welfare. Make them understand. Tomorrow, the next day, or next week, whenever we sortie again, the Mustangs and Spitfires will be waiting for us, and no doubt in much greater numbers than our own. These young men could die by the score," he cocked his head toward the long tables of happy Luftwaffe pilots. "Many of them have soloed only a few weeks ago and yesterday was but their first combat sortie."

"True," Major Weise nodded, his face suddenly sober.

"The Green Hearts have a long, proud tradition," Rudorffer continued, "both in the West and on the Eastern Front. If we do not instill caution in these young pilots, the Green Hearts could die in disgrace."

Robert "Bazi" Weise looked at the dense fog beyond the dining hall window and he then turned to Rudorffer. "What you say is correct, Erich, but no aircraft are going anywhere today. Let the young pilots enjoy their day of glory. This evening, after the evening meal, we will speak to them."

Rudorffer nodded and then sighed. The JG 54 Commodore had seen many Luftwaffe pilots die over the years and each death had brought a new pain into his heart, for he never got over the loss of a flieger. He now feared for these young men, feared that many of them would not celebrate Christmas Eve and more would not live to see the new year.

Other pilots in other Luftwaffe West airbases expressed the same happiness as the young pilots at Badenheisen.

Perhaps no elation reigned so openly on this zero visibility morning as at the jet aircraft base at Aschner, where ME 262 and AR 234 airmen loitered in the mess hall. Many of the KG 7 and KG 51 pilots huddled about the radio, listening to the continual reports of German advances through Belgium. When the radio commentator reported that the 26th SS Panzer had isolated St. Vith and was now rolling toward Vielsam, a shout went up from the flyers. Then, when the commentator, a few moments later, said that St. Vith was expected to fall within hours, a second chorus of cheers rocked the mess hall.

"They can thank us, thank us," a pilot from KG 7 shouted. "We destroyed the Americans on the road to St. Vith and the panzers needed only to move on like traffic on the Autobahn."

"You only began the destruction of American resistance," a pilot from KG 51 grinned, "but we finished the job."

"Yes, your Aredos made a contribution," the first jet pilot admitted.

"I wish we could fly today," another pilot said, staring out of the fog clouded window. "Perhaps we could open the way for other Wehrmacht and panzer units who do not move as swiftly as the 26th Panzer."

"Tomorrow, perhaps," the KG 7 pilot said.

The pilots of these jet units had been hand-picked from volunteers. All of them were experienced pilots with exceptional ability. All had superior physical stamina and high intelligence so necessary to handle the speedy, complicated ME 262 and AR 234 jets. These men, in fact, were the elite of the Luftwaffe. The Luftwaffe had even assigned a geschwader of ME 109s to protect Aschner so the 262s and 234s could take off and land without interference from Allied fighter planes.

The Aschner base was probably the most heavily defended base in Germany. More than twenty-four anti-aircraft guns surrounded the airfield and a battalion of grenadier combat troops protected the base. Only twice had American 9th Air Force attack bombers struck Aschner, but on both occasions German 109s and anti-aircraft fire had driven the American planes off before they could do much damage. B-17s of the 8th Air Force had bombarded the base from high altitude, but the raid had only destroyed or damaged a few jets and left a few craters in the runways, which German engineers had quickly repaired.

"When do you think we will fly again?" one of the pilots asked.

"The sooner the better," a KG 7 pilot answered. "I am eager to strike our enemies again. When you consider our record, we have nothing to fear. How can we be afraid when we shot down four or five of them for every one of our jets they shoot down?"

"But they have four or five times as many aircraft as we do."

"The Führer has promised more," the KG 7 pilot said, "and I believe him. We will soon have enough jet aircraft to deal with the Allies. Come, let us have some more coffee."

At the other end of the mess hall, Colonel Johannes Steinhoff sat quietly at a table with his deputy commodore, Major Theo Weissenberger, and with Oberst Lieutenant Walter Kowalaski, the commodore of JG 51, the Aredo bomber geschwader. Weissenberger had earned his reputation as a pilot with JG 5 in the Arctic wing, spending two years in the frozen north. He had already downed more than 200 planes before joining the Nowotny KG 7. Kowalaski, though a mere oberst lieutenant, had spent most of his career as an ME 110 light bomber pilot. He had then trained with the new

AR 234 jet twin engine bomber and his adept ability and leadership qualities had come to the attention of General Dietrich Peltz himself. So, when the Luftwaffe formed the first jet bomber unit, Peltz had asked Kowalaski to assume command of KG 51. Kowalaski had thus become the least ranking leader of any geschwader, although with only twenty-five aircraft, KG 51 was not much larger than a staffel. Kowalaski's promotion to captain seemed imminent.

"See how they bathe themselves in glory," Major Weissenberger scoffed. "You would think they are winning this new offensive by themselves."

"They have reason to feel proud," Oblt Kowalaski said. "They did well yesterday and they have left the Allies awe-stricken with their efforts."

"But they must not become too sure of themselves," Steinhoff said.

Johannes Steinhoff, the commodore of KG 51, had joined the Luftwaffe in 1936 and he had risen swiftly to staffel leader. The colonel, athletically built, maintained a perpetual look of determination in his gray eyes. He had begun his service in 1937 in Spain where he had downed fourteen enemy planes. By 1939, when war broke out, Steinhoff had already served in four different geschwaders. The strapping Steinhoff build had gained him a reputation as an incorrigible, a man who insisted on thinking independently and this trait irked his superiors. Thus, he was frequently transferred from one unit to another. Still, he had won the admiration of General Galland, who was somewhat of an insurgent himself.

By the fall of 1944, Steinhoff had scored more than 150 kills and he had won both the Knights

Cross and the Iron Cross, despite his disfavor with Herman Goring who had once commented: "An unruly flieger like Steinhoff deserves no medals from the Reich."

When Walter Nowotny formed the first jet fighter unit in October of 1944, Steinhoff accepted Nowotny's invitation to join KG 7 as a jet fighter pilot. JG 7 did well, frustrating the Spitfire and Mustang pilots with their superior ME 262s. Then, when Nowotny was killed in a crash in mid-November of 1944, Steinhoff was promoted to colonel and placed in command of the jet unit, over the objections of Herman Goring.

The jet pilots of JG 7 approved of their new commodore, however. They considered him a man of honesty, independence, courage, and compassion. Steinhoff would never knowingly endanger a man's life, and he continually refused to conduct missions that might bring sure death for no purpose. Steinhoff, in turn, had respect and confidence in his unit.

Now, on this December 17 morning, he looked at Kowalaski. "Yes, Leutnant, you can be proud of your Aredo pilots, but do you think that we can always do what we did yesterday?"

"I am sure we can succeed with this new offensive," Kowalaski said. "If we do, we will certainly postpone for many months the Allies ability to mount a new offensive against the Fatherland. In six months, I am told, we will have another five or six hundred Aredo bombers and trained crews to fly them. Who will stop such a force, Herr Steinhoff? And think of your ME 262s. I understand there are more than six hundred of them available at this very moment."

"But no pilots," Major Weissenberger scoffed.

"These too will come in time," the oblt said. "If we succeed in this Ardenne offensive, we will gain that time. Even the American 8th Air Force chief of staff is worried about the increasing strength of our jet units. I have heard that the Americans are considering as a first priority the destruction of our jet airbases. No," Kowalaski shook his head, "I have no doubts, and neither should you, Major, or you, Colonel."

"Perhaps not," Weissenberger answered.

The KG major, despite the overall success of the jet aircraft, had been a pilot too long. He had seen the fortunes of the Luftwaffe change from uncontested air superiority to a struggling inability to compete with Allied air superiority. He could not quite believe that Germany could change this trend.

At the German airbase in Wesel, Colonel Gunther Lutzow of JG 3 and Major Heinz Pritzl Bar of JG 1 sat at the table reserved for commodores in the Wesel airbase dining hall. They listened to the joyous shouts of their pilots, who had also been listening to the radio. Gunther listened with a solemn face, for he was a serious man, skeptical of any chance for victory in this war, and totally opposed to the leadership of the 3rd Reich. Heinz Bar, in turn, despite the years of fighting, looked at the jocular pilots with a grinning, optimistic face.

"They are under a delusion," Colonel Lutzow said to Bar.

"Why shouldn't they be happy?" Major Bar said. "They have a right to boast of their successes yesterday."

"We both know, Pritzl," Lutzow said, "that our victories yesterday were momentary triumphs. We could have had more such successes, I admit, if we did not have such asses as the Reichmarshal telling qualified air commodores how to run the Luftwaffe. By now, I believe it is too late."

Major Bar grinned. He admired Colonel Gunther Lutzow, whose baby face countenance was quite deceiving.

Colonel Lutzow was a man who rarely spoke to anyone except to issue orders or to give a reprimand. He had descended from an aristocratic Prussian family, steeped in the military, and he embodied all those qualities of honesty, dedication, and sternness so apropos to the Prussian stereotype. Lutzow's integrity was beyond question and he faced life's challenges without a flinch. He accepted suffering, death, disappointment, or defeat without a whimper—whether tragedy struck one of his men or Lutzow himself. But, he found hard to accept the blundering egotism of Hitler or the submissive ignorance of Goring, who would never question the Führer. Lutzow considered Hitler and Goring the principal incompetents who were responsible for the deterioration of the Luftwaffe.

By 1941, Lutzow had already scored one hundred aerial victories and he had won three Knight Crosses to become one of the most popular men in Germany. When men saw the tall, stiff necked Lutzow with the somber look on his narrow face or in his blue eyes, they instinctively retreated in awe. They knew of no man in Germany who possessed the courage, intelligence, and strong character of the JG 3 commodore. Lutzow could not tolerate hypocrisy, inefficiency, or shoddiness. If a ground crewman or a pilot failed to fulfill his duty, the man would surely suffer the wrath of Lutzow.

Further, the JG 3 commodore never hesitated to unleash his wrath to superiors.

The colonel never hid his total abhorrence for Goring whom he considered inept, cowardly, and squeamish. Once, at Goring's luxurious quarters in Karinhall, after Goring praised Lutzow for his fine record as a fighter pilot, Lutzow looked squarely into the Reichmarshal's eyes and said: "Herr Reichmarshal, for the good of the air force, you should resign at once. The Luftwaffe has enough problems; we did not need your inept interference."

The officers present had been stunned to silence by the biting insult. Goring, utterly embarrassed, had merely walked away, not answering or threatening the stiff Prussian with the oval, boyish face that so deceived his true character.

Now, in the Wesel dining room, Bar spoke again to Lutzow. "Our units did well yesterday and they will do well again."

Lutzow shook his head before he answered the JG 1 commodore. "You have been in this war a long time, Pritzl, and you have seen what the idiots did to our Luftwaffe and to so many of our brave pilots. How can you still believe that we can succeed?"

"Anything is possible if we have the will and if we have the hope," Bar said.

Now, it was Colonel Lutzow who looked at Bar with a tinge of admiration. No man alive was meant to fly more than the huskily built, square-jawed Heinz "Pritzl" Bar. He had begun flying in 1928 at age fifteen with a glider flying club and by 1930 he had earned a pilot's license. By age twenty-one, he found himself in the still clandestine German Air Force, training as a German fighter pilot. When war broke out, Bar was already trained.

Bar had been among the first to shoot down French aircraft in World War II, when in the fall of 1939, he shot down French flown Curtis P-36s. Over the next few years he had fought on the Western Front and Eastern Front, until by 1944 he had racked up 161 kills and earned the Knights Cross with two clusters. By the fall of 1944, when he scored his 175th kill, he took command of JG 1 in the defense of the Reich. Within a month, he had shot down a phenomenal 21 four-engine bombers.

Probably no geschwader commodore showed a more friendly, outgoing, and warm personality than did Heinz Pritzl Bar. Further, his strong physical appearance, his chiseled face, and his hawkish nose gave him a heroic look that prompted subordinates to follow him unwaveringly. He also had a sense of humor, a sparkling wit, and an amiability that impressed all who met him. He was a dynamic leader with a sense of fairness almost unparalleled among geschwader commodores. His men not only respected him; they worshipped him.

Now, Lutzow looked at Bar with near reverence. "Perhaps you are right, Pritzl. Perhaps it is those like myself, with our pessimism, that hasten our defeat. We need the optimists like you if we are to continue this war with honor and if we are to win the respect of our enemies."

Bar smiled, reached over the table and touched Lutzow's shoulder. "You are the best, Gunther, the pride of the Luftwaffe and the Fatherland. Men like you bring respect from our enemies, not my optimism. But, you must have hope. Without hope, we cannot survive. Let them celebrate," Bar cocked his head toward the boisterous pilots listening to the radio. "They will accomplish more if they are hopeful than if they wallow in despair."

"You are correct, Pritzl," Lutzow nodded.

"Drink your coffee," Bar said, "and we shall have another cup."

At the German base in Rheims, the young pilots of JG 2 who had met no enemy interceptors on escort missions yesterday, echoed a curious sing song, a reverse of "Where is the Luftwaffe?" As they loitered about their rest hall on this foggy morning, they chanted: "Where is the Allied Air Force? Where is the Allied Airforce?" Then, they grinned and cheered anew with each new report that told of more advances into Belgium by the Wehrmacht and panzer units.

JG 2, the Richthofen Unit, had established one of the best records in the Luftwaffe since it was formed on the Western Front in 1939. In 1940, when they became heavily engaged in the Battle of Britain, they downed more than 300 RAF planes. Their commodore, Helmut Wick, had scored 56 British kills before his own death off the Isle of Wright. Subsequent commodores were also great aces, like the renowned Walter Oesau and Egan Mayars. Oesau had scored over 100 victories before he left JG 2 for the Eastern Front. Mayars had scored 102 victories, including 25 four-engine bombers, before P-51 pilots killed him in 1944.

The tradition of outstanding JG 2 commodores continued with the appointment of Colonel Hans "Assi" Hahn in mid-1944. By December of 1944, Hahn had scored over 90 kills, mostly against P-51 pilots. He had won three Knights Crosses and no less a man than Gunther Lutzow had called Hahn the best leader in the Luftwaffe.

Hahn had first seen action in 1939 as a twenty-five-year old pilot and later shot down two Hurricanes during his first mission in the Battle of Britain. By the time he went to the Eastern Front in 1942, he had downed 68 RAF planes. In the East, he had downed 47 Russian planes on a mere seven missions.

Like Pritzl Bar, Assi Hahn also projected a bon vivant, optimistic, outgoing look. He wreaked with self-confidence and, despite the recent ill fortune of the Luftwaffe, he still believed they could succeed. The victories yesterday had bolstered this belief and he shared the sentiments of his pilots. He rose from his breakfast table and walked over to his pilots.

"I share your happiness, Fliegers," he told them. "The reports are indeed encouraging. Let these victories assure us that we can still win."

"Yah, Herr Commodore," one of the pilots grinned.

However, in one of the sleeping barracks, Leutnant Otto Kindes, a staffel leader, did not share this elation. He sat on his bunk playing solitaire while at a nearby table sat two comrades, Leutnant Josef Zwernemann and Sergeant George Kell. Leutnant Kindes had seen too many disappointments over the years, especially in the futile attempts to stop the big bombing raids over Germany. Kindes had shot down eight of the four-engine bombers, but he recognized that these efforts had barely dented the continued strategic bombing strikes by the 8th Air Force. He saw the successful strikes yesterday as a mere interlude in the declining fortunes of the Luftwaffe.

"Listen to them," Kindes scowled. "You would think they had won the war yesterday. 'Where is the Allied Air Force' indeed," Kindes sneered. "When they see the Allied air forces, they will know."

"It is hard to make them understand," Leutnant Zwernemann said.

"Will we see them when we fly again?" Sergeant Kell asked the staffel leader.

"You will see them, Kell," Kindes answered, slamming a card on his bunk. "You and those young pilots will see more than you care to see. We struck with surprise yesterday and caused them much harm, more than we did since the days of North Africa when we first met the American enemy. But now, they are the tigers," Kindes pointed, "and we stepped on the tiger's tail. They will strike back with a vengeance."

"Don't be so pessimistic, Otto," Leutnant Zwernemann said. "Perhaps the Reichmarshal is right; perhaps we do have the aircraft now to compete with the Allies."

"I wish I could share your optimism, Josef," Leutnant Kindes said.

"So long as the ground units continue to advance, we will gain time to become stronger," Zwernemann said.

Leutnant Kindes stared out of the barracks and looked at the dense mist. "The ground units will continue to succeed so long as we have this mist, for the Allies cannot mount swarms of aircraft to stop them. I pray this fog never lifts, even if it means we cannot fly ourselves. If the skies clear, the Allies will send hundreds of aircraft to decimate our Wehrmacht and panzer soldiers in

Belgium. With our fewer aircraft and with our many inexperienced pilots, we will not be able to stop them."

"Do you really believe they have so many aircraft?" Sergeant Kells asked.

"They can blacken the sky with them," Kindes said, slamming another card on his bunk.

"Perhaps you are right, Otto," Leutnant Zwernemann said, also looking out at the heavy mist. "Perhaps we are better off if the fog does not lift."

Chapter Four

Throughout France, Belgium, and Holland on this December 17 day, Allied air commanders and Allied airmen loitered at their bases with agonizing frustration. They stared at the dense fog that had grounded all aircraft, leaving the Allied flyers restless and disappointed. The Americans and British listened irritably to the radio reports that continually brought more bad news—the German Wehrmacht and panzer units were still advancing deep into Belgium. American troops were threatened at St. Vith, Clerveaux, Bastogne, and a dozen other important towns that lay along the roads to the Muese River.

By now, twenty-four hours later, the Allies had guessed the German plan—cross the Muese River and drive to Antwerp. If they could take the Belgium seaport, the Germans would surely destroy any Allied plans for a new offensive—like Operation Varsity.

At Evere in Belgium, flyers of 127 Wing sat in their recreation room and listened to the radio reports in disbelief. Squadron Leader George Buerling of the Canadian 414 Squadron sipped tea at a table with F/O Frank Hanton and Lieutenant Charles "Smokey" Stover. Stover looked at the 414

Squadron commander.

"I can't believe it, George, I can't."

"You can never tell with those Jerrys," Buerling said. "The commander should have let us go out. We might have spotted them if we did; maybe verified the reports of those American reconn pilots."

"They're mad; the Germans are mad," F/O Hanton shook his head. "They can't really expect to get away with this, can they?"

"They can if they won't let us go out after them," Buerling said.

Lieutenant Charles Stover looked out of the recreation room window. "There's no way we can go out in this fog. We'd only get ourselves cracked up."

Buerling only scowled.

The 414 Squadron leader had been in the war since 1940 when he joined the RAF's 402 Squadron and flew Hurricanes out of Malta in the Mediterranean. At the time, the Luftwaffe had many more aircraft. Still, Buerling shot down thirteen German planes during his tour at Malta. He had then joined the Battle of Britain where he again shot down more than a dozen German planes. By late 1944, he had raised his score to thirty-one kills. He had been given command of 414 Squadron when the unit moved to Evere to join the RAF 127 Wing.

George Buerling was a sober faced, serious man, quite anti-social, with pale blue eyes. But, he was a brilliant pilot and thus highly respected by his squadron personnel. But, this 414 Squadron leader from Montreal, Canada, was quite reckless, too, prepared to seek out the enemy at any time, under any circumstances, and in any kind of weather. He would go out today if he got permission.

"We'll be out soon enough," Stover told Lieutenant Buerling, "Maybe as soon as we see the runway. I heard we'd be helping the Americans in the northern sector, around Malmedy and Monschau." Stover shook his head. "Where the hell did the Germans get so many aircraft to support something like this?"

"They were holding them back that's what," somebody behind the three men suddenly spoke. When Buerling, Stover, and Hanton turned, they faced the 127 Wing commander, Captain Johnnie Johnson, one of the most successful and renowned pilots in the RAF. "Looks like General Vandenberg was right after all," Johnson told his pilots.

The tall, narrow faced air commander of 127 Wing was the son of a police inspector in Mobray, England, but law enforcement had never appealed to him. Flying did. He had joined the RAF and won his wings in early 1940. He had shown exceptional ability and leadership qualities, and he was a most determined pilot; a hunter, who often stalked his prey in cold, ruthless combat. By the summer of 1940, Johnson made squadron leader and by mid-1944, Johnson had become Britain's leading air ace with thirty-eight kills.

After the Normandy invasion, John Johnson led his squadron on sweeps over Holland to knock out German communications, rail heads, and highway junctions. On one foray in August of 1944, Johnson had met one hundred FW 190s. In the ensuing clash, one of the greatest dogfights of World War II, thirty-seven of the Spitfires and Hurricanes went down along with fifty-three of the FW 190s. In the aerial brawl, that had lasted for two hours, Johnson had downed six enemy planes, a record for any Allied airman in Europe.

The feat had earned Johnson the DFA, the Victoria Cross, promotion to captain, and command of 127 Wing.

Johnson was as outgoing and pleasant as George Buerling was sober and introverted. He now smiled at his famous subordinate who led 414 Squadron. "George, you must learn to relax. It's not fit for man or beast out there and all you'd do by going out is to waste petrol and put your lads through a futile exercise."

"We can do something, Captain," George Buerling insisted.

"Not until this fog lifts," Johnson answered.

"The Germans didn't wait for the fog to lift," Buerling scowled.

"That was yesterday when the mist was hardly noticeable," Johnson said. "I doubt if they're out today. Besides, those are the orders from Leigh-Mallory. Just 'ave patience, Lad, we'll get them soon enough."

"Yeh, we'll get the Jerrys soon enough," Buerling said scornfully, taking another sip of tea.

To the northeast, at the 122 Wing base in Volkel, Holland, Lieutenant Peter Hearne and F/O Bob Weighill sat at a small table playing cribbage. These flyers from 19 Squadron were usually in a happy-go-lucky frame of mind, but no such cavalier looks radiated from their clean faces now. The sudden German offensive and the massive Luftwaffe tactical air support for the offensive had sobered the pilots of 19 Squadron, as the event had stunned other Allied airmen.

19 Squadron had been supporting the Tommies along the Maas River, but in recent weeks, they had done little supporting since the Germans had obviously been in hiding. 19 Squadron had also

conducted sorties against German ships in the channels between Denmark and Norway, but the seas had been strangely lacking in German vessels of late. Now, both Lieutenant Hearne and F/O Weighill felt disappointed. The fog had ruled out any chance of hitting the fat German ground targets that were now exposed in Belgium.

"The Jerrys timed this right, they did," Lieutenant Hearne said. "The bloody bastards must've 'ad some damn good weather reports."

"'Ow long do you think this soup can last?" F/O Weighill asked.

"Our own weathermen say the poor weather will be 'round for at least a week," Hearne said. "Then they expect a Russian high to clear the skies. By then, the damn Jerrys could be all the way to Antwerp. Then, we'd 'ave a fight on our 'ands, a real 'ell of a fight."

"It wouldn't be any worse than those days over England," Weighill said.

"Maybe not," Hearne answered.

Hearne, although quite outgoing and debonair shared the same desire as Lieutenant George Buerling when it came to flying combat. He had developed an obsession to strike the Germans, perhaps brought on by the heavy damage to England during the Battle of Britain. Hearne, from Coventry, never quite forgave the Germans for the destruction to his home town. He and his 19 Squadron had escorted Mosquitos for strikes around and in Norway for many months. They had often run into enemy interceptors and Hearne himself had scored eight kills in these Norway forays. Now, the recent near inactivity in Holland had aggravated Peter Hearne, and he felt particularly frustrated because he had not been able to strike back at the sudden German offensive.

F/O Bob Weighill grinned at the now sour-faced Hearne. "Peter, we'll be out after those Jerrys. I'm sure we will."

"But it may be too late," Hearne said again.

"Forget the Jerrys for a while," Weighill said. He pointed to the cribbage board. "It's your move."

"The 'ell with this game," Hearne gestured abruptly. "Let's get us some rum and toddy."

In the West, at the American base in Asche, Belgium, Major George Prader deputy commander of the 366th Fortune Hunters Fighter Group, and Captain Floyd Benson, the commander of the group's 387th Squadron, sat at a small table in a quonset hut barracks. They listened to the radio and frowned with each new report of new American ground troop withdrawals in Belgium before the heavy German onslaught.

"Goddamn it," Captain Benson cursed, "would I like to have a P-47 over some of those Kraut tank columns right now, especially with a couple of dozen of armor piercing rockets under my wings."

Benson had first gained fame as pilot with the 8th Air Force, flying long range escort missions out of England for the B-17s, making strategic bombing raids over Germany. Benson had knocked down some fourteen enemy interceptors during the six-month period. As recently as October, Benson had shot down four enemy planes on one escort mission. He had then joined the 366th Group as a squadron commander.

Benson, from Huntington, California, was quite friendly, a trait he had developed as a youngster. When he became a squadron leader, he got on well with his pilots, for he only asked that they do their job efficiently, and his own personal record was enough to encourage his pilots to follow his orders.

However, Benson did not have to remind pilots of their duty, for the pilots of the 366th were proud of their unit. The 366th Fortune Hunters, with their P-47s, were specialists in fighter-bomber tactics against German communications. The 366th had been the first Allied air unit to use the delayed fuse bomb in low level bombing attacks against German targets when they destroyed German bunker positions in France in the spring of 1944. A month later, the group joined the new 9th Air Force and began escorting medium bombers over Western Europe. The Hunters had also supported invasion troops during the landings in Normandy, conducting as many as one hundred sorties a day. They had struck German communications, troops concentrations, roads, defense positions, and motorized columns. Three days after the invasion, the 366th with two other groups destroyed 133 German planes on the ground at the Luftwaffe bases of Cognac and Dijon, France.

The group's efforts in the invasion had earned them its first DUC. Then, during the battle of St. Lo, the 366th had destroyed 83 German tanks in a single mission to earn their second DUC. Since the fall of 1944, when the 366th moved to Asche, the P-47 fighter-bomber group had knocked out more than 500 pieces of rolling stock, 147 locomotives, and 17 bridges. They had also knocked down more than a hundred German planes.

Captain Floyd Benson had been a part of this success, and now, he was disappointed because they could not go out today and roll up their score. "What do you think, George?" Benson asked the major.

"You may as well calm down," George Prader said. "Colonel Holt says the 366th stays grounded until this fog lifts, and what he says goes."

Benson knew well enough that what Holt said did indeed go. Holt was a by-the-book man who always insisted that his ground crews spare no effort in serving the group's P-47s to a honed degree. He also insisted that his pilots follow orders at all times. In some ways he resembled Colonel Johannes Steinhoff with his desire for efficiency and dedication. However, Holt could always smile and joke with his pilots, although he maintained a line that reminded all in the group that he was the commander and they were the subordinates.

Still, the tall, lanky colonel, with a rugged face and penetrating blue eyes, had totalled more than a thousand hours in the air and he had flown thirty-five combat missions. He had downed six planes to become an ace. So, the men respected Holt and much of the success of the 366th Fortune Hunters could be traced to the group commander.

"Jesus," Benson now screwed his face. "How long can this soup last? Those Krauts could be across the Muese before we get a chance to hit them."

"I hear they're sending British troops down from Holland to help out," Major Prader answered. "They're also sending a couple of Patton's armored divisions up from Luxembourg."

"Hell, they can't do any good without air support. They need air support."

"There's not a goddam thing we can do," Prader

said. "But, we'll get the bastards sooner or later, don't worry."

"I feel sorry for those poor GIs," Benson said. "Those panzers might run right over all of them before we can help out."

"You know the colonel," Prader said, "if the fog clears enough so we can see the other end of the runway, he'll let somebody go out." Benson merely nodded and Prader sighed. "How about a little two man pinochle? Hell, we haven't got anything else to do."

"I'll get the cards," Captain Floyd Benson said.

At Lille, France, far to the West, Lieutenant James Lonely and Lieutenant Ed Steinburge were in the quonset hut recreation room of the 322nd American Bomb Group, "Nye's Annihilators." The two men were playing pool on a rickety table with a ripped cushion. Somebody had found the table somewhere and brought it to the American airbase. Outside, the B-26 bombers of Colonel John Samuels' 322nd Group stood forlorn and dormant, in straight wing tip to wing tip lines, and all but enveloped by fog. Steinburge had just made a neat carom to put a ball in the side pocket, and he then looked up at Lonely with a grin. "How was that shot?"

"Too bad you can't drop your bombs on those goddamn bridges like you dropped that ball in the side pocket," Lieutenant Lonely huffed.

"I hit my share of bridges," Steinburge protested. "Just ask the CO. Colonel Samuels is putting me in for the Air Medal." Then, Steinburge squinted at the fog beyond the window. "Fat chance of hitting any goddamn bridges today, though."

"Yeh, but that's what we have to do," Lieutenant Lonely said. "Knock out bridges to stop those Krauts from sending supplies to their panzer divisions."

The two men looked up from their pool table as Colonel John Samuels and Major Tom Stanton of the group's 449th Squadron walked into the recreation room. "Don't let us interrupt," Samuels gestured. "Get on with your game."

"When are we going out again, Colonel?" Steinburge asked.

"As soon as the fog lifts," Samuels answered. "The major and I were just discussing that," Samuels cocked his head toward Tom Stanton.

"Don't be so anxious," Major Stanton grinned. "You got a whole war left."

Steinburge and Lonely watched the two men move on, staring at them, for both Samuels and Stanton had been in combat for nearly two years, both having flown close to a hundred missions—far beyond the requirements for rotation back to the states. Samuels had won a DFC and a Silver Star while leading squadrons of B-26s through intense anti-aircraft fire and enemy interceptors to knock out an important rail center. Stanton had also won a Silver Star for leading a squadron of Marauders against canal locks on the Rhine against intense antiaircraft fire. They had proven their worth and thus had the respect of the newer and younger pilots of the 322nd.

When the colonel and major were gone, Steinburge leaned over the pool table and shot again—sending the eight ball neatly into a corner pocket. He straightened and looked at his companion. "That's how I'm going to hit that goddamn Euskirchen Bridge if I ever get another chance."

"Maybe," Lonely said.

"I win," Steinburge grinned. "You get the coffee."

"Yeah, I get the coffee," Lonely scowled. "I'd rather be getting myself one of those Kraut armored columns."

At Orcantes, in East Central France, the pilots of the 354th U.S. Fighter Group had recovered from the initial trauma of the Germans' sudden offensive in Belgium. Now, like other Allied airmen, the flyers of the 354th Valor in Combat Group felt the same urge to strike back at the Luftwaffe.

At a small rec room, a somewhat luxurious small chateau that served as the officers club, Lieutenant Glen Eagleston and Lieutenant James Daglis sat at one of the ornate marble top tables. The two men simply drank coffee and ate Danish pastry on this foggy morning. The pastry had come from a local bakery in Orcantes, a village miraculously recovered from the war, thanks to the liberal flow of American dollars from 354th Group airmen.

"Jesus, Eagle," Daglis said to Eagleston, "can you believe the German Air Force could do all that damage? We didn't see a goddamn enemy plane for weeks."

"I guess it proves that Vandenberg was right," Eagleston answered. "Those bastards were holding back, all right, but not for an advance on the Rhine. This drive into Belgium," Eagleston shook his head, "who the hell figured they'd try something like that?"

"Amazing," Daglis said.

"I just wish I was out today over Belgium," Eagleston said, sipping his coffee. "Christ, we'd have a field day."

Lieutenant Glen Eagleston was hoping to do

what the 354th airmen did best—wallop German ground troops and communications in fighter-bomber attacks. The group had begun its career in 1942 in England as an escort unit for B-17s. The group had been the first to escort Flying Forts on long range missions when the Forts attacked Kiel and Bremen nearly a year ago. 354th fighter pilots had knocked down thirty German interceptors on that mission, an accomplishment that won them a DUC. In June of 1944, the group won another DUC for escorting gliders into France on D-Day. By December of 1944, the Valor in Combat group had downed some 225 German planes, one of the highest scores of any fighter group in the 9th Air Force. They had also conducted countless support missions, like their sorties at Aachen that enabled American troops to capture this first major German city.

In the Orcante rec room now, Lieutenant Jim Daglis took another sip of coffee and looked at Eagleston. "I'd go out today if they let us."

Then, suddenly, Colonel George Bickel, CO of the 354th, and Major James Howard, CO of the 36th Squadron, sat next to the two pilots. "You boys don't mind, do you?" Bickel grinned. "It's kind of crowded in here."

"No, sir, Colonel," Lieutenant Jim Daglis answered. The young pilot stared at his two superiors with a tinge of awe for both Bickel and Howard had achieved long lists of accomplishments as fighter pilots. Both men had started their combat careers as fighter pilots in the Pacific against the overwhelming odds of the Japanese Air Force, and with inferior P-40s against the Japanese Zero.

Colonel Bickel himself had served for a year in

the Pacific where he had downed four enemy planes before returning to the United States. He had then come to Europe as a squadron commander, rising to deputy commander, and finally making group commander in mid-1944. Bickel had shot down five German planes to achieve the goal of ace. The short, triangular faced colonel treated his pilots like men, listened to them, and he had thus gained respect from them.

The tall, lanky, narrow faced Howard had been in combat for nearly three years, but he was still taking a toll against German aircraft. He had been a former Flying Tiger in China where he had downed six Japanese Zeros before returning to the States. He had then joined the 8th Air Force in England to escort bombers on long range missions over Germany. Howard had accomplished one of the major feats of the war when, on January 11, 1944, he had waded into a formation of German fighter planes that were trying to attack an American bomber formation. Singlehandedly, he had shot down three planes and damaged three more. The feat had won Howard the Congressional Medal of Honor.

The tall American major could have returned in the States and wallowed in this fame, but he elected to return to Europe and fight on.

"You boys enjoying your rest?" Bickel asked Eagleston and Daglis.

"To tell the truth, sir, I'd rather be out hitting some of those Kraut tank columns," Lieutenant Eagleston said.

"Not in this soup," the 354th commander said. "We just got word from 9th Air Force Tactical Command. Everybody stays grounded until further notice."

"But sir," Daglis now spoke, "that means those Germany infantry and tank units can keep right on barrelling through Belgium."

"Lieutenant," Major Frank Howard now spoke, "nobody'd like to be out there right now more than me and the colonel. But, take a look," he cocked his head toward the fog shrouded window of the small chateau. "How can we take off in that? Hell, we couldn't even get out of the hardstand areas."

An enlisted man steward arrived and placed two cups of coffee before Colonel Bickel and Major Howard. "Can I get you or the major something, sir?"

"How about some Danish like those fellows have," Bickel pointed to the half-eaten pastry on the plates of Eagleston and Daglis.

"Yes, sir," the steward said before he moved off.

"Sir," Daglis asked the colonel, "have you heard the latest in Belgium?"

"The Germans are still advancing," Bickel said, "but I understand our own ground troops are moving up fast to close some gaps. I think a couple of armored divisions from Patton's 3rd Army are on the way and some units from the British 21st Army Group are coming down from Holland." Now, Bickel shrugged. "I think we're a little overrated. If we can't give air support because of this soup, than neither can the Germans. And," he pointed out, "if this thing becomes strictly a ground war, our own ground troops will turn this thing around soon enough."

"You really think so, sir?" Daglis asked.

"It's going to be a ground war slugfest so long as this soup holds," Major Jim Howard now spoke. "The weather people expect this fog to linger for a few more days, at least." Howard sighed. "We're going to be sitting on our cans listening to radio reports, and German airmen will be doing the same thing."

"Yes, sir," Daglis answered, a tinge of disappointment in his eyes as he looked again at the dense fog outside.

For the next several days, low clouds and dense fog lingered over Eastern Belgium and both Allied and German airmen remained grounded. Meanwhile, Eisenhower worked furiously to get his army units into Belgium to fill the gaps. The question was whether or not the SHAEF commander could do so before the Germans crossed the Muese River. The Germans might then have a good natural defense to hold their Belgium gains.

But, the battle worsened for the Americans. On December 18, Stavelot fell. On December 20, St. Vith fell. The Germans had taken Malmedy. In the center, the Germans had cut off and isolated the major American base at Bastogne. In the South, Clervaux had fallen and panzer tanks growled toward the Muese River.

During these several days, whenever the fog lifted slightly, both American and German air units made air strikes. However, the Allied air units had made less than 300 sorties and the Germans under a 100. In truth, these limited air sorties had not altered the ground conflict. The Germans continued to advance and the Americans continued to retreat. In reality, both General Omar Bradley and Field Marshal Walter Model had written off air support as a factor in the hard fighting. Model turned his panzer units loose to run brazenly over open, exposed terrain so they could reach the Muese as soon as possible. Bradley, meanwhile, pushed men, vehicles, and tanks almost to exhaustion to halt the Germans before Army Group B reached the Muese.

By December 24, airmen on both sides had resigned themselves to idleness and they now devoted their time to decorating trees in their barracks and quarters for Christmas Eve. Americans looked forward to turkey dinners, a traditional treat for holidays. The British waited for their plum pudding, and the Germans looked forward to sauerbraten, a rare treat considering the shortage of beef in Germany. By 2000 hours on Christmas Eve, when Christmas Eve revelries had reached their heights at Allied and German air bases, a strange phenomenon emerged outside their recreation and living quarters. Stars, hundreds of them, now twinkled overhead, including the Star of Bethlehem that was so apropos for a Christmas Eve night. But, with the cleared skies, all Christmas Eve celebrations ended abruptly.

In every Allied wing, group, and squadron area, commanders issued the same sudden order: "Pilots and air crews will report for morning briefings. Ground personnel will prepare and load aircraft for dawn take-offs."

In Western Germany, geschwader, gruppe, and staffel commodores issued essentially the same order. "Air crews and warts will prepare for sorties at first light."

A/C Johnnie Johnson issued orders to pilots of his 127 Wing; Peter Hearne issued orders to his 19 Squadron pilots. At American bases, Norman Holt issued orders to the pilots of his 366th Fighter Group, Colonel George Bickel issued orders to the pilots of his 354th Fighter Group, and Colonel

John Samuels alerted the crews of his 322nd Bomb Group. At other Allied airbases, other air commanders did the same thing.

In Germany, Colonel Erich Rudorffer alerted the men of his JG 54, Colonel Johannes Steinhoff issued orders to the jet pilots of KG 7 and KG 51, Colonel Gunther Lutzow called early morning briefings for the pilots of his JG 3, Major Heinz Bar issued orders to JG 1 pilots and Colonel Hans Hahn issued commands to his JG 2 pilots. In other geschwaders, commodores issued the same orders.

Tomorrow was the day of "Peace on earth, good will toward men." But, there would be no peace over the skies of Western Europe on Christmas Day, 1944.

Chapter Five

By the evening of December 24, ground troops hardly celebrated. The Germans had penetrated almost fifty miles beyond the Ghost Front, with Jochen Peiper's spearheading tanks taking Rochefort, the last defense bastion to Dinant, only five miles from the Muese River. Ligneuville, Vielson, and Manhay had fallen, Bastogne was isolated, and Sepp Dietrich's panzer divisions were driving toward the big city of Liege, where rear troops were packing boxes for evacuation. Colonel George Bickel was probably wrong in assuming the Americans could stop the Germans from crossing the Muese without air support.

Now, on Christmas morning, as both sides prepared to send up their air units, the Allies held a decided advantage. First, Vandenberg had twice as many planes as Luftwaffe West. Second, Luftwaffe West could only send out fragments of their geschwaders because of lack of fuel, despite the promises of General Alfred Jodl. Finally, the German air units included hundreds of green, untested pilots, whereas the Allies had an oversupply of experienced airmen who by now were fully confident of disposing of any German air units.

And true enough, on this Christmas day, the Allied air forces would make believers of those Luftwaffers who thought they could still deal with the U.S. and RAF air forces.

When the orders came to prepare for morning sorties, most of the Allied flyers went to bed early, for they would be up at 0500 hours. Some ground mechanics and ordinance men did not sleep at all on Christmas Eve. They spent the night servicing and loading aircraft with rockets, bombs, and .50 caliber strafing belts.

Throughout the Allied air bases in Western Europe, the roar of aircraft engines welcomed the first light of dawn on Christmas day. Residents in dozens of towns were rudely awakened by the whines and roars: 122 Wing at Vokel, Holland, including 19 Squadron; 127 Wing at Evere, Belgium, including 414 Squadron; the 322nd Bomb Group at Lille, the 366th Fighter Group at Asche, and the 354th Fighter Group at Orcantes. Similar pre-flighting aircraft engines roared and whined in other Allied bases in Western Europe.

In Western Germany, the whines and screams of aircraft engines also awoke residents early on Christmas morning: JG 54 at Badenheisen, JG 2 at Rheims, JG 1 and JG 3 at Wesel, and the screaming jet engines of KG 7 and KG 51 at Aschner. In a dozen other German air bases, similar pre-flighting aircraft engines also awoke residents in the towns east of the Rhine. Unfortunately, many of the geschwaders would take off in reduced numbers because of the fuel shortage.

The Luftwaffe pilots had a special goal in mind: stop the Allied air forces from interfering with the drive through Belgium by the German ground forces. The Allied air forces had their own goal in mind: crush the onrushing Wehrmacht and panzer units in Belgium, or drive them back to the Ardennes.

The Allied air effort began at the surrounded American base at Bastogne in the center of the Bulge. The American commander of the trapped 101st Airborne Division, General Anthony MacAuliffe, had given his now famous answer of "nuts" to the German demand for surrender. So, the 116th Panzer Division had begun a siege with a systematic bombardment with 88 and 155 guns.

On Christmas morning, C-47 transport planes droned toward Bastogne. The transports of the American 439th and 440th Troop Carrier Groups—160 Gooney Birds—were loaded with supplies, ammunition, food, and other necessities for the defense of Bastogne. Even as German antiaircraft gunners sent up barrages of flak, the 116th Panzer Division troops watched in awe. These Deutschland soldiers had never seen so many transport planes in one formation. Inside the Bastogne defenses, American troops and Belgium civilians cheered as thousands of descending white parachutes floated into Bastogne.

And, as the Germans watched the falling parachutes, they suddenly heard the scream of P-51 and P-38 fighter-bombers, more than a hundred Mustangs and Lightnings from the 354th and 358th American Fighter Groups.

In a lead P-51, Colonel George Bickel of the 354th cried into his radio. "Okay, let's get those Germans. We don't want them to interfere with the air drop."

Then, one P-51 after another zoomed into the 116th Panzer Division positions, swishing high explosive rockets and laying armor piercing bombs on the enemy. Several German gun positions exploded in fragments, killing their cannoneers. Rockets raked sandbag positions of machine gun and mortar crews, and one after another the armor piercing bombs slammed into the rows of Tiger tanks that soon belched fire and smoke. Then came murderous strafing fire from .50 caliber wing guns, killing dozens of German soldiers. Within a few minutes, Colonel Bickel and his pilots had left a wake of death, destruction, and fire within the German ranks.

Then, as dazed German survivors stumbled about their macerated positions, an officer of the 116th Panzer scowled and then shouted angrily. "Where is the Luftwaffe? Where is the Luftwaffe?"

Before the officer got an answer, the whines of P-38s echoed through the clear sky. The twin engine Lightnings of the 358th Group also unleashed rockets and armor piercing shells into the holocaust created by the 354th Fighter Group. More tanks erupted in fire and smoke, more gun positions disintegrated from accurate low level rocket streams, and more troops died. Meanwhile, the C-47 Gooney Birds successfully dropped 1,500 tons of supplies into Bastogne before veering away in a long 180 degree arch to return to base.

But the attacks had not been without losses. Four of the P-38s, two of the P-51s, and eight of the C-47s fell to German anti-aircraft guns.

On Christmas afternoon, the troop carrier groups, again under escort by the 354th and 358th Fighter Groups, droned toward the beleaguered American positions in Bastogne with 1,500 more tons of supplies. This time, German fighter planes were waiting for them, and those in Bastogne as well as the German 116th Division troops got a spectator's view of an aerial dogfight between the

American fighter planes and some 47 190s under Lieutenant Colonel Erich Rudorffer and his JG 54 Green Hearts. Only one gruppe of JG 54 had arrived, for Rudorffer did not have enough fuel to mount any more planes. The young Luftwaffe pilots who had recently crowed in smug satisfaction would now get a sobering lesson in aerial warfare.

The 354th pilots had carried out more than 200 escort missions over Europe in the past year and they had counted more than 600 enemy kills by late 1944. The American pilots would now treat the young, inexperienced Luftwaffe pilots like the Americans owned them.

"Salvo bombs and prepare to meet interceptors," Colonel George Bickel said when he saw the formations of FW 190s in the distance. "Bandits ahead. They're after the Gooney Birds."

Soon, a skyfull of 100-pound armor piercing bombs tumbled from the wings of the P-51s, dropping to earth like chunks of huge confetti before exploding in thunderous, useless concussions on the cold, snowy fields beyond Bastogne. The fighter-bombers had suddenly become plain fighter planes who would dogfight this afternoon instead of attacking the 116th Panzer positions again.

"Let's go," Bickel cried into his radio, "and protect your wingmen."

"Lead the way, Colonel," Major James Howard of the 36th Squadron answered.

Soon, in pairs, the P-51s roared upward to tangle with JG 54. Lieutenant Colonel Erich Rudorffer, who wanted to hit the C-47s, soon enough saw the Mustangs far ahead of the lumbering transport planes. Now, he must take on the American fighters before he could attack the Gooney Birds. He cried into his own radio to his Green Heart pilots.

"Enemy fighter planes at six and four o'clock high. Attack in pairs! In pairs! Horrido!"

"Victor!" Major Robert Bazi Weise of II Gruppe answered.

In moments, the sound of roaring, whining planes echoed through the clear Christmas day. Soon, the sky shuttered from the chatter of machine guns and the explosions of whooshing rockets—American 40mm and German R4M. Aircraft dived, swerved, climbed, banked, and zoomed at full throttles.

"On your tail! On your tail!" Major James Howard cried.

Lieutenant Glen Eagleston reacted quickly and banked away, barely escaping the streams of rockets that whooshed past him. The modest, friendly native of Farmington, Utah, had experienced plenty of close calls during his career as a fighter pilot for the past two years. He had already flown over 50 missions and he had downed 16 planes to make him the top ace in the 9th Air Force. His best day had come on May 27, 1944 when he shot down three ME 109s while leading his flight on a mission across the Rhine to Manheim, Germany.

Now, he sighed in relief, even as Major Jim Howard came behind the unsuspecting 190 pilot and unleashed some rockets of his own. The missiles slammed into the German plane and the 190 exploded. Fragments of the Folke-Wulf tumbled to earth along with the dead pilot.

"17! 17!" Major Weise now cried into his radio. "You have two enemy fighters on your flank—

coming at three o'clock!" The young German pilot stared to his right and gaped at the two Mustangs. For a moment he stiffened in horror, unable to maneuver his machine. Major Weise then arched his FW 190 and zoomed on the attacking P-51s. Weise unloaded a half dozen rockets along with a barrage of .50 caliber machine gun fire. One of the P-51s exploded and its pieces fell to earth. The other Mustang pilot arched swiftly to the right, forgetting the FW 190 target.

"Idiot!" Weise cried into his radio. "Stay alert! Alert! I cannot come to your aid each time."

"Y-yes, Herr Major," the young Luftwaffe pilot answered.

Thus did the dogfight continue over the Bastogne area. Those on the ground stared up at the melee, watching planes explode, or spin to earth, or veer away with a wake of smoke or fire. Damaged aircraft, afire or wobbling, struggled out of the fight. More than a dozen parachutes drifted earthward, most of them carrying German pilots, the majority of whom fell into Bastogne to become American captives.

A half hour after the dogfight began, the battle was over. The Germans were outnumbered in aircraft two to one by the two American fighter groups. Further, the 354th and 358th pilots were more experienced and more confident. At 1500 hours, Leutnant Colonel Erich Rudorffer cried into his radio. "Break off! Break off and retire from engagement."

Rudorffer knew that his JG 54 had taken a beating from the American pilots. Twenty-four aircraft, half his complement, had been lost or badly damaged, while he and his own pilots had only downed nine enemy fighter planes. If the JG

54 commodore stayed here much longer, he could lose his entire gruppe.

By 1504 hours, the Green Heart survivors were zooming swiftly eastward in a tight formation. Colonel George Bickel scowled. He and his pilots of the 354th, as well as the pilots of the 358th, had enjoyed a feast. They would have loved to chase after the retreating FW 190s. But they could not pursue for their first duty was to protect the C-47 transport planes. Still Bickel could feel pride. The American pilots had driven off the Luftwaffe intruders before the German pilots could score a kill against a single C-47 Gooney Bird.

The American C-47 pilots, hanging far to the rear during the dogfight, now droned over Bastogne. At 0517 hours, hundreds of pint-sized parachutes again floated into the American positions at Bastogne—another 1,500 tons of supplies, food, medicine, and ammunition. Cheers echoed from the GIs of the 101st Division and from the Belgium civilians. Beyond Bastogne, the Germans of the 116th Panzer again looked on with sober faces. Their Luftwaffe had failed.

By the next day, December 26, the 4th and 26th American Armored Divisions would push through the shredded 116th Panzer ranks to relieve Bastogne. The effort would ignite the beginning of the end for Operation Herbstnebel.

On this same Christmas Day, some 400 9th Air Force aircraft droned eastward on a bridge busting mission. Their targets: the railroad viaduct at Ahrweiler, Germany, the highway bridge at Mayen, and the railroad bridge at Euskirchen. All were supply lines that funnelled supplies to Hasso von Manteuffel's 5th Panzer Army, whose 2nd SS Panzer Division had come within five miles of the

Muese River. In the huge mile long American air formations were 40 B-26s of the 391st Bomb Group, 30 B-26s of the 386th Group, 40 B-26s of the 387th Group, 33 B-26s of the 394th Group, 48 B-26s of the 397th Group, and 48 B-26s of Colonel John Samuels' 322nd, Nye's Annihilators. Hovering above and around them were 150 Mustang and Thunderbolt fighter planes, all out of Asche, Belgium, Colonel Norman Holt's 366th Fighter Group, along with the two attached groups from the 8th Air Force, the 352nd and 361st Fighter Groups.

When the scores of American aircraft crossed the German border, they split up into three formations. The 391st and 386th Bomb Groups headed for Ahrweiler with the 361st Fighter Group as escort. The 387th and 394th Bomb Groups headed for the highway bridge at Mayen along with escorting 352nd Fighter Group Mustangs. The 397th and 322nd headed for Euskirchen with their B-26s, with the 366th Fighter Group as escort.

The Marauders of the 391st and 386th came over Ahrweiler without a single enemy interceptor and with only minor ack ack fire, thus leaving the escorting P-51s with little to do except to loiter in the sky. Although anti-aircraft fire shot down two B-26s, the Marauders easily layed their bombs on target and knocked out the middle span of the bridge.

Meanwhile, the 387th and 394th Bomb Groups droned over Mayen to hit the important highway bridge. They were not as lucky as the B-26 units that went to Ahrweiler. The Marauders dropped to 4,000 feet and then droned over target. But as the first whistling bombs exploded along the length of spans, 25 ME 109s from JG 77, all the geschwader could mount because of gasoline shortages, jumped the Marauder formations. Within minutes, the German pilots sent four B-26s down in flames. However, the P-51 escorts, 53 Mustangs from the 352nd Fighter Group, pounced on the bandits. In moments the American fighter pilots knocked six of the 109s out of the sky, forcing the German pilots to break off their interception.

Many of the green, untested German pilots had panicked and scattered in a dozen directions, violating the critical need to stick by wingmen. American P-51 pilots chased after them, knocking six more of the 109s out of the air. The dozen remaining JG 77 pilots considered themselves lucky to escape.

Now, with the German planes driven from the sky, the Marauders droned through ack-ack fire to drop their bombs. Another B-26 fell out of the air from anti-aircraft fire, but the Marauders succeeded. By the time the last 387th and 394th plane left the target, they had knocked one span of the Mayen Bridge into the river and left a second span partially submerged in the rushing waters of the Rhine River.

Meanwhile, the 391st and 322nd Groups reached the Euskirchen railroad bridge. Colonel John Samuels, the 322nd commander, could not believe his eyes. He saw dozens of vehicles, jammed bumper to bumper, stretching across the entire four spans. "We've got a barrel of fish," Samuels cried into his radio. "We'll go in at 4,000 feet, in pairs." However, as Samuels led his Annihilators toward the bridge, the Marauder formations ran into a flight of 109s and 190s, 30 of them from the JG 2 Richthofen geschwader under Colonel Hans Assi Hahn.

Colonel Norman Holt saw the German planes coming and he cried into his radio. "Bandits at twelve o'clock. They don't look like too many. In pairs—straight ahead."

The P-47 pilots of the 366th quickly responded and zoomed swiftly eastward to deal with the enemy fighter planes. Colonel Holt himself was fully confident and he saw an opportunity for the 366th Fortune Hunters to raise their scores.

Colonel Hahn hoped to make the job difficult for the Americans. But, like so many other geschwaders, Hahn could only mount thirty planes because of the fuel shortages. The JG 2 commodore was obviously overmatched today. His thirty fighter planes would be too few against fifty-two Thunderbolts of the 366th Fighter Group and the countless gunners of nearly one hundred Marauders. Still, the JG 2 commodore tried to reach the B-26s. However, before Hahn and his Luftwaffe pilots reached the bombers, Colonel Norman Holt and his P-47 pilots were on top of him.

"Don't let the bandits get near the bombers," Holt cried into his radio. "Attack in pairs! In pairs! Stick to your wingmen."

"Lead the way, Colonel," Major George Prader cried.

Holt then arched his P-47 downward and the plane screamed like an angry falcon. In moments, the colonel opened up with a chatter of .50 caliber machine gun fire and whooshing rockets. His fire struck a 109 that had been zooming into the B-26 bombers. The Messerschmitt exploded and its pieces fell to earth.

Colonel Hahn now cried into his radio. "We must stop the enemy escorts. Two Staffel must stop the American fighter planes."

"Yeah, Colonel," Leutnant Otto Kindes cried. He led his two Staffel toward the American P-47s. In the early going, Kindes knocked one of the P-47s out of the air and Colonel Hahn knocked one of the B-26s down in flames to increase his score of kills. The B-26 simply fell like a burning rock before exploding in a ball of fire. None of the crew survived.

But the fight was really no contest. The P-47 pilots soon enough knocked down five of the 2 Staffel planes, while other T-bolt pilots shot down six of the ME 109s trying to attack the bombers. B-26 aerial gunners knocked down three more, while young, adventurous Floyd Benson shot down two planes to bring his score to sixteen kills. The Germans had lost over twenty planes, the worst slaughter yet on this Christmas day. Conversely, the Americans had only lost three P-47s and four B-26s.

Now, overwhelmed and badly beaten, Colonel Assi Hahn had no choice. He must quit the action to save the rest of his pilots and aircraft. "Break off! Break off!" he cried into his radio. "We will retire."

Moments later, the survivors of JG 2 jelled into formation and scurried eastward. Frustration and anger radiated from the round face of the usually optimistic Assi Hahn. Why couldn't they have enough fuel and enough aircraft and enough experienced pilots to deal with the American intruders? Behind the JG 2 lead flight, Leutnant Otto Kindes, leading 2 Staffel's battered formation, felt the same frustration. He had seen too many young pilots die before the experienced Mustang pilots and Kindes knew there was nothing he could do about it. And, he was most upset because JG 2 had brought out a mere handful of their more than a hundred planes for lack of gasoline, fuel that Jodl had promised so adamantly.

Despite the heavy German losses, Colonel Norman Holt would not allow his pilots to run after the limping JG 2 geschwader. "Stay with your wingmen and hang close to the bombers," he cried into his radio.

Now, the B-26s, with no further losses, droned over the railroad bridge, with Colonel John Samuels leading the way. The 322nd Group skillfully cut both the eastern and western approach spans, plopping both bridge segments into the river. Among the elated B-26 pilots was Lieutenant Ed Steinburge. He had dropped his bombs as neatly on one of the bridge spans as he had dropped the billiard ball into the corner pocket. Steinburge smiled; he would make Jim Lonely eat crow when they got back to Lille.

Then, Steinburge looked from the cabin of his Marauder and stared at the P-47s hanging next to the returning B-26 formations. Yes, he told himself, they had the means and the weather now, and they would break the back of the German offensive in Belgium.

The B-26 pilot had guessed right. The destruction of the three bridges would not only shut off supplies to the 5th Panzer Army, but the German ground troops were left with fewer means to escape eastward from Belgium. American and British armor units, inevitably, would launch a counteroffensive over the next few days. The fewer escape routes left to the Germans, the more the chances for the Allied units to snare whole divisions of Germans in a trap.

To the north, the RAF 205 flew out of Eindhoven, Holland with four squadrons of Mosquito and Typhoon bombers, along with three squadrons of Spitfire fighter planes from Evere. Captain Johnnie Johnson led the squadrons of 127 Wing Spitfires. Among all those who flew with 127 Wing, no one had charged himself as much as the sober Lieutenant George Buerling of 414 Squadron. The RAF formations from Holland and Belgium droned southward to strike German panzer columns of the north prong of Herbstnebel. Two panzer Divisions of Sepp Dietrich's 6th Panzer Army had overrun Ronzen and Monschau and the units were now driving toward Ardeene on the Muese River.

At 0900 hours, Johnson spotted two long columns of motor vehicles and panzer tanks. "There they are," the 127 Wing commander shouted into his radio. "We'll need to 'ang high and let the bombers 'it. If we don't meet interceptors, I'll give you lads permission to get in a few licks yourselves."

The anxious Spitfire pilots groaned in disappointment. These were luscious targets below, but the fighter pilots could only loiter in the sky while the Mosquitos and Typhoons roared in pairs over the enemy columns, laying a staccato of armor piercing rockets and bombs on the Germans. A length of fire and smoke soon erupted through the columns as the RAF aircraft riddled the exposed panzer divisions.

Then, suddenly the roar of 190s: 40 FWs roared toward the RAF attackers to break up the assaults on the German columns. Johnnie Johnson cried into his radio. "Jerrys at twelve and two o'clock—

high. Wingmen 'ang close."

The Spitfires jelled into pairs, banked and then arched upward to meet the 190s. In moments, another melee ensued over Belgium. And, once more, the odds were too high and there were too many inexperienced German pilots.

George Buerling got on the tail of a pair of Folke-Wulfs and cried to his wingman over his radio. "Stover, hang close while I get me a couple of Jerrys." Buerling unleashed a half dozen rockets and streams of chattering machine gun fire. His accurate fire blew apart the first 190 and the second FW tried to arch away. Wingman Charles Stover sent a stream of his own rockets at the fleeing plane and the 190 exploded. Its fragments tumbled earthward.

Captain Johnson himself zoomed down on an unsuspecting 190 pilot and caught the German fighter plane in the fusilage with two rockets that blew the plane in half. Both portions dropped to earth like distorted rocks. "Stay close, stay close," Johnson cried to his wingman. "There's a lot more of those Jerrys around."

Within five minutes, the dogfight was over. The Spitfires of 127 Wing had knocked down twenty German planes of JG 3 to a loss of two Spitfires. The harsh British fighter plane attack, outnumbering the Germans more than three to one, had stopped the German JG 3 Udets from downing a single Typhoon or Mosquito.

As the mauled JG 3 broke off the fight and fled, Colonel Gunther Lutzow cursed under his breath. He had downed one of the Spitfires, but the kill was small consolation. His worse fears had materialized. The skies had cleared of dense clouds and now the skies were dense with Allied aircraft.

When the surviving German fighter planes were gone, Johnnie Johnson cried into his radio. "Okay, lads, you can take a bit of a punch yourselves now at those Jerry columns below."

Soon, the Spitfires were also roaring over the German columns, whooshing unspent rockets into the trucks, gun carriers, and tanks. Chattering machine gun fire raked German troops who tried to escape the holocaust. By the time the 205 and 127 Wings were gone, devastation remained. The two crippled panzer divisions would never reach the Muese. In fact, they would become easy prey for the British 6th Airborne Division under Sir Bryan Burrocks. The Tommies could come down from Mastricht in northeast Belgium and finish the job on the German units, killing or capturing the survivors of the two panzer divisions before most of them could retreat out of Belgium.

The RAF's 122 Wing out of Vokel, Holland, sent five full squadrons of Spitfires to the Monschau-Echborn area to rake German supply columns with murderous rocket and strafing fire. The British left a mile long column of burning vehicles and flaming railroad boxcars in their wake. Lieutenant Peter Hearne and F/O Bob Weighill, out of any real action for weeks, had finally found themselves a fat target. The pilots of 19 Squadron expended almost every rocket and every round of ammunition. In fact, 122 Wing completed some 340 sorties on this Christmas day, knocking out 80 boxcars, 170 trucks, and 36 armored vehicles. Lieutenant Hearne and his debonair 19 Squadron pilots would have cause to celebrate on this Christmas night.

More 9th Air Force and 2nd Air Force units also went out on Christmas day to cut up panzer and

Wehrmacht units that had made such spectacular gains in the past eight days. American fighter-bombers struck German units in the Marche-St. Vith area with battering rocket, bomb, and strafing fire. They decimated the Germans so badly that newly arrived 3rd and 9th American Division units forced the Germans into full retreat. Other P-51 and P-47 fighter-bomber units struck roads and rail points at Nohfelden, destroying more than one hundred motor vehicles and some twenty panzer tanks.

On the late afternoon of December 27, 1,430 heavy bombers of the 8th Air Force, with an escort of 736 fighter planes, droned over the German air fields at Rheim, Wesel, Merzhausen, and Badenheisen. Runways at all five bases became lengths of deep craters. Buildings burned and collapsed. The attackers also destroyed fifty planes on the ground and damaged fifty more. Then, in the dead of night, while Luftwaffe West commodores reeled from the daylight misfortunes, 485 RAF heavy bombers droned over Western Germany from England to smash the railroad and marshaling yards at Koblenz to seriously deprive the 5th Panzer army of more help.

On the morning of December 28, the 9th Air Force launched a total of 1,391 fighter-bomber sorties that blasted more German motor and tank columns all the way from Monschau to St. Vith, and from Stavelot to Prum. Near St. Vith alone, P-51s of the 373rd Fighter Group destroyed 170 motor vehicles, six armored vehicles and 57 tanks. More medium and light bombers, B-25s, B-26s, and A-26s smashed German communications at LaRoche and at Houffalize. By noon time, American bombers had conducted a staggering total of 2,243 sorties. 667 medium U.S. bombers had unleashed 1,277 tons of bombs on bridges, railheads, road junctions, defended positions, and defended buildings. The fighter-bombers had destroyed 690 German motor vehicles, 703 tanks, 301 railroad cars, and 131 gun positions; and they had made 31 road cuts and 69 railroad cuts.

By the afternoon of December 28, the 2nd SS Panzer Division, only five miles from the Muese River had ground to a halt for lack of gasoline and supplies, thanks to the massive air assaults by the Allied air forces during the past four days. Now, American armored divisions were closing a ring around the ill fated 2nd SS Panzer. To the south, Colonel Jochen Peiper found himself cut off within six miles of his goal at Marche. He could only move about in stunned disbelief. How could his fortunes have changed so dramatically in four days?

Air power! Real air power; overwhelming air power had shattered the German offensive during these four days and the German dreams of renewed glory. The Allied air force, further, had unlimited supplies of fuel while the German air units and ground units found themselves almost out of fuel.

Reports filtering into Field Marshal Walter Model's headquarters told of thousands of vehicles, including tanks, standing bumper-to-bumper and waiting to retreat eastward. Thousands of Wehrmacht soldiers also struggled through the cold to reach safety before hordes of advancing Allied ground troops from every part of France, Belgium, and Holland. The Allied air forces had cut supply lines, roads, towns, and railheads, threatening to leave thousands of infantry and panzer troops stranded in Belgium to die or surrender.

General Richard Metz, chief of staff of the 5th Panzer Army, sent an urgent report to Field Marshal Model. "The Allied air attacks are too powerful. Every road is clogged. Not even a motorcycle can find room to move. We have no ammunition, no food, and no gasoline. I am not sure we will ever escape from Belgium."

"I will talk to the Luftwaffe," Model answered. Model immediately called General Dietrich Peltz, but got a discouraging reply.

"We have been overwhelmed," Peltz said. "We have lost 271 aircraft during these recent air battles and from the Allied air attacks on our bases. Also, we have no gasoline. We simply do not have the means to help you."

"General Peltz," Model said somberly, "if the Luftwaffe does not do something, I could lose the entire Army Group B. Already, we have lost 100,000 men killed, wounded, and captured. Surely, we must do something to save the other 200,000 brave German troops. They cannot possibly escape if the Allied air forces continue to destroy bridges, roads, and railheads; and if they continue to attack our columns of men, tanks, and motor vehicles."

"I will see what can be done," Peltz said.

Then, by the evening of December 28, the dense clouds and thick fog closed over Western Europe, stopping at least temporarily the horrendous Allied aerial attacks for the past four days. The respite gave General Dietrich Peltz time to "see what could be done."

Peltz, from an idea of Herman Goring himself, now came up with a daring plan to save Army Group B, a plan called Operation Bodenplatte.

Chapter Six

By mid morning of December 29, Field Marshal Gerd von Rundstedt met at his headquarters in Osnabruck with Field Marshal Walter Model, General Hasso von Mantueffel, General Sepp Dietrich, General Ernst Brandenberger, General Dietrich Peltz, General Adolph Galland, and the Reichmarshal himself—Herman Goring.

"Gentlemen," von Rundstedt began, "in the past twelve hours, neither General Peltz, Field Marshal Model, the Reichmarshal, nor myself has enjoyed a wink of sleep. These hours were among the busiest hours I can ever recall. We must now admit that Operation Herbstnebel has failed. Unfortunately, the clearing weather enabled the Anglo-Saxons to mount superior numbers of aircraft to badly hurt our ground troops in the Belgium battle. Our problem now is to extricate our brave soldiers who are in danger of annihilation."

"Many of the highways, railroads, and bridges have been damaged or destroyed," Field Marshal Model said. "The suffering men of Army Group B are now threatened with death or capture unless they can escape advancing American and British forces. Unless we can gain a respite from Allied air power, the enemy air forces will surely take a terrible toll on our retreating columns."

"At the moment," Peltz now spoke, "inclement weather again covers the Western Front to forestall new massive Allied air sorties. But, when the weather clears, as it surely will, our thousands of soldiers in Belgium face destruction from superior enemy air forces." Peltz looked at Herman Goring and then looked at some papers in his hand. "We have a chance. The Reichmarshal and I, with the approval of Field Marshal von Rundstedt and Field Marshal Model, have drawn up a plan."

"What plan?" Adolph Galland asked.

"A plan we have code named Operation Bodenplatte," Peltz said, "since the plan involves a surprise attack on the Allied airfields. The Reichmarshal himself conceived the idea."

"An attack on the Allied airfields?" Galland huffed. "The idea is incredible."

"Such an air operation may save the bulk of Army Group B," Model said.

Galland squeezed his face irritably. He felt little compassion for Model since he had opposed the Ardenne offensive in the first place, and felt certain that such a strategy was doomed to failure. Further, Galland was somewhat piqued with Model who never considered air power more than a mere support arm in war. Model had been a product of the old Prussian school that believed war strategy entailed land battles: the movement of armies, tanks, and artillery. Model believed in captured bridges, wrested road junctions, and occupied cities. Model, in fact, would have been perfectly content to leave aircraft out of Operation Herbstnebel and let the two land armies decide the issue.

Galland also felt cool toward the field marshal, because Model had been a close supporter of Hitler and, like the Führer, Model had not shied away from military gambles. Since he had won the respect of Hitler, Model was one of the few men with any influence on the Führer, and Model had convinced Hitler to pull the troops out of Belgium, rather than lose them. Hitler had apparently conceded that Operation Herbstnebel had failed.

Now, ironically, Model called on the Luftwaffe to save his defeated land armies, for there was no where else to turn.

"We have been assured, Herr Galland," Model said, "that you will get all the replacement aircraft and pilots you will need to carry out the plan devised by General Peltz and the Reichmarshal. General Jodl further promises to furnish Luftwaffe West with all the fuel it will need for this operation."

However, Galland was unimpressed. Jodl had also promised all the fuel they would need for Operation Herbstnebel. Yet, after the initial December 16 assaults by Luftwaffe West, most air units were already short of supplies and by Christmas the German air units could only mount limited aircraft, and then, only by taking the most restrictive measures.

Galland remembered his conversation only yesterday with Major Robert Weise of JG 54 in Badenheisen.

"Herr General," Weise had told Galland, "how could we deal with the massive Allied counterstrikes with our lack of fuel? We did not deal with combat strategies, but with subterfuge in trying to obtain gasoline. After the mid-December strikes I was forced to send my trucks on constant journeys to pick up 200 gallons of gasoline here, another 500 gallons there, and perhaps 300 more somewhere else. We forged requisitions, forged names, or used any other ruses to obtain fuel. Other geschwaders did the same thing. And, when trucks finally brought us all the gasoline they could, we often did not have enough fuel for a single gruppe operation."

During the same tour, Galland had stopped at Wesel, where Captain Werner Specht had made similar complaints. "Only a week after we began Operation Herbstnebel, we had practically no more fuel. We used horses and oxen to drag our aircraft to take off points and back to revetment areas after the aircraft landed. I issued orders to all my ground crews to spend minimum time on preflighting engines, and I have instructed my pilots to shut down engines as soon as their aircraft touch down on the runway. Even in these most stringent circumstances to conserve fuel, we have gasoline now for perhaps a single staffel to make two or three sorties."

Remembering these comments from his air officers, Galland glared at Model. "Field Marshal, we had nowhere near the fuel we should have had for Operation Herbstnebel. And, when the Allied air forces struck back, we did not have enough gasoline to send out more than half of our available aircraft to oppose them."

"I assure you, Herr Galland," Herman Goring suddenly spoke, "the Führer himself has approved this plan and he himself has promised that you will get all the fuel you need. The Führer has assured us that nothing will be spared to give us what we need for this operation." He then handed some papers to the 1st Fighter Corps Commodore. "Adolph, I would like you to read this plan yourself."

Galland glanced quickly through the several sheafs of paper and then gaped at Herman Goring. "This plan is insane! Totally insane! We do not have the means for such an operation. Do you realize how many airbases the Allies have?"

"You will have ample means," Goring insisted. "I have been assured by General Jodl that two million gallons of gasoline will be available for aircraft since the Führer has ordered this fuel allocation. You will also have more pilots and many new aircraft, including more jet fighters and bombers. You will also have an additional 15,000 tons of ammunition and bombs."

"Even if we had all you say," Galland said, "We could not carry out this plan. The Allies have a strong web of radar installations, along with good warning systems at their airfields themselves. They would have swarms of fighters pouncing on our formations before we came anywhere near their airbases."

Now, General Peltz grinned. "Adolph, our agents have done a remarkable job of pinpointing every Allied radar site in Europe. We have only to mark out a careful route to avoid these radar units. We will use Colonel Streib's NJG JU 88 units. The pilots and navigators of these units are the best in the German Air Force. Streib has assured us that his JU 88 crews can map out a route to avoid the Allied radar systems and the Allied airbase warning systems."

General Adolph Galland did not answer.

"Herr Galland," Field Marshal Model said, "this proposed Operation Bodenplatte represents our only chance to save Army Group B."

"Why was I not consulted?" Galland barked. "This is the second time I was ignored on a planned air operation."

"There was no time," Field Marshal von Rundstedt said, looking hard at the 1st Fighter Corps commodore. "Believe me, Herr Galland, if we had time, I would have insisted that you be present. But, you have the commendable habit of always being in the field to encourage and help your combat fliegers. We brought you here as soon as we could locate you. Please forgive us, General, and please believe me when I say we earnestly need your cooperation for this plan to succeed."

Galland nodded, softening his irate countenance.

"You have no idea, Herr Galland, how badly we have suffered from the massive Allied air attacks for four days," General von Manteuffel suddenly spoke. "Six of my 5th Army divisions are trying to cross the Our and Saur Rivers. There are traffic jams for miles west of these rivers. If the skies clear, American and British air units may destroy thousands of good German soldiers as one destroys dense colonies of ants. Surely you must feel a sympathy for my soldiers as you do for your fliegers."

"Of course," Galland said.

"Manteuffel speaks the truth," General Brandenberger said. "The same situation prevails to the south with our 7th Army. Many bridges, railheads, and roads have been cut. I have four divisions isolated. We cannot get supplies to them and we cannot untangle the jammed columns of vehicles and foot soldiers to retire out of Belgium. If the Allied air forces destroy all means of escape, these fine German soldiers could be exterminated, not only by the Allied air forces but also by the Allied ground forces who have now joined the battle."

Adolph Galland shook his head. "You have seen what happened to our Luftwaffe over the past few days. In not a single instance could our geschwaders mount enough aircraft to stop Allied bomber and fighter attacks on our troops, supplies, and communications. We simply do not have enough aircraft and fuel, and too many of our pilots are inexperienced. We cannot compete with the thousands of trained Allied airmen and the thousands of planes in the enemy's ranks." No one answered Galland and he tapped the sheafs of paper in his hand. "What you propose here could destroy whatever is left of Luftwaffe West."

"Yes, it is a gamble," General Peltz said, "but a gamble we must take. Adolph, whatever dangers lie in these plans cannot compare to the peril facing Army Group B, especially if the Allies strike again as they did for the four day Christmas period."

Galland pursed his lips. "What you say is true, Dietrich, but still—"

"Our fliegers will not balk, I'm sure of that," Dietrich Peltz said, "and remember this, Adolph," he gestured, "we were very successful in the initial phase of the Herbstnebel Operation. Why? Because we surprised the Allies. Only when they recovered from the shock did they react. I believe this proposed Operation Bodenplatte will be even more surprising to them. By the time the Allies recover from this strong blow, perhaps the bulk of Army Group B can escape swiftly from Belgium." He leaned close to Galland. "Would you want another Stalingrad on the Western Front, Adolph?"

"No, no, of course not," Galland said. "All right, I will help however I can with this plan."

"Thank you, Herr Galland," Field marshal Model said. "I am in your debt."

Adolph Galland merely nodded. He knew he had no choice.

Herman Goring widened his moon face with a grin and tapped Galland on the shoulder. "Adolph, your willingness to help in this endeavor will assure success. I would like this operation conducted as soon as every available aircraft on the Western Front can be loaded and ready. I leave the details to you and to General Peltz."

"Whatever you do," Field Marshal von Rundstedt gestured, "if you save one company of men, one tank, one gun, one box of supplies, or one loaded vehicle, we will have something with which to defend the Fatherland from our enemies."

Galland nodded again.

"Good," von Rundstedt grinned, a rare phenomenona for his perpetually sober face.

Still, Galland felt uneasy when he scanned again the sheets in his hand, for Operation Bodenplatte was indeed a daring plan. The operation called for the destruction of all Allied airbases in Western Europe, a massive knockout blow that would stop the Allied air forces from launching any air attacks against German ground units of Army Group B, while the dozens of panzer and Wehrmacht divisions escaped back to Germany. Herman Goring, who seldom conceived an intelligent idea, was initially responsible for this plan. He had met at once with von Rundstedt, Model, and Peltz at Osnabruck to offer the strategy. Von Rundstedt and Model had been delighted with the idea and Peltz believed that Luftwaffe West could pull it off—if they got the needed fuel and supplies. These leaders had then brought in the other leaders for consultation. Before they could find Galland, they had completed their initial planning.

Despite rumors to the contrary, the Germans had plenty of agents in Allied occupied Europe, and German reconnaissance planes had been quite active over Europe. So, the Germans knew the locations and general complement of aircraft at every Allied airbase, 11 British and 17 American. The British had three bases in Holland: 205 Wing at Eindhoven, 116 Wing in Tilburg, and 122 Fighter Wing in Volkel. The eight RAF bases in Belgium included three bases around Brussels that housed the Polish Volunteer Wing, the RAF 137 Wing, and the RAF 127 Wing that included the Canadian squadrons. The 121 Wing of Mosquito bombers was in Ghent, two tactical bomber units were in Melsbroek and Westem along the North Sea coast outside of Ostend. The 114 Wing was at Antwerp, and the 116 Wing was at Hasselt with light bombers.

The Americans maintained 9th Air Force units at Lille, Cambrai, and St. Dizier in northern France that were under the jurisdiction of Air Marshal Leigh-Malloy's 2nd Tactical Air Force. The 9th also maintained fighter groups at four Belgium bases: the 363rd, 373rd and 36th Fighter Groups at Leculot; the 370th, 371st, and 474th Fighter Groups at the sprawling base in Florennes; the 48th and 404th Fighter Groups at St.

Trond; and the 366th Fighter Group with its two attached 8th Air Force fighter groups at Asche.

In France, a reconn and bomb group were based at Juvincourt, while four bomb groups were based at the huge airfield in Coulimers. Single bomb groups were at Bretigny and Chautedon. In central France, three bomb groups were at Melvun, and two troop carrier groups were at Ciastres and Conflans. Three more French bases housed two fighter groups at Toul, the 354th Fighter Group at Orcante, and the 365th Fighter Group at Frescaty, outside of Metz.

In the scattered air bases of Western Europe, the Allies based more than 2,500 combat aircraft. The Luftwaffe would indeed need a herculean effort to knock out all twenty-eight Allied bases and their hundreds of aircraft. Galland and Peltz decided at once that they would probably need to ignore some of the smaller bases that only housed single groups or were too remote to interfere with troop withdrawals from Belgium.

The two Luftwaffe West generals worked during the remainder of December 29 and into the next day, December 30. Herman Goring, as soon as the meeting at Osnabruck had ended, immediately ordered the shipment of arms to all gruppens in Luftwaffe West: R4M rockets, SC spitterbombs, MG 1000-pound demolition bombs, and TSC incendiary bombs that could cause destruction and fire within a fifty-seven feet radius. He also ordered endless boxes of .50 caliber machine gun belts. The arms were expected to reach all units before Galland and Peltz finished their detailed planning.

Galland and Peltz took a quick survey of their resources. Since the advent of Operation Herbstnebel, and especially for the four days of clear weather, Luftwaffe West had taken a bad beating and most of the geschwader ranks were quite depleted.

General Beppo Schmidt's Jagdivision IX at Ostheim had been hit hard in the B-17 air raids. The two attack bomber units, SG 4 and SG 20 had a mere ninety operable 110s left for service. At the suggestion of Goring, and despite their reluctance, Peltz and Galland agreed to accept twenty-seven ME 110s of I/JG 104, a training unit, for Operation Bodenplatte. Goring ordered I/JG 104 to fly immediately to Furth, a small base near Ostheim. Schmidt did have his KG 7 and KG 51 jet units still pretty well intact at Aschner, twenty-five AR 234s and seventy-one ME 262s, although six of the 262s were unfit for duty. JG's 26, 54, and 77 had a total of 216 planes.

Adolph Galland took a count in his own Jagbabschmidt Mittelrheim. JG 2 had suffered badly between losses on interceptor duty and by attacks from the American heavy bombers at Rheims. The geschwader had lost a whopping 54 aircraft, and a mere 60 FW 190s remained between JG 2s two gruppen. JG 4 was down to 58 serviceable aircraft after losses during the 8th Air Force heavy bomb attack on Rheims, and the three gruppen of JG 11 and 115 109s and 190s left after bad interceptor sorties and destruction by 8th Air Force B-17s. JG 27 had lost 16 of its aircraft in futile interceptor sorties for three days and they were down to 51 serviceable 109s. JG 53 was down to 46 serviceable FW 190s after losses in dogfights with American P-51s.

Oberst Colonel Wilheim Moritz of Jagdivision 3 took a survey of his own units. Moritz's JG 1 was down to a mere fifty-two 190s after the Allied bombing attack on Wesel and after the losses against American fighter planes. JG 3 was down to sixty 190s after the air attacks and after the unsuccessful fights with P-47s in the attempt to stop the 322nd Bomb Group's attack on the Euskirchen Bridge. JG 6, the famed Horst Wesel attack geschwader, still had 133 of its ME 110 attack bombers.

Colonel Werner Streib, commodore of the 1st Nachtkorpst that who had moved west for Operation Bodenplatte, had suffered the least with his night fighter planes. His NJG 4 at Lichtenseim had forty-eight 110s and his NJG 9 at the same base had forty JU 88s. Streib did not know how useful these night tactic aircraft would be on daylight sorties. Streib also had fifty JU 88s in the NJG 101 which he proposed to use as pathfinders for Operation Bodenplatte.

"Please prepare the night fighters also," General Peltz told Streib. "We will need every aircraft that can carry bombs and rockets."

"I would need a few days to acclimate the night fighter airmen to prepare themselves for day operations," Colonel Streib said.

"Colonel," Peltz said, "Major Schnaufer commands those 110s of NJG 4, does he not?"

"Yes."

"With Schnaufer in charge of the crews, you will need no more than a few hours. Tell him to prepare his 110s for day operations at once and he will be back to you by dusk to tell you that he and his crews are ready."

"You are a sly one, Herr Peltz," Streib said. "I will speak to him."

If RAF airmen knew anybody in the Luftwaffe,

they knew Major Heinz Wolfgang Schnaufer. The twenty-three-year-old German Air Force pilot had more nerve and stamina than any airman alive. When the British began their regular night time bombing raids over Europe in late 1942, the Luftwaffe had faced the severe problem of finding good night fighter interceptor pilots. Most pilots wanted no part of the nerve-wracking night duty, where you often became a victim of your own anti-aircraft guns. Most night pilots needed arm twisting persuasion, and sometimes a commodore assigned a flieger to NJG staffels as punishment for some infraction.

But Schnaufer had volunteered freely for night service.

No one had regretted Schnaufer's choice more than the RAF night bomber crews. The strikingly handsome, powerfully built, dark haired German pilot had joined Captain Helmut Lent's NJG 1 at St. Trond, Belgium, in the fall of 1942. The unit had conducted interceptor missions against the swarms of Lancasters and Mosquito bombers that droned over France and Belgium before reaching Germany. Within a month, Schnaufer had shot down 17 Lancasters, and within a year his score had reached 97. Before the war ended, Schnaufer would get his 121st night time kill, an incredible statistic.

British airmen had called Schnaufer the "night ghost of St. Trond." A ghost he was, for who but a ghost could knock down so many Lancasters and Mosquitos without getting shot down himself? Because of Schnaufer's astonishing effort, Air Marshal Harris had offered a Victoria Cross to any RAF flyer who brought down the Ghost of St. Trond. No British flyer ever did.

In September of 1944 the British captured St. Trond. In October, on the anniversary of the ghost's first kill of an RAF night bomber, RAF airmen held a birthday party for the unknown as yet Ghost of St. Trond. Such was the British respect for Heinz Wolfgang Schnaufer.

When Colonel Werner Streib asked Schnaufer if he could prepare his NJG 4 for a daylight mission, the major answered soberly: "It makes no difference to me whether I strike our enemies by day or by night. I will call my crews and by the time you have our aircraft armed with bombs and rockets, we shall be ready." Then, Schnaufer called on his two ME 110 crewmen, Gunner Fritz Rumpelhardt and Radio man Wilheim Gaenstle. "We must prepare our geschwader for a day mission. I want you to find the oberst and unter fliegers as well as all warts of this geschwader. They are to report to the briefing barracks within a half hour."

"Yes, Mein Major," Sergeant Rumpelhardt said.

Flight crews and ground crews moved at once when Sergeants Rumpelhardt and Gaenstle relayed the message from the NJG 4 commodore. No man dared balk or lag when Schnaufer called. The old Ghost of St. Trond was not only a determined and aggressive flyer, but also a stern, no nonsense commodore. He maintained strict discipline in his geschwader and no JG commodore got more respect from his men, except perhaps for Colonel Gunther Lutzow.

Throughout December 29–30 the Germans continued their preparations for Operation Bodenplatte. Loaded freight trains and truck convoys streamed through the foggy weather, under low hanging clouds, all through the daylight hours of

December 29 and into the night. By midnight, bombs, rockets, munitions, and other supplies had reached their destination at a dozen Western airbases. By this same midnight hour of December 29, engineers and laborers had repaired the runways at Rheims, Ostheim, Wesel, and Badenheisen; they had also carted away damaged or destroyed aircraft. By the morning of December 30, every combat ready aircraft, 109s, 190s, 110s, and jets, were ready for loading. Galland had designated some gruppen as potential escort aircraft. They would salvo their bombs to protect the fighter-bombers in the event of interception by Allied fighter planes.

Alternate schwarms (four plane formations) in each staffel would carry four spitterbombs and twenty-four high explosive R4M rockets, while the next schwarm carried four TSC incendiary bombs along with twenty-four R4M rockets. Some staffels and even entire gruppen would carry two MG 1,000 pound demolition bombs to chop up runways. The heavier twin engine 110s would carry four MG bombs for demolishing runways.

By the afternoon of December 30, Peltz and Galland had determined that they could count on some 1,130 aircraft for the mission, including some 90 jets and some 300 of the heavier ME 110s. The two generals worked with Luftwaffe West staff, all of whom had come to Peltz's headquarters in Ostheim. These leaders in turn would carry instructions back to their geschwaders.

General Peltz had invited to the top briefing Colonel Wilheim Moritz, commodore of Jagdivision 3 and Colonel Werner Streib of the 1st Nachtkorps night fighter wing. Both Moritz and Streib had served in the Luftwaffe for more than five years and both had grown into inspiring leaders. Moritz had taken command of Jagdivision 3 some three months ago to direct tactical support strikes against the British in Holland and Belgium. Streib had been with the night fighters for nearly two years and had won command of the 1st Nachtkorps earlier this year.

"We should send our heavier aircraft to the major bases at Eindhoven, Ghent, Coulimiers, St. Dizier, and Florennes," Pelt told the assembled commodores. "SG 4 may go to Coulimiers, SG 104 to St. Dizier, and SG 20 to Florennes. I would like the 110s of the JG 6 Horst Wesel geschwader to hit the British bases."

"I will send the JG 6 gruppens to these British bases," Colonel Moritz said. "JG 6 has 133 ME 110 attack bombers. Half will go to Eindhoven and half to Ghent."

"I would suggest that the KG 7 jet planes strike Volkel," Peltz said. "JG 77 can strike the British Typhoon bomber base at Antwerp and JG 1 can make the long flight to strike the bases at Westem and Melsbroek near Ostend on the North Sea coast. The JG 26 gruppen can strike the British bases around Brussels and the JG 54 units can strike the American bases in Belgium. General Schmidt's KG 51 jet bombers can strike the British base at Tilberg."

"Good," Moritz said.

Peltz now looked at Galland. "And what of your geschwaders, Adolph?"

"The gruppen of JG 2 will strike the American base at Lille," Galland said. JG 4 will attack the American base at Chateudon and JG 11 will strike the American bases at Bretigny and Juvincourt. I will send JG 27 to strike the American base at

Cambrai and JG 53 to strike the American fighter base at Frescaty, outside of Metz. Perhaps we can send JG 3 to the American bomber base at Melvun.

"Fine," Peltz nodded before he looked at Colonel Werner Streib. "Colonel, since your units are not accustomed to daylight attacks, they can strike the American transport bases at Conflans and Ciastres."

"Both Major Wohlers of NJG 9 and Major Schnaufer of NJG 4 have assured me that their crews can perform as well in daylight as at night," Colonel Streib said. "Still, I am not so certain. So it is best that the NJG units attack transport aircraft that cannot strike back."

"I would also ask that your NJG 101 be the eyes for our mission," General Peltz said. "We have planned to leave our bases and rendezvous in four columns, one for the bases in Holland and Antwerp, another for the bases in Belgium, a third for the bases in northern France, and the last for the bases in central France. I would like to assign a JU 88 as a pathfinder for each gruppe and two JU 88s as pathfinders for each of the four fliegercorps. Do you have enough Junkers for this?"

"We have fifty of them and that should suffice."

"I will ask Colonel Moritz to lead Fliegercorps Holland himself and I will ask Colonel Priller to lead Fliegercorps Belgium. Is that all right, Adolph?"

"Fine," Galland nodded. "Colonel Priller is a capable leader."

"Beppo," Peltz now looked at Schmidt, "I would ask that my own deputy, Colonel Wolfgang Falch lead Fliegercorps North to strike the American bases in Northern France. And you, Colonel," he looked at Streib, "You would do us an honor if you lead Fliegercorps South to strike the American bases in central France."

"I will not fail you, Herr Peltz," the 1st Nacktkorps commodore said.

"As soon as we have made enough copies of Operation Bodenplatte, you will all return to your units to work out details with gruppen commodores," Peltz said. "We have already notified gruppen commodores and geschwader commodores where they are to meet with the four fliegercorps commandos. Colonel Streib, be sure to assign your JU 88 pilots and navigators at once to the various gruppen and fliegercorps so they can participate in the briefings of their assigned units."

"I will do so as soon as I have copies of the operation," Streib said.

Peltz now looked at his watch. "It is time for the evening meal. I will give these operation orders to my clerks and ask them to make them up immediately. They should have them ready when dinner is over."

So, the plan was completed. Luftwaffe West would now take a daring gamble. Fliegercorps Holland under Colonel Wilheim Moritz would include I/JG 6 to hit Eindhoven, KG 7 to hit Volkel, JG 1 to hit Melsbroek and Westem near the North Sea, JG 77 to hit Antwerp, and KG 51 to hit Tilberg.

Fliegercorps Belgium under Colonel Josef Priller would include the JG 26 gruppen to hit Evere, Duerne, and Grimbergen, the RAF bases around Brussels. JG 54s three gruppen would strike LeCulot, St. Trond, and Asche. II/JG 6 would hit Ghent.

Fliegercorps North under Colonel Wolfgang

Falck included SG 20 to hit Florennes, JG 27 to hit Cambrai, JG 2 to hit Lille, SG 4 to strike Coulimiers, and SG 104 to hit St. Dizier.

Fliegercorps South under Colonel Werner Streib included JG 4 to hit Chateudon, JG 11s two gruppens to hit Juvincourt and Bretigny, JG 3 to hit Melvun, JG 53 to hit Frescaty, near Metz, while NJG 9 and NJG 4 would attack the American transport air groups at Conflans and Ciastres.

The massive air attack would miss only three of the Allies' twenty-eight bases, the British base at Hasselt, the 354th American Fighter Group base at Orcante, and the American fighter plane base at Toul. But Luftwaffe West simply could not hit them all.

By 2100 hours on the evening of December 30, each staff member had copies of Operation Bodenplatte. They would hurry back to their headquarters and call for briefings early in the morning. On this same evening of December 30, General Peltz, OKL of Luftwaffe West, sent the following directive to all units:

> Luftwaffe West will conduct a very important multiple strike on January 1, 1945, an appropriate New Year's gift to our enemies. Take off times will vary with each gruppe since all units will strike simultaneously at a variety of targets. You will begin loading aircraft at once, as soon as bombs, rockets, and ammunition arrive at your airbase. Alternate Schwarms will carry 4 SC spitterbombs and 24 R4M rockets, with other swarms carrying 4 TSC incendiary bombs and 24 R4M rockets. At

least one staffel from each gruppe will carry two MG 1,000 pound bombs, with ME 110s carrying four MG 1,000 pound bombs. All aircraft will carry fully loaded .50 caliber strafing belts.

The commodores of I/JG 6, JG 77, JG 1, KG 7, and KG 51 will report to a briefing with Colonel Wilheim Moritz at Eschborn by 1100 hours, December 31, commodores of II/JG 6, JG 26, and JG 54 will report to Colonel Josef Priller at Verrelbusch at this same hour. Commodores of SG 20, JG 27, JG 2, SG 4, and SG 104 will report to Osthem by 1100 hours, December 31, to meet with Oberst Colonel Wolfgang Falck. Commodores of JG 4, JG 11, JG 3, JG 53, NJG 9, and NJG 4 will report to Lichtenseim to meet with Colonel Werner Streib. If any geschwader or gruppen commodore cannot make his briefing, he will send a designated officer in his place.

At the JG 26 base in Verrelbusch, Colonel Josef Pips Priller read the directive with surprise. "I am to lead several geschwaders," he frowned, looking at one of his gruppe leaders, Major Peter Eder. "What is this all about? What kind of gift would Herr Peltz like us to give our enemies on New Years Day?"

"I don't know," Major Peter Eder answered, "but tomorrow you will find out."

Chapter Seven

On the morning of December 31, at the JG 26 base in Verrelbusch, Colonel Josef "Pips" Priller prepared his aircraft. He did not know yet the details of Operation Bodenplatte. Of all the German air units assigned to Luftwaffe West, none had begun with more aircraft than JG 26, eighty-four 109s and one hundred eighteen 190s. Further, no unit had more capable leaders: Major Anton Hakl of II Gruppe and Major Peter Eder of I Gruppe. Colonel Priller himself usually led IV Gruppe. The geschwader's III Gruppe served on the Eastern Front.

JG 26 was probably the most famous air unit in the German Air Force. Known as the Schlageters (sluggers), JG 26 had done more damage during the Battle of Britain in 1940 than did any other Luftwaffe geschwader. The British called them the Abbeville Boys, for JG 26 had operated out of Abbeville, France, for more than three years, from 1940 through 1943. The Abbeville Boys had thus far in the war knocked down more than 3,000 Allied aircraft over England and Europe.

Some of the greatest flyers in the German Air Force had served with JG 26: Captain Friedrich Geisshardt, who shot down 102 French and British planes before Spitfire pilots shot him down in June of 1943; Hauptman Emil Long, who shot down 117 aircraft before enemy pilots killed him in March of 1943; Leutnant Alfred Gross, 52 victories before a P-38 pilot killed him in the fall of 1944; Captain Hugo Dahmer, 56 kills and then death in the summer of 1944; the famed Major Joachim Muencheberg, with 135 air victories before Allied pilots shot him down; and Leutnant Waldsmer Radener, who shot down 36 four engine Allied bombers, a record, before P-51 pilots finally shot him down in the fall of 1944. The list of honored aces with the Schlageters goes on and on.

Many of the famed German pilots still living had served with the Schlageters: the renowned Adolph Galland, now in command of the 1st Fighter Corps; the famed Major Walter Krupinski, a Knights Cross winner with Oak Leaf, already with 197 enemy kills, and currently the commodore of JG 52 on the Russian Front; three time Great Cross winner Captain Heinz Kemethmueller, with 90 confirmed kills, and now commanding a staffel in Fliegercorps Reich.

Among the current assigned personnel of JG 26 were several German aces. Priller himself had shot down 101 enemy aircraft, including 30 four engine bombers and he had already won two Knights Crosses and an Iron Cross. Major Peter Eder, commodore of I Gruppe, had already scored 70 victories, including 26 four-engine bombers. He held two Knights Crosses and an Iron Cross. One of the greatest living aces, Major Anton Hakl, commanded II Gruppe. Hakl had won Three Knights Crosses, with some 190 enemy kills, including 32 Allied four-engine bombers.

Colonel Josef "Pips" Priller, only 150 pounds

and a mere five feet, two inches tall, had risen far above his physical stature. Fellow pilots had dubbed him Pips early in his career because of his small height, and Priller himself had pulled strings to join the Luftwaffe in 1936 because they had considered him too small. But the quick witted, ever smiling, highly intelligent Priller soon proved more than worthy as a pilot and leader. By 1939, he was a staffel leader and he served through the Battles of France and Britain with distinction under the famed Daddy Moelder of JG 51. By January of 1944, after 80 kills, and three high decorations, Priller won promotion to colonel and command of the famed JG 26 Abbeville Boys. Since his appointment, the 26 geschwader had specialized in Allied heavy bomber interception and Priller himself had already shot down six B-17s and five B24s.

Like so many other of the geschwaders now in Luftwaffe West, JG 26 had been pulled out of Luftwaffe Reich to the West German bases for Operation Herbstnebel.

Priller, huddled inside his storm coat, now walked across the airfield on this snowy, chilly December 31 morning. He watched the warts, maintenance and ordinance men in black coveralls, as they checked II Gruppe's aircraft: electrical systems, engines, and aerilon systems. The warts had been working throughout the night in some cases to prepare these planes for tomorrow's as yet unknown mission.

Pips Priller watched the men load SC spitterbombs on some aircraft and thousand pound MG bombs on others. Other armorers loaded .50 caliber machine guns in the wings. Major Hakl's II Gruppe would also carry rockets and TSCs.

Priller's own IV Gruppe would include two staffels with SCs, TSCs, and R4Ms, while the other staffel of IV/JG 26 would carry heavy MG thousand pounders to hit runways.

The colonel stopped at one of the 109s and looked up at a tall wart noncom. "How does it go, Sergeant?"

The sergeant snapped to attention. "Mein Colonel."

"Does it go well?" Priller asked.

"We are on schedule, sir," the sergeant answered. "By this afternoon, every aircraft in II Gruppe will be fully armed and checked out."

Priller looked at the fighter plane and then turned to the ordinance man again. "We have never carried such heavy bombs on Messerschmitts. Sergeants, do you think it will be all right?"

"The 109 is a fine aircraft, sir. She can do anything." Then, the sergeant frowned. "Mein Colonel, I know it is none of my business to ask, but you must forgive me. I and the other warts have burned with curiosity. Why are we loading such heavy bombs on some staffel aircraft if we are to carry out tactical air support for our troops in Belgium?"

Pips Priller squeezed his face. "I wish I could tell you, Sergeant. I only know that tomorrow all of our JG 26 aircraft, every 109 and 190, will fly on some important mission."

"But sir," the sergeant persisted, "the weather is unfit for flying and the weather is expected to remain poor for some days. Yet, we are preparing over 150 aircraft in this geschwader. I understand, Mein Colonel," the sergeant leaned closer to Priller, "that other warts in other geschwaders in other bases throughout west Germany are doing the same thing."

"Sergeant, neither you nor I can question OKL," Priller said. "I only know that more than a dozen geschwader and gruppen commodores will be meeting with me in a few hours here at Verrelbusch."

"Yes, sir."

The sergeant stood for a moment and watched the short, wiry colonel move away. Then, he turned to a fellow wart. "The colonel says he knows no more than we do."

"Something big will happen, Hans," the corporal said, "something we have not seen in months, perhaps years."

Priller continued his tour over the remainder of the JG 26 area at Verrelbusch. Most of the aircraft, of course, were hidden under trees or camouflaged with brush for Priller knew that low flying Allied light bombers and fighter-bombers were constantly seeking German airfields. Both the light Typhoons and heavier Mosquitos of the RAF's 2nd Tactical Air Force and the A-20s and P-47s of the 9th Tactical Air Force continually prowled over western Germany, seeking targets of opportunity. Priller did not expect Allied planes out today in this cold, gloomy, low cloud morning. Still, perhaps from habit, Priller maintained his camouflage.

Pips Priller soon met Major George Eder of the JG 26s I Gruppe. The stocky, sturdy, blond-haired Eder was scolding a wart mechanic. "Dumbkoffe! How can you say this engine is fine when oil leaks from one of the connections? Achtung!" He threw his head upward in disgust and then glared at the mechanic, his blue eyes burning and his round face tight with anger. "Are none of you dependable? Where is your sergeant?"

"D-down the line," the mechanic stammered.

"Report to him at once," the major cried, "and tell him to send a man who can properly check out this aircraft."

"Y-yes, Mein Major." The mechanic snapped to attention, bowed his head, and then scurried away.

Eder moved close to the aircraft and peered at the engine behind the open cowling. He ran a finger over the connection and then scowled when he saw the blot of oil on the tip. "Dumbkoffe!" he growled again.

"Peter," Pips Priller suddenly came next to the major and grinned, "why are you so upset?"

The major turned, looked at Priller and then sighed. "Colonel, we have too many shoddy warts among our mechanics. They do not always inspect the aircraft carefully. Look," he pointed at the engine, "a leaking oil connection. How, with a leaking engine, can a pilot fly this aircraft with a heavy load of two MG bombs?"

"You should scold the line chief, not the poor corporal," Priller grinned again. "The line chief is responsible."

"I will do that, too, Colonel," Major Eder nodded. Then he looked hard at Pips Priller. "I do not understand. Why have we been asked to load heavy MG bombs on a full staffel of aircraft?"

"I have been asked that question all morning, Peter, and I can only say I have no idea. I only know we will conduct some kind of tactical mission tomorrow. Our orders will not be here until this morning and I will not open them until I meet with the geschwader and gruppen commodores at 1100 hours."

"I see," Eder said.

"Certainly, whatever our mission, I'm sure you will succeed as will the pilots of your gruppe who have so much faith in you."

Major Eder lowered his head to hide a blush. Priller had embarrassed the major with his flattery.

Priller's praise for the I/JG 26 commodore was totally warranted. Major Peter George Eder had been a dynamic fighter pilot throughout his career that began in 1937 as an eager seventeen-year-old who had lied about his age to join the German Air Force. At age nineteen, when he finished training, he had joined the famed JG 51 Moelder along with other pilots like Priller.

However, during the first ten months of combat, Peter Eder had been unable to shake his fears, always tense, nervous, and uncertain whenever he went into combat. He had not scored a single hit against enemy planes, although he had been shot down twice. Luftwaffe brass had just about decided to dismiss him when the incomparable Werner Moelders took a special interest in the nervous young pilot.

Moelder had taken Eder aside and told him: "None of us would be pilots if we listened to those who said we were unfit to fly. Just remember, the ME 109 is a great aircraft. It will do whatever you ask. Once you believe this, you will no longer have any fears."

Eder had taken Moelder's advice and by 1940, the native of Frankfurt had become one of Germany's aces, scoring ten kills on the Russian front. After Moelder's death, Eder had joined JG 26 as a squadron leader. During the Battle of Britain, Eder had shot down an additional 56 planes. Eder's aircraft always carried a big #13 on the fuselage and RAF pilots came to admire the unique number among the Abbeville Boys, for Eder would never knowingly kill the pilot of a disabled aircraft. In fact, downed RAF pilots who survived Eder's guns had thanked the Lord that their conquerer had been "Lucky 13."

Most amazing, Eder himself had been shot down seventeen times during four years of combat, suffering wounds on four occasions. But always, the vigorous Eder returned to combat. His stocky body and ruddy face were laced with scars by this December day in 1944. Still, he eagerly looked forward to another engagement with the enemy, whatever it was.

Eder, after the glowing praise from Colonel Priller, grinned at the JG 26 commodore. "We will do our best, Colonel."

Priller tapped Eder on the shoulder and then smiled. "Do not be too hard on the warts, Peter. They have been overworked for many months, and we can be grateful for the miraculous job they have done to keep so many aircraft in combat condition."

Major Peter Eder nodded and watched his commodore walk off. Then, the major sighed. He would still scold the line chief of II Gruppe and complain about the dumbkoffe who had missed the small oil leak.

Some seventy miles to the south, at Wesel, Colonel Gunther Lutzow stepped from his commodore's office and squinted first at the gray clouds and then at the light morning mist hanging over the field. The ground was still white as were the tops of trees and camouflage nets that hid the sixty 109s of his JG 3 Udet geschwader. Lutzow tightened his coat, pulled up the collar and ambled toward the length of trees that obscured the 190s of his assault unit. JG 3 had done pretty well on the Western Front during the past two years—until he ran into the swarms of fighter planes of the RAF 127 Wing on Christmas day.

Lutzow knew, of course, that he could probably count only a dozen or so experienced pilots in his JG 3 and he feared for the many green flyers of his unit. His fears had been well founded, indeed, and he only hoped that more of these novice pilots would not meet the same fate as so many had on that Christmas mission. He wondered about this upcoming mission, as curious as so many others. Why were entire staffels carrying thousand pound MG bombs while the other aircraft carried the usual rockets, SCs and TSCs for ground support?

As Lutzow ambled along the parked FW 190s, glancing at the warts who serviced the aircraft, he said nothing to them. The ground crews in turn quickly stiffened to attention and then relaxed when Lutzow gestured them to ease. When the colonel was gone, one of the mechanics turned to a gritty sergeant.

"Is it true what they say about Herr Lutzow? Did he really scold the Reichmarshal himself? Berate Herr Goring to his face?"

"Yes, it is true," the sergeant nodded. "The colonel has always spoken his mind without hesitation. He even complained of the Reichmarshal to the Führer himself."

"But he seems so aloof, so far off from everyone; like he is insulated from those around him."

"If you do something wrong," the burly sergeant grinned, "he will come to you, but I would not want to be in your boots when he did."

Now, as Lutzow continued his tour on this cold, humid morning along the parked FW 190 aircraft of his JG 3 Udet unit, he merely glanced at others working in their black coveralls, or he squinted at the leaden skies. Lutzow did not really care what kind of mission he carried out tomorrow, nor did he care about the low clouds. He cared only for the young pilots who were so eager, but also so naive. He hoped again that most of them would be spared.

Near the end of his tour, he ran into Major Werner Specht of III Gruppe, a man who had already scored thirty-two kills, including fifteen four-engine Allied bombers. Lutzow's eyes reflected a glint of pride for the muscular Specht, who was among the few men the colonel admired, one of the few men the colonel would speak to without issuing orders or a reprimand. When Specht commanded a staffel in JG 11, he had nurtured such aces as Heinz Knoke, Sieg Simsch, and Bruno Stolle. He and his staffel had shot down more than a hundred four-engine bombers before Specht took command of a gruppe in Lutzow's JG 3.

"Major," Lutzow said in his somber voice, "is your gruppe ready?"

"Yes, Mein Colonel," Specht answered. Then he looked hard at Lutzow. "You have been moving about vigorously since dawn, Colonel. Should you not get ready for your appointment at Verrelbusch?"

"I will be leaving soon," Lutzow said. "My aide will shortly arrive to pick me up. It is mere two hour drive from here."

"Colonel," the major leaned forward, "when you return from Verrelbusch, you should rest this afternoon, for I suspect you will have a busy evening and a most busy day tomorrow."

"You are right," Lutzow answered. He tapped the major on the shoulder and sighed. "I wish I had fifty pilots like you."

"We will do our best, Colonel," Specht said.

Lutzow nodded and walked away. Major Werner Specht watched the colonel disappear into the slight mist and he then pursed his lips. He knew that Lutzow felt concern for his pilots, even though he showed no emotion. The major only hoped he would succeed in the upcoming mission tomorrow, whatever it entailed.

On the other side of the airbase, Major Heinz Pritzl Bar and his I/JG 1 commodore, Waldemar Woitke, had just finished inspecting their aircraft.

"I cannot understand the use of the large MG bombs," Woitke said. "What could we possibly be doing with such heavy explosives? You would think we are preparing to attack British aircraft factories."

Heinz Bar grinned. "When I know what they plan for us, I will tell you. I should return from Eschborn sometime this afternoon."

"But can our single engine aircraft even get off the ground with two of these one thousand-pound monsters under their wings?" Captain Woitke asked.

"I hope so," Bar said. "I will admit, I too am confused by these bombs. I would suspect that this mission has something to do with helping the Werhmacht and panzer troops in Belgium. Perhaps they expect us to knock out bridges or railroad pikes to stop advancing Allied armies."

"Strange, Heinz, quite strange," Woitke said, shaking his head.

Bar shrugged. "We will know soon enough. I will be driving to Eschborn within an hour." Then, the major pulled the collar of his coat closer to his neck. "Come, Waldemar, we are finished here. Let us go inside where it is warm."

At Rheims, Colonel Hans Assi Hahn of JG 2 looked at the low clouds. He had hoped the weather remained bad, so he would not need to face the merciless Allied superiority again too soon, not after the beating he had taken at the hands of the 366th U.S. Fighter Group. But now, he learned he was going out tomorrow, with some of his staffels carrying MG bombs. He was simply confused. He must wait a few hours, until he met with Colonel Falck, before he had any answers.

At Aschner, Colonel Johannes Steinhoff viewed the inclement weather with a sour face. His ME 262 jets always succeeded and he was ready to take the Snowbirds anywhere. But the KG 7 jets took off best on long, dry runways. He doubted that the runways would be dry tomorrow and he worried more about the take-off than he did the enemy or the expected poor weather.

At Ostheim, the commodores of SG 4 and SG 20 looked at the gloomy skies with uneasiness. These ME 110 twin engine bombers would be more heavily loaded than usual and slowed down considerably. They would be easy targets for enemy fighter planes. The SG commodores only hoped that, whatever the mission tomorrow, they would hit with the same surprise they did on December 16.

At Badenheisen, Colonel Erich Rudorffer walked along the parked aircraft of his JG 54 with Major Robert Weise and Major Alfred Keller. They had pushed their warts hard and their 109s and 190s were ready to go. The three men, however, had not yet recovered from the near knock-out blow by the U.S. 354th Fighter Group during the air battles over Bastogne. Whatever their mission, they hoped there would be no repetition of that Christmas day debacle. Still, the three JG 54 officers were grateful for one thing—Goring had indeed come through with plenty of gasoline supplies.

At Lichtenseim, Major Heinz Schnaufer had already given his crews of NJG 4 a quick all day lecture on conducting daylight attacks. He hoped his pilots had understood, so he could carry out his boast to Werner Streib: "It makes no difference to me whether I strike our enemies by day or by night." Still, Colonel Streib had not told Schnaufer that his unit would be hitting the helpless American transport plane base.

On this raw December 31 morning, General Peltz himself looked out of his headquarters window at Ostheim and pursed his lips. He had never sent out aircraft in this kind of weather, and certainly not with overloads. He was not sure his geschwaders could get off the runways without mishaps.

And, at his headquarters in Treuenbritzen, General Adolph Galland stood by a window and stared at this dismal December 31 morning. Then, when he turned and stared at the thick, sealed envelope on his desk, he scowled. The Führer, the Reichmarshal, Peltz—they were all crazy. They could not possibly expect to avoid the dozens of radar stations. The Allies would guess the Luftwaffe West mission soon enough and send hordes of fighter planes after them. They could decimate the German formations before any gruppe even reached an Allied airfield.

Galland turned to an aide. "Here are the orders," he picked up the envelope. "Get them to Colonel Priller at Verrelbusch at once."

"Yes, Herr General," the aide said before he bowed and left the room.

Colonel William Moritz, of course, already had his orders, as did Colonel Wolfgang Falck and Colonel Werner Streib. They would merely wait in their headquarters for the commodores to arrive for the briefing.

Now, Galland, Peltz, Schmidt, Goring, and the Armies of the West generals would wait tensely for thirty-six hours, until a multiple of geschwaders and gruppen took off from their bases to conduct what seemed like an impossible task—knock out twenty-five Allied air bases. The Germans hoped the JU 88 pathfinders truly avoided Allied radar stations. Only if they caught the Allies with surprise again, could they succeed with Operation Bodenplatte.

Chapter Eight

German pilots and ground crews of Luftwaffe West had prepared for a period of inactivity during the expected several days of poor weather. But, the freight trains and truck convoys had rolled toward the airbases all during the night of December 29–30 and into December 31. Ammunition and bombs had arrived at Rheims, Verrelbusch, Badenheisen, Ostheim, Wesel, Aschner, and other Luftwaffe West airbases. By the late morning of December 31, the warts had pretty well finished their work and gruppe and geschwader commanders had reached their designated Fliegercorps areas for briefings. Commodores from I/JG 6, II/JG 77, JG 1, KG 7, and KG 51 met with Colonel Wilheim Moritz at Eschborn. Moritiz's units of Fliegercorps Holland would hit the British bases at Eindhoven, Volkel, Tillberg, Antwerp, and the distant bases near Ostend. The commodores of II/JG 6, the gruppens of JG 26, and the gruppens of JG 54 met with Colonel Josef Priller at Verrelbusch. Fliegercorps Belgium would hit the three British bases around Brussels, the RAF base at Ghent, and the American bases on Belgium—LeCulot, St. Trond, and Asche.

To the South, gruppen and geschwader commodores of SG 20, JG 27, JG 2, SG 4, and SG 104 met with Colonel Wolfgang Falck of Fliegercorps North at the Luftwaffe West headquarters in Ostheim. Falck's units would strike the American bases at St. Dizier, Florennes, Coulimiers, and the smaller bases at Cambrai and Lilli. Finally, the last array of commodores, those of JG 4, I/JG 11, II/JG 11, NJG 9, NJG 4, JG 3, and JG 53, met with Colonel Werner Streib of Fliegercorps South at Lichtenseim. They would assault the American bases at Chateudon, Juvincourt, Britigny, Conlans, Melvun, Ciastres, and Frescaty near Metz, all in France.

Streib had already sent his NJG 101 crews to the other fliegercorps briefings, except for those who would accompany the units of Fliegercorps South. The 101 pilots and navigators needed to join these various gruppen and geschwaders to get all details on their assignments as target pathfinders.

The pilots and navigators of JU 88 units had already met with Peltz's IC intelligence officers and TO technical advisers to map out routes the JU pathfinders would follow to avoid radar. The JU 88 crews had also been warned to bring the gruppe units under the clouds to ground level at least fifteen to twenty kilometers from targets to avoid warning installations at Allied airbases. Here at Lichtenseim, Colonel Werner Streib had assigned two JU 88 pathfinders to Fliegercorps South and one JU 88 to each gruppe, as Streib had assigned two Junkers to each of the other fliegercorps and one Junker to each of the other gruppen.

Major Heinz Schnaufer expressed an air of contempt for the JU 88 assigned to his NJG 4. "If I cannot find my target after all my experience in night flying, I may as well ground myself." Still,

Schnaufer accepted the Junker pathfinder for his geschwader.

By late afternoon, all geschwader and gruppe commodores had returned to their units and they immediately posted notices for local briefings of their staffel and schwarm leaders, with most of the briefings to commence immediately after the evening meal.

At 1830 hours, December 31, Colonel Josef Pips Priller called his air leaders of JG 26 into a briefing. By now, every officer had heard of the proposed air strikes tomorrow. Their only question: what were the targets? What were the assignments for the JG 26 Abbeville Boys? As the flieger leaders seated themselves, they noted a sober look on the face of the usually smiling Pips Priller.

"Gentlemen," Priller began, "tomorrow the Luftwaffe West launches a massive attack against the Allied airfields in Holland, Belgium, and France. The effort is a daring and dangerous one, for we have seen what happened when the Allies launched their own counterairstrikes. Their victories only confirmed their superiority in numbers—overwhelming. They came in countless schwarms to not only destroy the Herbstnebel offensive, but also to drive our aircraft from the battle fronts, with heavy losses. Now, we find the soldiers of Army Group B in a most dangerous position and we have been asked to save them."

No one answered Priller.

"Thousands of good Wehrmacht and panzer troops could be captured or annihilated," Priller continued, "for the Allied air forces have seriously cut their supply lines and communications. The problem we face is how to extricate these thousands of German troops from Belgium." He nodded to an aide who lit up a map behind him. Then, the aide, Deputy JG 26 commodore Hanz Goetz, spoke himself.

"You can clearly see the identified Allied airbases in Holland, Belgium, and France," Major Goetz said. "There are nearly thirty of them. Every gruppe in Luftwaffe West is assigned a target. Our targets are here," the major tapped his pointer on the map, "Brussels. The British have airbases at Grimberghen, Duerne, and Evere. We know the British air units from these bases around Brussels caused the most damage to the panzer and Wehrmacht units of General Dietrich's 6th Panzer Army. Now, entire divisions of this army face destruction unless we can assure them a means of escape. If we destroy the airbases around Brussels, the British cannot launch strikes against our retiring troops."

Colonel Priller now took the pointer and moved toward the lighted screen. "Gentlemen, you know the targets for JG 26." He looked at Peter Eder. "Major, I would like your staffels to attack the Polish wing at Duerne."

Major Peter Eder nodded.

"I myself will lead IV Gruppe to attack the British wing at Grimberghen." Then, the colonel looked at Major Anton Hackl. "Major, you had the honor of a visit from Reichmarshal Goring himself this afternoon, and I hope his words of encouragement will be inspiring to you and your fliegers."

"The Reichmarshal was most sympathetic," Hackl said. "Be assured, Colonel, we will do whatever is necessary."

"Good," Colonel Priller said. "I would ask that

the aircraft of II Gruppe attack the Evere airfield with its two British wings. You can decide for yourself how you want your staffels to conduct their strikes."

"We will not fail, Colonel."

"They have assigned a JU 88 pathfinder to each gruppe," Priller continued. "The pathfinder crews who sit at this briefing know their responsibilities. They have been thoroughly briefed to lead us along a path that will avoid the Allied radar installations. Our safety is in the hands of these pathfinders, so be certain you do not stray from them." Priller paused. "Since our target is exactly two hours from our base here in Verrelbusch, we will take off promptly at 0800 hours to reach our destination by 1000 hours."

"Will all Luftwaffe West units leave at the same time?" a staffel leader asked.

"No," the colonel answered. "We have coordinated take off times so that every gruppe will reach its target at exactly 1000 hours for simultaneous attacks."

"Colonel," another staffel leader asked soberly, "you must permit me to express doubt. Are you certain we can carry out this plan before countless Allied fighter planes take to the skies to intercept us? Could we not lose our entire Luftwaffe West in such an event?"

"General Galland himself raised this question when the plan was proposed," Colonel Priller said. "All possibilities were weighed carefully and they came to the same conclusion. If we do nothing, there will certainly be disaster—the loss of thousands of soldiers in Belgium. But, if the plan succeeds, we will stop Allied air assaults on these ground troops and their lines of escape back to Germany. I ask you Leutnant," he looked hard at the staffel leader, "is this plan worth the risk?"

"I'm sorry, Herr Colonel," the Leutnant said, "I spoke like a coward."

Priller grinned, cracking the sober look on his face. "The recreation hall is open. There is schnapps, beer, and pastry. Enjoy yourselves, but make the evening short. You must get a good night's sleep for we have a busy and dangerous day tomorrow."

An eruption of ad libs exploded through the briefing hall before the JG 26 leaders moved off.

To the south, at the big German base at Rheims, Colonel Hans Assi Hahn held a briefing with his own gruppen, staffel, and schwarm leaders of JG 2. He saw before him only sober faces, men obviously uneasy. However, optimism had returned to Hahn's lively blue eyes. The anticipation of stunning multiple strikes in Operation Bodenplatte had made him forget the Christmas day losses to the U.S. 366th Fighter Group.

"Do not look so uncertain," Hahn grinned. "We did suffer losses a week ago, true. But," he gestured, "tomorrow is another day, another chance to succeed as we did two weeks ago. I firmly believe that tomorrow we will strike our enemies a blow they will long remember."

The sober faced audience did not answer.

Now, Hahn nodded to an aide who lit a screen with a map on it. The colonel then took a pointer and tapped a point on the map—Lille. "Here sits the worst culprit of all, the American B-26 gruppen that have been responsible for destroying the bridges at Ahrweiler and Euskirchen to bring so much distress to the 5th Panzer Army. Our Richtofen unit has been given the opportunity to extract vengeance against these American air units at Lille."

Hahn, of course, was referring to the American 332nd Bomb Group, Nye's Annihilators and the 386th Bridge Wreckers Bomb Group. He might also have mentioned the 36th P-47 Fighter Group, also at Lille, that had destroyed an entire 5th Army motorized column.

"We have, unfortunately, found ourselves reduced to sixty operable aircraft," Hahn continued. "Still, if we attack with vigor and resolve, we can destroy the enemy base at Lille. I will personally lead I Gruppe over the revetment and taxi areas where we will likely find the American planes parked. II Gruppe will concentrate on the two runways. I expect II Gruppe to leave so many holes in the runways that not even a mountain climber will be able to move across them."

"Who will go in first, Herr Colonel?" Leutnant Kindes asked Hahn.

"You, Leutnant," the JG 2 commodore answered Otto Kindes. "You will take your 2 Staffel and attack the P-47s, so they cannot interfere with our attack. I will follow with 1 and 3 Staffels to strike the bombers. II Gruppe can follow to attack the airstrips. 4 Staffel will strike the smaller runway, while 5 and 6 Staffel will strike the bomber runways." He paused. "Any questions?"

None.

"Since our target lies two and one half hours from our base in Rheims," Hahn said, "we will take off at 0730 hours to make certain we arrive at Lille precisely at 1000 hours. As you know, this massive strike tomorrow will be coordinated so that each gruppen reaches its target at 1000." He scanned the men again. "Let us hope we can make the first day of the new year a successful one." Then, Hahn grinned. "I do not like to see so many solemn faces among you. This mission will succeed, I know it will. I can feel it in my heart. Do not think of past misfortunes; think only of the opportunity that awaits us tomorrow. Leutnant," he looked at Josef Zwernemann, "where is that beaming smile I used to see on your face?"

"I'm sorry, Herr Colonel," Zwernemann answered with a grin. "You are correct. If we are determined, we cannot fail."

"Good," Assi Hahn said. "Now, you may retire to the recreation hall, but your New Year's Eve celebrations must be short. We need a good night's sleep."

As the men rose from their benches, they broke into an ad lib of conversations before they shuttled out of the briefing hall.

Wesel, Germany, along the Rhine River, was one of the bigger airbases of Luftwaffe West. Eschborn, just outside of Wesel, was the headquarters of Jagdivision 3, while Wesel itself and nearby Badenheisen based three full geschwaders of aircraft. No wonder, then, the American 8th Air Force strategic bombers had singled out Wesel and Badenheisen as targets during the Herbstnebel offensive. The B-17 raid on the afternoon of December 27 had caused widespread damage. Besides the destruction of buildings and runways and the death of some fifty fliegers, the B-17s had destroyed or damaged thirty-nine at Wesel and sixteen at Badenheisen.

However, by December thirtieth, as they had everywhere else, the Germans had repaired the airfields. JG's 1, 3, and 54 were back in business. Both Lutzow's aircraft and Bar's aircraft were ready to go by the evening of December 31. And, probably no geschwader commodore was more anxious to participate in Operation Bodenplatte than Heinz Pritzl Bar, despite a most perilous assignment.

Bar's JG 1 Oesau unit would attack the two British bases at Melsbroek and Westem, outside Ostend near the North Sea coast. His fifty-two 109s would carry auxilary gas tanks for the long flight, and JG 1 would be the first Luftwaffe West unit to take off tomorrow. JG 1 would leave at 0630 hours, for the unit would need three and one half hours to reach its targets.

Gruppe, staffel, and schwarm leaders had arrived at the JG 1 briefing hall by 1830, December 31, to listen to their commodore. They sat quietly and curiously as Bar lowered a wall screen and then grinned. "I do not know how far we have flown before, but tomorrow we will be in the air for at least seven hours. We will be off at 0630, before the sun rises—if there is any sun tomorrow morning."

An ad lib of chuckles radiated through the hall.

"They must think we have not had enough flying time," Bar continued, "and they must wish us to catch up in one day." He paused and then slapped the map with his finger. "Here are the targets, near Ostend on Belgium's North Sea coast. JG 1 has the task of destroying the British bomber bases at Melsbroek and Westem. I would have preferred revenge on the Americans who showed us little compassion during their raid on Wesel. But, who are we underlings to question the Luftwaffe high command?"

Another simmer of chuckles echoed through the hall.

"Perhaps we can knock some of the egotism out of these Britishers who crow so loudly, while they are carried by the Americans." He paused. "Unfortunately, the Americans destroyed many of our aircraft, but we still have fifty-two Folke-Wulfs among our gruppen. We will divide our staffels into two groups. I will lead the staffels of I Gruppe to strike Melsbroek and Captain Waldemar Woitke will lead the staffels of II Gruppe to strike Westem."

"But, Colonel," one of the men said, "is it possible to make such a long flight without detection? Are we not likely to meet interceptors?"

"Anything is possible," Major Bar said, "but whoever promised any certainties in war? Our pathfinder pilots and navigators have laid out a course along a remote route in order to avoid the enemy's radar systems. It is our hope that neither Belgium civilians nor Allied observers detect us. We must simply trust the pathfinders."

"But what if we *do* meet enemy interceptors?"

"I have designated one staffel from each gruppe to immediately salvo bombs and auxiliary tanks to act as escort. The other staffels will continue to targets. I must warn you," he gestured, "do not expend more than half of your strafing ammunition over targets as you may be tempted to do. We may encounter British fighter planes on the way back to Germany and we will need to fight them off."

The men in the briefing hall did not answer.

"Now," Bar asked, "are there any questions? Obviously, the staffels carrying the MG bombs will attack the runways, while other staffels attack parked aircraft."

Still no questions.

"Fine," Major Bar grinned. "The recreation hall is open. We have lagar, coffee, schnapps, pretzels, and some pastries. We also have some sausage delicacies. But, make your celebrations short and keep your drinking moderate, for I want you fully awake and with a clear head tomorrow—no later than 0500. If all goes well," Bar grinned again, "we will have a real celebration tomorrow night." He paused. "You are dismissed."

Chattering erupted among the crowd of JG 1 fliegers as they rose from their benches and left the briefing hall. Only Captain Waldemar Woitke remained and he looked soberly at the JG 1 commodore.

"Major," the captain said, "they are asking the impossible. I must agree with the young leutnant. We cannot possibly reach the North Sea coastal area without detection."

"Our lives are in the hands of the Junker pathfinders," Major Bar answered. "It is my understanding that these crews have spent many hours with the IC men of Luftwaffe West to learn the location of every Allied radar installation."

"I am most skeptical," Captain Woitke answered, shaking his head. "These targets are so far away. Why must we make such a long flight to the northwest coast? Enemy aircraft there cannot possibly cause us much damage."

"Suppose we destroyed all the other Allied bases in Western Europe except for the bases near Ostend," Bar gestured, "then what? British light bombers from the Ostend area would attack us at once. But worse, Allied aircraft from England would stage through Melsbroek and Westem to continue their devastating assaults on the Wehrmacht and panzer troops. No, Captain, these bases must be destroyed. Remember, nothing is impossible if we have the will to succeed."

"Perhaps," the captain said.

A solemn look suddenly replaced the amiable look that usually radiated from Bar's face. "We have no choice," the major said. "Someone must fly to Ostend. They selected JG 1. True, there is the possibility of failure. But, if we do not try, failure will be a certainty. Come, Waldemar, let us have some schnapps and then we will get a good night's sleep."

"Yes, Mein Major," Woitke said.

Heinz Pritzl Bar obviously did not relish the long flight he must make tomorrow. Still, he drew strength from within himself, determined to succeed. He sighed and then walked off with Woitke to the JG 1 recreation hall.

In a dozen other geschwader briefing halls, other JG commodores briefed gruppe, staffel, and schwarm leaders. Also, at Wesel, the fliegers of JG 3 learned from Colonel Gunther Lutzow that the Udet unit would hit Antwerp. The JG pilots reacted with a mixture of uncertainty and enthusiasm.

At nearby Badenheisen, Colonel Erich Rudorffer of JG 54 told his Green Heart pilots that their targets were perhaps the most dangerous of all in Operation Bodenplatte. The three gruppen of JG 54 would strike the string of American fighter plane bases at St. Trond, LeCulot, and Asche. Nine American fighter groups based dozens of P-51s and P-47s at these bases. The pilots of JG 54 had already tasted the devastating stings of swarming P-51s. When Green Heart pilots had tried to intercept some of the American B-26s a few days ago, the Mustang pilots of the U.S. 354th Fighter group had knocked a dozen of their planes out of the air and had badly damaged another dozen.

Now, the pilots of JG 54 were worried. If these Mustang pilots got off the ground before the Green Hearts destroyed their runways, JG 54 could suffer an even worse disaster than the Christmas day losses, especially since their 190s would be carrying heavy loads and thus slowed down. Still, the pilots at Badenheisen understood the importance of their mission, and they owed the Americans something after their aerial beating and after the B-17 raid on Badenheisen. If they could knock out the American fighter bases, American bombers could make no more bridge-busting attacks. Without escorts, the B-26s and A-26s would suffer badly from German interceptor planes. And finally, these fliegers of JG 54 did not forget the peril of the troops in Belgium.

"We must be extremely alert and fully determined," Colonel Erich Rudorffer told his fliegers. "The prestige and the reputation of the Green Hearts flies with us tomorrow."

Nobody answered the JG 54 colonel.

At Wesel, Colonel Gunther Lutzow had briefed the pilots of JG 3, that special Udet assault unit. Lutzow's pilots had long conducted tactical support missions instead of interceptor sorties. JG 3 had been assigned to such duty in the west and had not been one of the units transferred from Luftwaffe West for Operation Herbstnebel and now Operation Bodenplatte. Still, Lutzow warned his pilots.

"There are many American fighter bases near our target at Melvun. We must be certain to attack with quick surprise and then retire quickly."

By about 2100 hours, December 31, all air

leaders and their fliegers had been thoroughly briefed. Meanwhile, the warts of Luftwaffe West had completed the preparations on the hundreds of 109s, 190s, 110s, ME 262s and AR 234s that would carry out the morning mission.

At his headquarters in Osthem, General Dietrich Peltz acknowledged one after another of the incoming briefing reports. He posted a pin on a map board behind him with each report. Peltz was satisfied. His subordinates had done a creditable job in preparing for the coordinated attacks. Like everyone else in Luftwaffe West, Peltz hoped that all would go well with Operation Bodenplatte. He prayed that the poor weather would hold, at least through tomorrow. If the poor conditions prevailed, Peltz was certain that Allied air commanders would expect nothing to happen on the morning of January 1, 1945.

The Luftwaffe West Obercommando had just studied the briefing board behind him again when Colonel Wolfgang Falch, his deputy, came into the room. "The latest weather report, Herr General."

Peltz studied the sheet in his hand and nodded. His prayers had apparently been answered. The poor weather was expected to continue for at least two more days and possibly longer.

"The Allies cannot possibly expect us to carry out a massive air attack in such weather," Colonel Falck said.

General Peltz nodded and then asked: "Is your Fliegercorps North ready?"

"Yes, Herr General," Falck answered, "and so too are all the other fliegercorps. All local units have had their briefing and all aircraft are ready."

"Good," Peltz said.

The Luftwaffe West Obercommando then peered into the night beyond his headquarters window and he now saw a slight mist in the evening darkness. Peltz frowned. If the mist worsened, they could have zero visibility by morning. That's all he needed, a heavy fog that would force a cancellation after the endless hours of preparation for Operation Bodenplatte.

"Can I bring you a schnapps, General?" Colonel Falck asked.

"I would prefer a brandy," Peltz scowled. "In fact, I would ask that you make it a double brandy . . . and pour one for yourself."

"Yes, Mein General," Falck said. "I will call our aide."

Chapter Nine

At his headquarters in Versailles, France, General Hoyt Vandenberg had met with General Elwood Queseda of IX Fighter Command and General Edward Backus of the 9th Tactical Bomber Command. The three men on the gloomy afternoon of December 31 shuffled through the array of papers on the desk before Vandenberg looked at Backus.

"German air activity has diminished to nothing."

"Our group commanders think they've pretty well knocked out the last of Luftwaffe West since Chrismas."

"Maybe," Vandenberg said. "Anyway, we've got to start thinking about Operation Varsity. I know we've still got to deal with the Germans in Belgium, but we should take care of that within the next couple of weeks. Eisenhower agrees that we'll have Army Group B pretty well macerated by then, so he wants us to go ahead with our planning for Varsity."

"I've anticipated that," General Backus said, "so I've made up some plans myself. We'll have the two bomb groups at Melvun support General Patton's 3rd Army to the south when his infantry and armor divisions drive toward the Rhine through Luxembourg. Patton expects to cross the Rhine at Koblenz. Our four A-20 and B-26 groups at Coulimiers will support General William Simpson's thrust toward Koblenz from the north. The 387th and 409th Bomb Groups will support Jim Deven's 6th Army advance through the center toward the Rhine city of Bonn. Finally, the 322nd and 386th groups will support General Hodges' 1st Army to the north. Hodges plans to drive beyond Aachen to capture the Rhine city of Cologne."

General Hoyt Vandenberg nodded.

"The various groups had already received coordination instructions for each infantry or armor division they must support," General Backus said. "They go as soon as this thing in Belgium is over and Bradley gives the word to begin Varsity."

"Good," Vandenberg said. Then he looked at General Queseda.

"The fighter units are ready," Queseda said. "Some of our P-47 groups like the 366th at Asche, Belgium, will give tactical support wherever they're needed. We'll also have some P-38 groups in reserve for tactical support if needed. Other fighter groups will escort the bombers on those communication and bridge-busting missions, but I don't think we're going to see any German interceptors. I'll work out a plan with Ed Backus here on escort assignments for his B-26s and A-26s."

Vandenberg nodded again and then looked out of his headquarters window at the leaden skies. "I wish this weather would break soon so we can get out more planes and finish this job in Belgium. If we don't knock out more bridges and communications, a lot of those Germans could get away and give Bradley some real trouble for Varsity. I know we've been sending out some units to hit roads and rail junctions to keep those German ground troops isolated. But, it's been a limited thing, and Bradley would like round the clock strikes against those German ground troops. But," Vandenberg sighed, "maybe the weather will break soon."

"Oh, one more thing," General Backus suddenly gestured. "I got a report from reconn pilots that the Germans have been quite busy at some of their western bases. The reconn pilots also report that there's been some unusually heavy rail and road traffic toward the Rhine river airbases. It's the first time the 67th Reconn Snoopers have reported anything like that in a week. The pilots have been out every day according to their group commander."

"They're seeing things," General Queseda huffed. "The Germans can't have a plane left in Luftwaffe West after what our fighters did to them. I think those reconn pilots need a rest."

However, Vandenberg screwed his face. "I remember a couple of weeks ago when we said the same thing about those Snooper pilots. But they were certainly right. I want their reports studied thoroughly," he gestured, "and I want a good analysis of any other reports they send to our headquarters."

"Okay, Hoyt," Queseda said.

On this same December 31 afternoon, at Lilli, France, Colonel John Samuels looked at the leaden skies and then stroked his narrow face. The commander of the 322nd Bomb Group felt uneasy. Two of his B-26 squadrons had left on a routine mission and now, three hours later, they had not yet returned. He looked at his other B-26s and those B-26s of the 386th Group that shared the Lille bomber base with his 322nd and the 368th Fighter-Bomber Group. Samuels, with a tightly buttoned, turned up coat and peak cap, paced about the taxi strip and then walked toward the control tower with his deputy commander, Major Tom Stanton.

"Where the hell are they?" Samuels growled. "The bridge target was less than an hour away. They should have been back by now."

"Maybe they ran into bad weather and decided to fly to some other airfield," Major Stanton said.

"Hell," Samuels said, "every field is just like our own today. No, it isn't the weather. They got jumped by the bastards."

If German pilots wanted to intercept somebody, that somebody was surely the B-26 group with the diamonds on their tails. Since arriving in England in mid-1943, the 322nd had destroyed more bridges, marshaling yards, enemy installations, and road junctions than any other medium bomb group. From England, the 322nd and four other 3rd Division groups constantly attacked targets in France, Belgium, and Holland. The 322nd had been the first medium group to use the new Hx4 blind bombing technique when they destroyed the German Air Force base of Coxyde in Holland in February of 1944 to win a DUC. The group had also supported the Normandy invasion by hitting roads, enemy motorized columns, and bridges in over 200 missions and dropping more than 4,000 tons of bombs. Her B-26 gunners had knocked more than a hundred German fighter planes out of the air. Most recently, of course, they had, with another group, knocked out the

Euskirchen Bridge.

So, if Luftwaffe planes were out today, their pilots would surely have loved to meet the B-26s of the 322nd and extract a little revenge.

However, Tom Stanton scoffed at the idea of interceptors. "My God," he told Samuels, "we haven't seen a goddamn Kraut plane for a week. Our fighters probably destroyed most of them during that four day mauling after Christmas Eve."

But John Samuels shook his head. "No, the bastards jumped them," he said again, before he and Major Stanton continued their stroll. When they reached the runway control tower, Samuels looked upward. "Sergeant," he cried, "have you got any word yet?"

"No, sir," the sergeant answered, "we haven't heard a thing."

Samuels scowled again and then looked at the slippery runway that had worsened since his 449th and 450th Squadrons took off early this afternoon. He called again to the sergeant in the control tower, and he told the NCO to order sanders out on the runway. When and if Samuels' two B-26 squadrons returned, they might be better off with de-iced runways.

Within a half hour, the sand trucks had done their job and only moments later, the drone of planes echoed from above the thick clouds. Colonel John Samuels hurried up the steps of the control tower, followed by Major Stanton.

"Sergeant," Samuels cried, "are those our two squadrons?"

"Yes, sir," the sergeant answered.

"What the hell happened to them?"

"They got jumped by bandits, sir, and they're bringing back a lot of wounded."

"Bandits," Samuels growled. "Goddamn it. I knew it."

"They must have wanted that bridge awfully bad to send up interceptors in this kind of weather," Major Stanton said, stroking his chin.

Within a half hour, just before dusk, the last of the 449th and 450th Squadron planes touched down on the Lille runway, with two of the B-26s skidding off the strip and nearly plowing into some trees before coming to a halt. Two more B-26s belly-landed for they had suffered damaged landing gears. A fifth Marauder hit the strip and simply spun off the runway, sending up eruptions of snow. Luckily, the B-26 did not explode.

At the post mission briefing, Colonel Samuels' eyes widened as he listened intently to the report from Captain Lynn Nelson, commander of the twenty-four B-26s on the mission. The twenty-four Marauders had just come within sight of the Our River Bridge, Nelson said, when a swarm of German interceptors, twenty or thirty of them, suddenly came through the clouds and jumped them. The 322nd had damaged the east span, but they never got a chance to finish the job. The ME 109s opened up on the medium bombers with murderous rocket and machine gun fire. Within minutes, Nelson had lost four of his B-26s and suffered damage to several more. For nearly an hour, the B-26s had played a running hide and seek in the dense clouds with the German fighters. Finally, the 322nd B-26s shook themselves loose of the persistent pursuers by zig-zagging themselves back to base. They had lost more than an hour in the process.

"Goddamn," Major Tom Stanton hissed. "We haven't seen any German interceptors around for a week. That's why we didn't even bother to ask for escorts today. Why the hell would those Germans come out this afternoon? Especially in this weather?"

"Something's up," Samuels said. "They want that bridge awfully bad."

True! The Germans had plenty of reason to intercept the attackers at the Our River Bridge, for the span was one of the few arteries left for both carrying supplies to Army Group B units and for bringing these same units out of Belgium. The Germans were determined to allow no more destruction of communications before Operation Bodenplatte, only some fourteen hours away.

To the east of Lille, at Asche, Belgium, Colonel Normal Holt, CO of the 366th Fighter Group, squinted at the low clouds and then he looked at the wing tip to wing tip array of P-47 fighter-bombers and the same lines of P-51s of the visiting 352nd and 361st Fighter Groups of the 8th Air Force. The ordinance men had not loaded bombs on the T-Bolts or Mustangs; nor would they until 9th TAC ordered them to do so. However, the strafing guns of the American fighter planes were fully loaded, with the barrels covered with tarps.

After his quick tour of the field, Colonel Holt returned to his trailer office where his deputy commander, Major George Prader, handed him a note. "I've got an interesting report from the 67th Reconnaissance Group," Prader said. "They say the German airfields at Wesel, Rheims, and a lot of other places east of the Rhine are bursting with activity. They think the Luftwaffe is up to something."

"We said those reconn pilots were crazy a couple of weeks ago when they told us the same thing,"

Holt said. "But they were right. We should have known better then. Colonel Peck's boys are pretty good. What do those 67th pilots say?"

"They said they saw over a hundred aircraft at Wesel alone," Major Prader said. "They also reported a mile long freight train of canvas covered flat cars west of the Rhine near the big German base at Ostheim."

"Did 9th Tactical get the report?" Holt asked.

Prader nodded. "General Vandenberg isn't taking the report lightly this time. He wants every reconn report that comes to be thoroughly analyzed."

Colonel Norman Holt looked out of his trailer window. "You know, this goddamn weather came on us suddenly, before we really finished off those German air units. They must still have a lot of planes, and they're planning something else."

"But what?" Major George Prader asked.

"I don't know," the 366th commander answered. "Just make sure our T-bolts stay on full alert and the same goes for those Mustangs from the 8th Air Force."

"Okay, Norm," George Prader said.

At the same base in Asche, Belgium, Captain Floyd Benson of the 366th's 387th Squadron sat in a quonset hut recreation room with Lieutenant Colonel John Meyers of the 352nd Fighter Group, one of the units on detached service to the 9th Air Force for Operation Varsity. The Asche base, one of the newest, still had primitive facilities, for the most part. Offices, mess halls, sleeping quarters, and support sections were still in tents. Only the headquarter's offices and the officer's recreation room were in quonset huts. And, of course, Colonel Norman Holt, had his quarters and private office in a trailer. So, the men at Asche shivered most of the time. Colonel Holt had thus given the enlisted men permission to use the rec room as well as the headquarter's quonset hut for comfort. Dozens of airmen spent every spare moment in one or the other of quonset huts for a bit of warmth.

Therefore, Benson and Meyers, sitting at a small table in the rec room, were amidst dozens of babbling officers and enlisted men.

"This is a busy place," Benson grinned at Meyers.

"Anyplace to keep warm, I guess," Meyers answered quietly.

"I guess this God-forsaken place must be hell after England with nice warm quarters and plenty of English lasses," Benson said.

"It can't be helped," Meyers said.

"They only set up this base for our own 366th," Benson said. "I guess they never figured to have two 8th Air Force fighter groups here with us. I'll bet you wish you were back in England."

Lieutenant Colonel Meyers shrugged. "I go where they send me."

Both pilots shared a common trait—both were American air aces. But here, the similarities ended. Benson was an outward, socializing person, while Meyers had a sober, introverted personality. Benson's amiability made him popular. He had, for example, made these visitors from the 8th Air Force to Asche feel at home with his welcome, as he was now trying to befriend the sober faced Meyers.

The quiet, reserved John Meyers so far had scored twenty-two kills, the last on that Christmas day escort mission on the Rhine River bridge. His fellow pilots considered the solemn, round face Meyers an excellent flyer with great skill in protecting bombers on escort missions. Meyers was a modest man, almost shy, and this trait prompted others to consider him snobbish. But, for men who knew Meyers intimately, they knew he would do anything for a fellow airman.

Meyers, tall and robust in built, with a moon face, rarely smiled. He took his job and the war very seriously, refusing to indulge in the often happy pleasantries of men who might fly out tomorrow and never come back. He had accepted the cold inconveniences of Asche as a mere necessity in the game of war.

"Colonel," Benson grinned again, "don't take this goddamn war so seriously. It'll soon end and maybe we'll still be around when it does."

"Maybe," Meyers said.

"Let me get you a drink," Benson said.

"We're supposed to go out in the morning."

"So are we," Benson answered, "but I'm not so sure anything is going to happen in this kind of weather. Anyway, we haven't seen a sign of the bastards for days. The Krauts must be finished. Christ, we must've knocked out half of Luftwaffe West ourselves on those bridge-busting missions."

Meyer nodded. "Okay, I'll have a drink with you."

Then, Meyers and Benson walked to the crowded bar of the rec room.

Far to the north, in Eindhoven, Holland, a calm had settled over the headquarters of the British 2nd Tactical Air Force. Sir Trafford Leigh-Mallory was completing plans for the British air effort of Operation Varsity. The British air chief had filled in his wing commanders who believed, like many of the Americans, that they had pretty well knocked out the Luftwaffe during the December 25–28 air battles. Meanwhile, the RAF personnel at Eindhoven, inactive for the past three days, were waiting for the weather to break and waiting for Vandenberg to give the word to start Varsity. The men at Eindhoven, with little to do now, thought wistfully of England and, as the new year approached, the British 2nd Tactical airmen were thinking about New Year's Eve parties.

To the northwest, at the RAF Evere airfield outside of Brussels, Belgium, Lieutenant George Buerling of 414 Squadron, 127 Wing, stood in the cold on this December 31 afternoon and watched ground crews load Mustang and Spitfire strafing guns. He studied the men carefully, but he said nothing while the ground crews threw occasional glances at the famed RAF pilot. Besides his exploits out of Malta, Buerling had been one of those Battle of Britain heroes who Winston Churchill had called the few to whom so many owed so much. He had been among those pilots who had met personally with Churchill and when the Prime Minister had asked how he could help, George Buerling had answered without hesitation:

"Send us more petrol so we can fly five or six sorties a day instead of two or three."

Buerling, the sober faced loner, who had an obsession to fight the Germans, was unable to temper his fervor for more combat. Now, despite the weather, Buerling had every intention of taking his 414 Squadron out tomorrow to hopefully destroy any targets of opportunity. When he caught a glimpse of disgust on the face of one of the ground crew, Buerling walked up to him and stared fiercely at the man.

"Sergeant, we're at war. We can't let a few clouds interfere, can we?"

"No, sir."

"Then get on with your job."

"Yes, sir," the sergeant answered.

When Buerling moved off, a lance corporal walked up to the sergeant. "Sarge, the man is a bloody devil, 'e is. 'Is mind is only on one thing—get Jerry. 'E ain't human, 'e ain't."

"Some flyers are like that."

The corporal looked at the dense clouds and now the slight mist of falling snow. "What the 'ell can he do with this weather, anyway? If there's any Jerrys left after that Christmas show, they must 'ave found some place nice and warm and decided to stay there."

"Get on it, Lad. I don't want no 'eat from the lieutenant. 'E's too much of a tiger, 'e is, and 'e'd chew me up without a blink."

"Sure, Sarge."

George Buerling continued on and then entered the rec room where the cheerful, extroverted Johnnie Johnson, commander of 127 Wing, met the lieutenant. "George, aren't you pushing your lads a bit? I 'aven't issued any orders for sorties tomorrow; it's volunteer, you know. Maybe you ought to give your 414 boys a bit of a rest."

"My pilots haven't complained," Buerling said. "I'd like to take them out tomorrow."

"No, they 'aven't complained," Captain Johnson admitted, "but we do 'ave this new offensive coming up. As soon as the weather breaks, we'll need to finish off the Jerry ground troops and then get right into this drive across the Rhine. Maybe your boys would be in better shape if they're rested some."

"Maybe," Buerling said.

"Sure I'm right," Captain Johnson said. "Come on, we'll get a spot of tea and brandy."

At Volkel, Holland, the British fighter plane base less than thirty miles from the Maas River, Squadron Leader Peter Hearne stood in the officer's club with some fellow pilots of the 19 Squadron. The stucco brick building, a former furniture warehouse, was the most popular spot on the Volkel airbase, even though its roof leaked, despite repairs after German air attacks.

On this raw, December 31 afternoon, Hearne and his pilots stood about an improvised bar, eating pretzels and drinking rum. Perhaps no squadron in the RAF included so many adventurers as did 19 Squadron. The flyers were almost throwbacks from the World War I debonair gentlemen pilots. Hearne himself always wore a smile on his oval face and a twinkle in his blue eyes. Perhaps his outward attitude was a mere cover for the tense job of aerial combat. But, more likely, the young RAF squadron leader had probably developed a love for combat.

Hearne and most of his squadron pilots had been former rugby players on the fields of Eton; thus they had brought a somewhat aristocratic and gentlemanly air with them when they joined the RAF. Still, the squadron had distinguished itself during the Battle of Britain, producing more than a dozen aces. Hearne himself already had thirteen kills. He and other pilots of the squadron had learned their trade well under Johnnie Johnson who had commanded 19 Squadron before becoming a wing commander.

Some of the pilots in the Volkel rec room were

singing one of the more risqué songs of the time: "Around her leg, she wore a yellow garter; she wore it in the springtime and in the month of May. . . ."

A smiling pilot sat at a totally untuned, old piano that somebody had found in Volkel to transport here in a lorrie. After another round of rum and the conclusion of another song, F/O Bob Weighill grinned at Hearne.

"If things are slow 'ere, maybe we can find some of those bloody Jerry ships off Norway."

"I'll go anywhere to 'it Jerry, anywhere I can find 'im," Hearne grinned.

19 Squadron, after the Battle of Britain, had spent considerable time escorting bombers that attacked German shipping in the channels and fjords between Norway and Britain. On many occasions 19 Squadron pilots ran into interceptors and subsequent vicious dogfights over the sea lanes. When the squadron moved to Volkel, here in Holland, Hearne and his pilots still spent considerable flying time in the attacks on German shipping.

"You think we'll fly out tomorrow, Peter?" F/O Weighill asked.

"No chance," Hearne said. "Nobody's seen Jerry around since we clobbered them a few days ago. And there 'aven't been any ships in the Skagerral or Kattagat Channels in months."

"What about the Yank reconn report?" Weighill asked. "The bloody Americans claim the Jerry airfields east of the Rhine are busy as beehives."

"Those Yanks 'ave 'ad too much grog," Hearne said. "Jerry can't 'ave a plane left on the Western Front. Anything they do 'ave, they'll need to use against the big bombers 'itting inside Germany."

"I 'eard Leigh-Mallory laughed for a full 'alf hour when he 'eard about those supposed Jerry buildups," Weighill said.

"The air marshal 'ad every reason to laugh," Hearne said. "The Yank blokes 'ave been flying too long. They need a rest, they do."

Weighill looked at the dreary day outside. "When the 'ell is this weather going to break? I'd like another go at those Jerry motor columns."

"Maybe the weather will never break," Hearne shrugged. "Anyway, w'o cares."

"If we can't sortie, what'll we do?"

"What'll we do?" Hearne grinned again. "We'll 'ave us another round 'a rum and we'll sing another tune. Jimmy, play something else."

The piano player nodded. "'Ow about Picadilly W'ore?"

"You play it and we'll sing it," Hearne said.

A moment later, the piano sent out another tune and the 19 Squadron flyers drank another mug of rum between their unsynchronized singing. None of the pilots worried about the Germans.

Thus, except for a few nebulous suspicions, American and British airmen settled into a December 31, 1944 complacency.

Chapter Ten

By 2100 hours, December 31, thick low clouds still hung over the Western Front. Temperatures hovered in the 20s, but the damp, misty air chilled the bones of American infantry and armored division dogfaces. They were cold and in no mood for New Year's Eve celebrations. The American GIs huddled in the open, trying to keep warm; or the lucky ones crowded around small fires inside of battered buildings, dank cellars, or bullet-riddled farmhouses. None of these GIs who had borne the brunt of Operation Herbstnebel were in a festive mood. At best, these troops might have a bottle of wine found in some cellar or perhaps a hot meal wherever company cooks had facilities to cook C rations.

Still, the GIs felt grateful. While artillery still rumbled in and around the battered towns, open fields and dense forests of Eastern Belgium, these American ground troops knew the Germans would not launch any more blitzing panzer attacks. The American infantry and armored troops had taken the offensive and on this New Year's Eve they could at least rest before continuing on.

However, at the Allied airbases, the airmen

enjoyed plenty of warmth, plenty of drink, and plenty of good food. British and American airmen alike warmed themselves around pot bellied stoves in recreation halls, comfortable commandeered buildings, hotels, frame structures, or even four-man canvas tents. Most of the airmen had been pretty well grounded for the past three days. They had thus prepared for New Year's Eve celebrations since the poor weather had stalled their December 25–28 aerial offensive and lessened considerably the possibility of flying missions tomorrow.

The Allied airmen reasoned they would be out soon enough, perhaps without rest, and conducting four or five sorties a day. So, they would take full advantage of the respite to enjoy New Year's Eve.

At Volkel, Holland, the debonair 19 Squadron pilots spared no effort. In fact, the RAF fighter pilots had begun celebrating this afternoon, drinking rum and singing songs while they decorated their stucco recreation hall. They had also shined the old piano, polished their makeshift bar, and even covered their tables with oil cloth. Several bottles of scotch, rye, and brandy, along with a variety of Dutch wines had lined the shelf behind the bar. Somebody had found a Dutch delicatessen in Volkel to prepare fish, chips, sandwiches, and sugar cookies. The 19 Squadron flyers had even invited pretty Dutch lasses to their New Year's Eve party, and by 2100 hours, the celebration was well underway.

More than a dozen 19 Squadron pilots jammed the bar, huddling about three or four of the cute Dutch girls as the flyers laughed and joked with their guests, who spoke little English. Other flyers sat at tables with other Dutch lasses, drinking high balls or wine and eating sugar cakes, fish, and chips.

When the man at the piano banged out "Picadilly Whore," the 19 Squadron flyers abruptly stopped their chit chat, exchanged grins, and then broke into a chorus:

"Oh, the Picadilly w'ore, she plied 'er trade in Soho,
When along came a Tommy who was 'uddlin in 'is coat;
When 'e saw the wench and asked to 'ave a go,
The wo're first asked to see 'is one pound note."

When the chorus ended and the airmen reverted to their drink and talk, one of the Dutch girls frowned. "Vot iss zis w'ore?" she asked.

The question brought an explosion of laughter from the airmen, a burst of guffaws that rocked the low ceiling of the stucco building.

The piano player grinned and then pounded even harder on the piano before he shouted above the din: "Another chorus, lads, another chorus," he cried to his fellow airmen. "We got all night, we 'ave. Sing out! Sing out!"

The men responded.

"Oh, the Picadilly w'ore, she plied 'er trade in Soho . . ."

At one of the tables, Lieutenant Peter Hearne and F/O Bob Weighill sat on either side of a Dutch girl, a pretty blonde, somewhat buxomy, but with a clean, round face. "Drink up, lass," Hearne gestured to the girl, "and eat your sweet cake."

"Yah," the girl smiled.

"We're 'ere for a time tonight, we are," F/O

Weighill said. "We got nothing to do tomorrow but sleep. With the soup outside, nobody's going anywhere."

"Ze Zoup?" the girl frowned.

"The clouds, the mist—fog," Bob Weighill gestured.

"Ah, yah, ze mist," the girl smiled.

"Drink up," Peter Hearne told the girl again.

The Dutch girl smiled and sipped the highball.

Hearne and Weighill grinned and then joined the chorus in the closing lines: ". . . The w'ore first asked to see 'is one pound note."

Later, when flyers saw by their watches that the New Year had arrived, some of them stole kisses from some of the Dutch girls. Then came dancing, more eating, more drinking, and more songs, especially the Cockney songs. During the long evening, the 19 Squadron airmen stayed up well into the wee hours of the morning. They ate too much, drank too liberally, and celebrated too long. Most of them weaved unsteadily and quite groggily back to their sleeping quarters, thoroughly intoxicated after this New Year's Eve jubilee. They fell quickly into deep sleep.

When, at 1000 hours, the first wave of ME 190s from Gunther Lutzow's JG 3 assault geschwader droned over Volkel, the 19 Squadron airmen would still be asleep.

At Evere, the pilots of 127 Wing celebrated as lively as their fellow RAF airmen in Volkel. In their quonset hut rec room, the airmen of 414 Squadron had also amassed an array of liquor along with sugar cakes, fried chips, and fish. Here too, the flyers gathered about an improvised bar to drink and sing the New Year's Eve away. These RAF airmen also managed to find women, a dozen

Belgium lasses from Brussels, to join their pleasure. By 2100 hours, December 31, laughter, loud talk, and plenty of drinking prevailed among the British flyers and their guests.

On an old wind-up victrola phonograph, somebody put a record on and the flyers broke into a vocal accompaniment of the scratchy, overused disc. The song was the same Australian piece that RAF airmen had picked up from their Down Under brethren during the North African campaign.

> "'Round 'er leg she wore a purple garter,
> she wore it in the springtime and in the month of May,
> And if you ask 'er why the 'ell she wore it,
> she wore it for an airman w'o was far, far away . . ."

Then came the echo of guffaws before the airmen settled once more to another drink, another sugar cake, or another round of conversation with their friendly Belgium lasses. F/O Frank Hanton had caught the ear of one Belgium girl, flattering her, extolling her on her beauty, or touching her. He danced with her when somebody put a slow waltz on the victrola, but he did not dance with her for long. With the women outnumbered at least ten to one, Hanton did not get halfway across the cramped dance floor before Lieutenant Charles Stover cut in.

"You don't mind, do you, Frank?"

"Why not," Hanton shrugged. He gave up his dancing partner to Stover and he then wandered off. Hanton spotted a solitary figure sitting at one of the small tables. The loner was George Buerling, that sober faced, all business squadron leader of 414 Squadron. Buerling sat rather glumly and quietly. Frank Hanton came over to him and slapped the squadron leader on the shoulder.

"Good Lord, George, why the hell are you so down? A good looking man like you? Some of these Belgium girls have been giving you a look. Why don't you grab one of them and have a time for yourself."

Buerling only scowled.

"It's New Year's Eve, man, a time to celebrate, especially after the job we did on those Germans."

"Don't drink too much," Buerling gestured, "we might go out tomorrow."

"What the hell do you mean, go out? We're closed in again; nobody's flying."

"We're not closed in that bad," Buerling said. "I understand Wing wants to have an armed reconnaissance unit out in the morning and that might be us."

"Damn! Won't you ever relax?"

"All I'm saying," Buerling answered soberly, "is that if the weather is any good at all, 414 Squadron will probably be out."

Frank Hanton shook his head. "One way or the other, George, this'll be the last New Year's a lot of us will likely spend together. Some of us may be dead before next New Year's or we'll all be back to Canada because the war will certainly be over by then. Those of us who do get back will not likely see each other again. We'll go our separate ways. You'll be lost somewhere in Montreal and I'll be lost somewhere in Toronto."

"Maybe," Buerling said, "but we've got a war on right now. If there's anything we can do tomorrow to make it easier for those American infantry boys, we sure as hell ought to do it."

Frank Hanton shook his head again and picked up George Buerling's half empty glass. He walked back to the bar, wiggling among the crowd until he reached the counter. Then, he ordered a refill. "For the squadron leader," he cocked his head toward Buerling. The bartender nodded and filled the glass. Then, while Hanton carried the drink in one hand, he led one of the Belgium girls with the other hand to Buerling's table. When they sat down, Hanton grinned to his squadron leader.

"She's a beauty, wouldn't you say?"

The girl smiled at the 414 squadron leader, and she leaned closer. "Voues es un joli gargon."

When Buerling frowned, Frank Hanton leaned close to him. "She says you're a pretty man. Now, did you ever expect anybody in Belgium to tell you that?"

"I guess not," Buerling answered, his face softening. Then, both Buerling and the girl turned as the other pilots broke into song again.

> ". . . 'Round 'er leg, she wore a yellow garter, she wore it in the springtime and in the month of May . . ."

George Buerling grinned. He struck up a quiet conversation with the girl, drank and ate with her, and even danced with her. Others in the quonset hut nodded in satisfaction. The 414 Squadron commander had finally broken down, forgetting the serious business of war, and agreed to relax.

The pilots of 414 and other 127 Wing squadrons at Evere celebrated well past midnight. Like those at Volkel, these RAF pilots at Evere drank, ate, caroused, and finally collapsed in deep sleep on their barracks beds. Most of them would still be sleeping soundly at 1000 hours tomorrow morning. Only George Buerling and twelve pilots of 414 Squadron would be airborne when fifty 109s of JG 26s II Gruppe under Major Anton Hackl droned unexpectedly over the Evere airfield.

To the southwest, the American bomber crews of the 322nd Bomb Group had gathered in their rec room at Lille. The airmen of Nye's Annihilators, who enjoyed considerable success after the weather cleared on Christmas day, enjoyed luxuries none that those in the RAF and Luftwaffe could ever afford. For the Americans, their drinks included the best champagne, the best Hiram Walker whisky, and top grade scotch. Their food included real potato chips, sliced turkey and ham, apple and blueberry pies, and every manner of party caps and favors. The Americans had plenty of money and a knack for ingenuity. These two items enabled the 322nd airmen, as well as American airmen from other groups in Europe, to get whatever they wanted.

Lille was a small French town, but the Yankee dollar from three American air groups had brought to Lille a burst of activities and an influx of people. Bars and cafes and houses of prostitution lined the narrow streets. Winemakers and spirit makers did a big business. And, on a milder note, the bakers, tailors, cabinetmakers, and farmers had found willing customers among the Americans, who had the price if the seller had the item.

The 322nd Bomb Group at Lille included a long, polished oak bar, with a mirror behind it and shelves jammed with liquor and wine bottles. The tables had smooth, clean tops, the phonograph played clearly, and the coffee urn was always filled with a fresh brew. On this particular New Year's

Eve, when the word went out to Lille for women to join Yank parties, females arrived in droves. Innocents to prostitutes flocked to participate, especially since the Americans sent vehicles to pick them up.

By 2100 hours, the 322nd quonset hut rec hall shook from the din of two hundred airmen and a hundred women: laughing, giggling, drinking, eating, and dancing. Sombody continually changed records on the phonograph as the night of revelry wore on and on.

An hour after midnight, both the bomber crewmen and their invited women had already become unsteady from too much drink, bloated from too much good food, wilted from heavy dancing, and hoarse from too much heavy singing. At 0130 hours, January 1 1945, the man at the phonograph put on a soft ballad. Nobody complained of the slow, quiet "White Cliffs of Dover," for the song gave the tired airmen a respite from the whirlwind celebration. They relaxed to sing quietly and softly.

"There'll be bluebirds over the white cliffs of Dover,
Tomorrow, just you wait and see;
There'll be love and laughter and peace ever after,
Tomorrow, when the world is free."

The song had come from England, but while Britishers had shown no great interest in the tune, both American soldiers overseas and civilians at home had popularized the melody. Americans sang the song during quiet moments in camps or during quiet hours before moving into combat. Back in the states, American wives, sisters, and sweethearts sang "White Cliffs" when they thought of their loved ones in far away foreign lands.

The song held rich meaning for Americans.

". . . The shepherd will tend his sheep,
And Johnny will go to sleep.
Tomorrow, when the world is free. . . ."

When the song ended, Lieutenant James Lonely and Lieutenant Ed Steinburge walked quietly to a table and sat down with two French girl companions. The B-26 pilots had been among the lucky ones to find girls for themselves.

"Have another drink?" Steinburge said.

"No, no," one of the girls gestured quickly. "Too much. Too much."

"They can't hold a hell of a lot, can they?" Lonely grinned at Steinburge.

"They aren't used to so many goodies," Steinburge returned the grin.

The pilots looked up as Colonel John Samuel stopped next to them and tapped Lieutenant Steinburge on the shoulder. "Are you boys treating our guests right?"

"Yes, sir, Colonel," Lieutenant Lonely said.

"Behave yourselves," Samuels gestured, "but enjoy yourselves, too."

"Are we going out tomorrow, sir?" Steinburge asked.

"I don't think so," Samuels answered. "We haven't got a thing from bomber command. Anyway, they say this bad weather will hang on. Not even fighter-bombers are likely to be out. So, I guess you can celebrate as long as you want," Samuels grinned.

"Day off tomorrow," Steinburge suddenly

shouted and jerked to a standing position. "A toast to the colonel!"

"A toast to Colonel Samuels!" a dozen voices responded. The 322nd commander lowered his head, somewhat embarrassed.

The 322nd Bomb Group party at Lille continued into the wee hours of the morning. The pilots and navigators and bombardiers (and gunners at their enlisted men parties) would sleep soundly tonight from too much celebration. Most of them would still be fast asleep tomorrow at 1000 hours when Colonel Hans "Assi" Hahn and sixty 190s of JG 2 roared over the sprawling American airbase.

At Asche, Belgium, more parties were in full swing on this New Year's Eve. The pilots of the 9th Air Force's 366th Fighter Group, in fact, had a real excuse to celebrate. They needed to play host to their visitors, the pilots of the 8th Air Force's 352nd and 361st Fighter Groups. A din at the Asche airbase radiated from the two quonset huts on the base, the only places to get warm. In one hut, some of the pilots of the 366th entertained the men of 361st, while in the other quonset hut, the remainder of the 366th pilots treated the airmen of the 352nd.

The men at Asche had no women as companions, for Asche was only a name and not a town. Besides, Asche lay too close to the combat zone and few civilians cared to be so near the Bosch. When the Germans launched Operation Herbstnebel two weeks ago, civilians who still remained in the Asche area had departed in a hurry. So, while the Americans here had plenty to eat and drink, they had no female companions. But they sang and they drank and they talked.

At the rec hall quonset hut, Major George Prader urged Lieutenant Colonel John Meyers of the 352nd to break down and enjoy New Year's Eve.

"I don't think you're going anywhere tomorrow," the major said.

"We're scheduled for an armed reconn patrol," Meyers answered.

"It's a little misty out and it might be worse by morning," Prader said. "I doubt if anybody'll be out."

"Maybe not."

"Anyway, we deserve a break," Prader said. "Have another drink and another cheese on rye."

"I'm stuffed."

"You can't stop now; it's only a few minutes to midnight." Prader leaned close to Meyers. "We've got plenty to celebrate. We've been in this goddamn war for three years and you and I are still alive. A lot of guys I knew last year at this time won't be able to drink a toast at the stroke of twelve."

"I can't argue with you there," Meyers said.

"A lot of pilots underestimate those Krauts," Prader said. "They may be outnumbered, their aircraft outclassed, their logistics gone to pot, but they've still got some goddamn good flyers."

"Yeah," Meyers said.

"Finish your drink," Major Prader said. "You need a fresh highball for midnight."

"Sure," Lieutenant John Meyers grinned.

At the headquarters quonset hut in Asche, Captain Floyd Benson, constantly friendly and outgoing, offered a drink to Lieutenant Urban Drew of the 361st Fighter Group that was also on temporary assignment to Asche from the 8th

Air Force.

"It is true, Lieutenant? You got yourself one of those jets?" Benson asked.

"I was lucky," Drew answered modestly.

"Lucky hell," Benson said. "I heard you've already got yourself eight kills."

"Nothing compared to you," Drew answered. "I hear you got over a dozen."

The captain from Lancaster, California, lowered his head to hide his embarrassment. "I'm the guy that was lucky. Anyway, I never got a jet."

The young 361st Fighter Group pilot felt an immediate admiration for Benson. The captain, despite his great record, showed no egotism or snobbishness of any kind. Drew himself had accomplished a rare achievement in downing a jet in October when his 361st Group had made a low level sweep over Aschner. Drew's unit had made an attack on the famed Nowotny JG 7, the first jet fighter unit in operation. Drew had come in at an angle to strike the ME 262 in the fuel pod and the jet had exploded. Then, moments later, Drew had caught an ME 109 in his sights and knocked this second German plane down.

Drew had felt uneasy among these 366th Group strangers, but Benson had made him feel at ease and Drew was soon drinking and celebrating. By midnight, he was also singing like everyone else.

"Let's have another drink," Benson said to Drew.

"Are you supposed to be going out tomorrow?" Drew asked.

"I'll be all right," Captain Benson said.

The men at Asche ate and drank well into the wee hours of the morning, and most of them would go to bed drunk. They would not even feel the cold of this winter night in their four-man canvas tents. Some, like Lieutenant Colonel John Meyers and Captain Benson, would be awake at 0900 for possible armed reconn missions. Most of the airmen in the three fighter groups, however, would still be asleep when Major Robert "Bazi" Weise of IV/JG 54 led fifty-seven 190s over the crowded American fighter base at Asche.

At Orcante, France, the pilots of the 354th American Fighter Group indulged in the same New Year's Eve pleasures as other Yank and RAF airmen. Except for their escort missions to Bastogne and other air sorties for the next three days, these men of 354th, far to the south of the Bulge, had been unaffected by the battle taking place in Belgium. At Orcante, everyone from group Colonel George Bickel to the lowest mechanic corporal enjoyed comfortable living quarters, good food, and frequent leaves to Paris, only a hundred miles to the west. The airmen at Orcante could only complain of one discomfort—they were away from their homes in the United States.

Orcante had been a permanent French airbase since World War I, a major Luftwaffe base after the fall of France, and now an American base. Big, comfortable barracks with soft beds housed the enlisted men and elaborate chateaus with rich ornaments, huge sitting rooms, and marble dining tables served the officers.

In one of the huge guest halls of a chateau, the pilots of the 354th Fighter Group held an elaborate New Year's Eve party. Women from Orcante packed the hall along with a paid band. At the two bars every conceivable liquor—from rare French wines to cognac lay on the counters. The richest foods—hams, beef, chicken, cakes, and rolls sat on inviting food tables. Pilots and women guests simply gorged themselves.

Even the enlisted men enjoyed a rich New Year's celebration in a small chateau that served as their rec room. Their own tables also held good food, plenty of drink, and ample women. Here in Orcante, as elsewhere in Allied bases, the men celebrated until well into the wee hours of the morning.

At the officer's chateau, the pilots and their women had petered themselves out by 0200 hours from heavy drinking, gourmet eating, and fast dancing. Now, in the wee hours of January 1, 1945, they merely loitered in tired groups to sing, with some of the songs quite risqué:

"Roll me over in the clover, roll me over,
lay me down and do it again. . . ."

Among the loudest of these voices was that of Lieutenant Glen Eagleston. When the last chorus ended, "Eagle" Eagleston flopped into a chair at one of the tables next to his fellow pilot, Lieutenant James Daglis.

"Some night, Eagle," Daglis grinned.

"Let's get another drink," Eagleston answered. "Hell, we got all night and all day tomorrow."

"Yeah," Daglis said. "Colonel Bickel says we might be grounded for at least a couple of more days."

Eagleston grinned and picked up a bottle on the table. "Then we may as well finish this. Two days is sure as hell enough time to sleep it off." He looked at the two smiling women sitting at the table with him and Daglis. "How about another drink, Ma'moiselle?"

"Oui," one of the girls smiled.

"Good," Eagleston nodded and then poured four more drinks. Before his trio of companions had finished their drink, Eagleston had downed his quickly and then poured himself another.

"Eagle," Jim Daglis grinned, "you better take it easy. Before you know it, you'll pass out. How will it look to enlisted men to see an officer pass out?"

"The hell with it," Eagleston said. "It's New Year's Eve, and who the hell knows where any of us will be next New Year's Eve?"

Daglis looked at his watch. "It's almost 0300."

"It doesn't matter; we're not going anyplace." Then, Lieutenant Glen Eagleston broke into a solo:

"Roll me over, roll me over, roll me over and do it again. . . ."

Those at the other tables chuckled at the fighter ace, and their guffaws echoed through the ornate hall of the chateau.

At 1000 hours on January 1, 1945, most of these pilots of the 354th Fighter Group would still be sound asleep, slumbering soundly after their night of revelry. For these airmen, no drone of Luftwaffe planes would interrupt their sleep at Orcante. However, a half hour later, Colonel George Bickel would rouse his 354th pilots out of bed on the double and get them airborne within fifteen to twenty minutes. Glen "Eagle" Eagleston, big head and all, would find himself caught in the middle of the greatest dogfight that ever took place on the Western Front.

Chapter Eleven

At 2100 on December 31, 1944, most of the pilots and crewmen of Luftwaffe West had begun a rather short, subdued New Year's celebration. For most of the Fliegers, their gruppen briefings had just ended and the airmen had been warned to retire early so they could arise fresh and alert the next morning. And, unlike the British and Americans, the Germans had found little time to prepare recreation halls and other quarters for New Year's Eve celebrations. They had been too busy since the start of Operation Herbstnebel two weeks ago, first in air support strikes for their panzer and Wehrmacht units, next in the losing fight against superior numbers of Allied planes, and then with preparations for Operation Bodenplatte.

On this chilly, cloudy night at Verrelbusch, at 2210 hours, the slow mellow refrain of the popular "Lile Marlene" drifted beyond the frosted windows of the frame structure recreation hall:

"Outside the barracks, by the corner light,
I'll stand and wait for you at night,
We will create a world for two, I'll wait for
you, the whole night through,

For you, Lile Marlene; for you, Lile Marlene . . ."

Inside the hall, only a dozen pilots still crowded around the small plank bar. The others of JG 26 had already gone to bed. The bar counter held a few half finished bottles of schnapps, some empty beer glasses, and four near empty bottles of wine that had come from somewhere in France a long time ago—when Germany still occupied Western Europe. The dozen pilots wore nostalgic looks on their handsome young faces. They knew that tomorrow they might again meet the swarms of enemy fighter planes, and they remembered too vividly the results of their last encounter with Allied air superiority.

The Abbeville boys of JG 26 had lost many of their comrades during the air battles of December 25–28, and they guessed that some here might not return tomorrow. So, the Schlageter pilots at Verrelbusch did not really celebrate; they reminisced. They remembered the days when the Luftwaffe ruled the skies over Europe, Russia, and Africa; when the ME 109 and FW 190 surpassed in ability all enemy aircraft; when they could walk through any German village or city and command respect in their Luftwaffe uniforms.

As these German airmen thought of those glory days, they sang Lile Marlene, for the song had been nurtured in Paris during the height of the German occupation, and at the height of Germany's good fortunes:

"Bugler, tonight, don't play the call to arms,
I want to know an evening with a charm,
Then we will say goodbye and part, I'll

always keep
You in my heart, with me, Lile Marlene,
Lile Marlene."

No optimism or anticipation shone from a single face here, for few of them looked forward to their dangerous task tomorrow. The JG 26 airmen had not enjoyed anything more to eat than pretzels, slices of brown bread, and a few weiners, nothing like the sumptuous banquet tables of the Americans. No female companions or glittery decorations adorned the drab recreation hall. The men here daydreamed more than anything else on this December 31 evening, thinking of happy homes when smiles still prevailed, or of fabulous Berlin in its beauty and energy before Allied bombers had turned the proud city into rubble; or of pretty Bavaria with its bustling holiday crowds, quaint hotels, and lively beer halls before a losing war had turned Bavaria into a drab, quiet state. The fliegers sipped their beer and ate their sparse food in almost quiet resignation.

At a table in the hall, Colonel Josef Pips Priller sat with his two gruppen commodores, Major Anton Hackl and Major Peter Eder. They drank beer and munched pretzels as they listened to the soft refrains of Lile Marlene. Priller squeezed his face as he looked at his pilots; many of them were so young and they reminded him of innocent children. When the airmen finished the next chorus of "Lile Marlene," Priller shook his head.

"They seem better suited for the choir loft of the Cologne Cathedral than to the controls of a fighter-bomber."

"But there is no more Cologne Cathedral," Major Anton Hackl said, a tinge of bitterness in his voice. "There is no more Cologne; the British have seen to that."

"Let us hope we can pay them back tomorrow," Priller said. He then looked at Major Eder. "Peter, I do not see any of your gruppe pilots here. Have they all gone to bed?"

"They are worried, Colonel," Eder answered, "and rightly so. They do not believe we can reach any of these Allied airbases before swarms of American and British planes jump our formations. I must admit, I am suspicious, too."

"If we are careful, we may surprise them as we did two weeks ago," Priller said. "The British in Brussels will be celebrating all night on this holiday eve. They are like that. They will sleep late, for they are overconfident, thanks to the industrial might of America." He looked at Hackl. "Is that not so, Anton?"

"Yes, the British do overestimate themselves," the slim narrow faced Anton Hackl answered.

"Most of these pilots are yours, Anton," Peter Eder cocked his head toward those singing at the bar. "The hour grows late, and these fliegers must be awake early tomorrow."

Major Anton Hackl shrugged. "I cannot deny them these moments together. Some may not be here tomorrow to sing again."

Neither Colonel Josef Priller nor Major Peter Eder answered. They sipped their beer again, munched their pretzels, and listened again to the soft refrain:

". . . Then we will say good-bye and part;
I'll always keep you in my heart with me,
Lile Marlene, Lile Marlene. . . ."

The quiet singing and soft talk that prevailed at Verrelbusch, also prevailed in other German bases on this December 31 evening. In Wesel, at 2200 hours, some two dozen men loitered around the bar in the recreation hall of JG 1. The airmen had been here for less than two hours for Major Heinz Bar had not finished his briefing until well after 2000 hours. The airmen did find refreshments in the recreation hall after the briefing, but the pretzels, grizzly sausage, dark bread, schnapps, and second rate beer could hardly be considered delicacies. Still, the pilots dug in until most of the food and drink was gone.

The somber faces of these pilots hardly reflected a festive mood. Among all of the geschwader fliegers of Luftwaffe West perhaps none felt the uneasiness of their mission as did the combat flyers of JG 1. They would fly three and one half hours one way tomorrow, and all of them were certain that enemy fighter planes would jump them long before they reached the British bases around Ostend. None relished the idea of flying across hundreds of miles of Allied occupied territory, and they could not feel much enthusiasm for the ordeal.

The JG 1 airmen here talked in low tones to each other, discussing their wives or families or sweethearts, or the good times that had once prevailed throughout Germany. They did not blame Hitler or the 3rd Reich for their fallen hopes and a ravaged Germany; they blamed simple ill luck or the misfortunes of war.

At a small table, Major Heinz Bar and Captain Waldemar Woitke drank schnapps and ate bread and sausage. They listened to the small talk among those at the bar or among small groups sitting at tables.

"The men are quiet," Captain Woitke said.

Major Heinz Bar nodded. Somberness had replaced the normally outgoing, bright look on his handsome, chiseled face. "They are worried, Waldemar. No matter how much I tried to encourage them, they are nervous and unsure."

"Who can blame them?" Woitke said. He paused and looked at his watch. "It is after ten o'clock. These fliegers must rise early. Perhaps we should tell them to go to bed."

"No," Bar answered. "On an evening such as this, and with perhaps the most dangerous mission of their careers awaiting them tomorrow, how can we tell them to go to bed, as we would tell little children? They are men, even the young ones, who must do more than we should ask from the bravest of men. No, they must be treated like men. They will know when it is time to stop their quiet talk and bid each other good night."

Before Captain Woitke answered, somebody put a record on a phonograph. After a few scratchy seconds, the Luftwaffe's favorite tune filled the recreation hall: the strains of "Auf Wiederseh'n." The men stopped talking to listen and to remember again the good times in Germany when the tune first became popular. Then, one man burst into song:

> "Auf Wiederseh'n, Auf Wiederseh'n, we'll meet again, sweetheart,
> This lovely day has flown away, the time has come to part . . ."

By the time he had finished the first two lines, others had joined in:

". . . We'll kiss again, like this again,
don't let the teardrops start,
With love that's true, I'll wait for you,
Auf Wiederseh'n, sweetheart. . . ."

Then, a silence descended over the JG 1 recreation hall in Wesel. The fliegers now sat or stood seemingly alone at the tables or near the bar, each man rapt in his own recollections of the past and its glory.

Finally, one of the fliegers rose from a table. "It is late; time to go to bed." His words burst through the quiet room like a short, blaring speech. He stood up, downed the last of his beer in a quick gulp, and then scanned his comrades. "Auf Wiederseh'n, Fliegers; till we meet again." Then, he walked from the room, the click of his boots echoing across the floor like the harsh, metronome beat of a drum.

Others in the recreation hall, alone or in pairs, slowly rose from the tables or left the bar and ambled out of the room. Soon, only Major Bar and Captain Woitke remained.

"You see, Waldemar," the major grinned. "They knew when it was time to leave."

Captain Waldemar Woitke nodded and rose from the table. "I too know when it is time to leave. Good night, Major."

"Sleep soundly, Waldemar," Bar answered.

Heinz Bar watched his gruppe leader leave the hall. Then, the JG 1 commodore walked slowly to the small phonograph, picked up the record, and placed the disc on the turntable. As he stood alone in the recreation hall and listened to the nostalgic tune of "Auf Wiederseh'n," his mind wandered to the past. He remembered his small farm near

Sommerfeld, outside of Leipzig: the laughter of his parents, sisters, and brothers, and the thrill of walking with that pretty girl he had once hoped to marry. He remembered the thrill of his first glider ride in 1930, and he remembered that day in 1941 on the Russian Front when they shot him down, and, half blind and badly injured, he had stumbled through Russian territory for two days to reach safety. And, Bar recalled his service in Italy, one of his pleasant memories with fine wines and emotional women.

Now, in retrospect, Bar realized he had flown almost one thousand combat missions and he wondered if his luck had run out. Tomorrow, he would fly the most dangerous mission of all. He did not mind for himself so much; he had enjoyed the good life. But the young pilots—how many would return to Wesel?

". . . With love that's true, I'll wait for you,
Auf Wiederseh'n, Sweetheart. . . ."

Now, the needle scratched. Major Heinz Pritzl Bar turned off the phonograph, snapped off the lights, and left the recreation hall.

The somberness at Verrelbusch and Wesel was repeated in almost all the other airbases in Germany's Western Europe. But, among the airmen of JG 2 at Rheims was a spark of optimism. The pilots of Hans Assi Hahn apparently relished their target for tomorrow—the bomber base at Lille. They ached for revenge against the B-26 bridge busters, the American air units that had brought so much distress, peril, and isolation to the panzer and Wehrmacht soldiers in Belgium.

At 2315 hours, December 31, nearly thirty pilots

of JG 2 still loitered in their recreation hall, drinking schnapps and lager beer. Their fears of enemy interceptors tomorrow had been subordinated to their eagerness to knock out dozens of American Marauders. No doubt, Hans Assi Hahn's optimism and confidence had rubbed off on many of his fliegers. And why not? They had carried out some important strikes during the early days of Operation Herbstnebl. Despite the losses on Christmas day to the U.S. 354th Fighter Group, the Richthofen unit had done considerable damage to American ground troops.

Lieutenant Otto Kindes had been among the few fliegers in JG 2 to view with suspicion the positive attitude here, for he had flown too long to easily become swayed by Hahn's optimism. He knew too well the power of the Allied air forces. At one of the tables, Kindes sat with Leutnant Josef Zwernemann and Sergeant George Kell. They had already finished a bottle of schnapps and they had begun a second bottle. Otto Kindes had just poured another round when Colonel Hans Hahn patted him on the shoulder.

"Leutnant, not so much; we have a long flight tomorrow."

"But you told us not to worry," Kindes answered, a tinge of disdain in his voice. "So, we are not worrying."

The colonel grinned. "Still, we need a clear head, do we not?"

"Join us, Colonel," Leutnant Zwernemann suddenly spoke.

"Why not?" Hahn shrugged. He flopped into a chair with his fliegers and took a drink. Then, he saw the uneasy look on Sergeant Kell's face. The colonel frowned. "Is something the matter, Sergeant? Are you so worried?"

Kell only shook his head; he did not speak. How could he tell the colonel that he was simply awe stricken in the close presence of the legendary Assi Hahn?

"Sergeant," Hahn grinned, "you just follow me tomorrow and you will be all right."

Sergeant George Kell only nodded.

Colonel Hahn tapped Kell on the shoulder. "You have a fine record. There is no need for a man like you to lack confidence in yourself. You have been in our Richthofen geschwader for a long time. Did you think I would keep you in this geschwader if you were not among the best pilots in the Luftwaffe? Just think what you have accomplished in your short career, and you will know that you can succeed tomorrow."

"Thank you, Mein Colonel."

"Kell," Hahn said, "I would wager that before another month has passed, you will be a leutnant, an officer with all the privileges of such officers."

Sergeant George Kell grinned, but he did not speak.

Hahn returned the grin, downed his drink, and then rose from the table. He lightly tapped Kell's face with his fingers and then looked at the others. "Not too much tonight, fliegers, and not too late. We have important work tomorrow."

When Colonel Hahn left the table, Leutnant Zwernemann leaned close and grinned at Kell. "He is human, just like the rest of us. He will not turn you to stone with a simple stare."

"But he is such a great man," the young sergeant said.

"He was once a nobody just like you," Leutnant

Kindes gestured. "You may one day rise to an oberst's rank, too, if the war lasts long enough."

Sergeant George Kell nodded.

By 2300 hours, the drinking and eating and chit-chat had somewhat diminished at the Rheims recreation hall and a quiet descended over the hall. In the subdued atmosphere, somebody put the ever popular "Lile Marlene" on the phonograph. The first note had barely come from the speaker when the men of the Richthofen unit broke into an almost simultaneous chorus:

> ". . . Outside the barracks, by the corner light,
> I'll always stand and wait for you at night;
> We will create a world for two, I'll wait for you, the whole night through,
> For you, Lile Marlene, for you, Lile Marlene . . ."

The Luftwaffe pilots also sang other slow, nostalgic tunes on this cold, damp night: "Nocturne," "Die Feldermous," "Blue Danube," and several more. Then, at 2300 hours, the airmen of JG 2 began leaving the hall, bidding each other a good night. By 2330, darkness had totally fallen over Rheims.

Soon, the sound of big British Lancasters broke the late evening silence of New Year's Eve, but nobody at Rheims worried. The RAF were interested in terror bombing of the large cities, not in strategic bombing against military targets. The four engine British planes were heading for some large German city, not a target like the Rheims airbase.

* * *

At 0630 hours, January 1, 1945, the last trace of night still hung in the sky over Wesel. But engines screamed across the black landscape and warts moved about like phantoms in the night as they helped fliegers into cockpits, checked parachutes, gear, and canopies. Only a blinking red light from the runway control tower marred the near total darkness in this gloomy, starless morning. Some of the pilots squinted at the low hanging clouds, barely recognizable in the darkness. The clouds offered a mixed blessing: they would leave Allied air commanders unprepared, but the low clouds would force the JG 1 flyers to fly blindly above the overcast during the long flight to the RAf bases near the North Sea coast.

Major Heinz Bar sat stiffly in the cockpit of his 190 and watched the twin engine JU 88s lumber lazily toward the head of the runway—without lights. The Junker pathfinders would leave first, setting the course for the Ostend area where half of JG 1s Folke-Wulfs would hit Melsbroek while the other half hit Westem. Suddenly, the blinking red light turned to a full green and an array of white lights exploded in a length of bubbled brightness along both sides of the runway. Then, the JU 88s roared down the runway and rose into the sky before disappearing into the darkness.

Now, Major Heinz Bar revved his 190 engine and taxied slowly to the head of the runway. He could feel the strain from the heavy weight of four spitterbombs under the fuselage and the twenty-four rockets under his wings. But the Folke-Wulf responded faithfully to Bar's touch of the controls. At 0635, the blinking light again changed to a steady green. Bar revved his engine again, released the brake, and then shot down the runway and into the darkness. Another twenty-five 190s followed him before Captain Waldemar Woitke zoomed down the runway. Then, twenty-five more loaded Folke-Wulfs of JG 1s I Gruppe followed Woitke. By 0645 hours, the last of the two gruppens of fifty-two aircraft left Wesel, following the JU 88 pathfinders that now droned above the clouds. Soon, JG 1 had also come above the clouds and then jelled into four plane diamond formations before droning westward.

Bar's JG 1, though part of Colonel Wilheim Moritz's Fliegercorps Holland, would not join the other formations set to hit Eindhoven, Volkel, Antwerp, and Tillberg. Bar's targets lay too far away. He would be deep into Belgium before the other geschwaders of Fliegercorps Holland formed over the Rhine and droned westward before breaking off to seek their own particular targets.

At 0730 hours, daylight had come to Western Europe. At the German airbase in Wesel, Colonel Hans Assi Hahn sat impatiently in the cockpit of his FW 190. He watched the JU 88s roar down the Wesel runway before he revved the engine of his own plane and roared down the airstrip to soar skyward. The other forty-nine 190s of JG 2 soon followed him. Over the battered city of Cologne, Hahn's Richthofen unit would join other geschwaders of Fliegercorps North before the formations droned westward. JG 2 and JG 27 would be the only single engine units among the ME 110 twin engine bombers that droned toward the bigger American bases at Florennes, Coulimiers, and St. Dizier. But, although Lille was much further than the other targets of Fliegercorps North, Hahn would reach his target at about the same time since his 190s were much speedier than the ME 110s.

For another two hours, engines whined and planes zoomed down runways throughout the Luftwaffe West airbases in Western Germany. Not until 0830 hours, two hours after JG 1 had left Wesel, did the last of the Luftwaffe West geschwaders leave their bases. The last to leave were I/JG 6, KG 7, II/JG 27 and KG 51 of Fliegercorps Holland who would hit the nearest bases in Holland and Antwerp.

By 0900 hours, more than 1,100 airborne German planes were flying westward above the thick clouds. They hung close behind the JU 88s, trusting the judgment of these pathfinders. Many of the fliegers, however, worried about the possibility of Belgium or French early risers who might hear the German formations and report them to the Allied military. But, by 0930, January 1, 1945, nobody had thus far detected the Luftwaffe West geschwaders and gruppen, not even those FW 190s of Heinz Pritzl Bar that had already been droning westward for three hours.

The air below the low hanging clouds was only slightly misty, so the Germans could make their strikes. And, the Luftwaffers had guessed correctly. Most of the Allied airmen, British and American, still slept soundly, still numb from too much food, drink, and revelries.

Some Allied airmen had been up by 0830. The ever eager, all business George Buerling of 414 Squadron had ordered his pilots out for an armed reconn mission. Buerling had volunteered for such an early sortie. The sober faced Lieutenant Colonel John Meyers of the 352nd Group at Asche was up, for he expected to make a low-level armed reconnaissance flight this morning. Also at Asche, the buoyant Captain Floyd Benson of the 366th Fighter Group was also awake, for he too expected to go out on an armed reconn mission this morning. To the north, a squadron from the Polish wing at Duerne and a squadron from the RAF wing at Grimberghen had been airborne since 0700 to seek targets of opportunity.

Most of the RAF wing leaders and the American group leaders, however, had forsaken missions on this January 1 day because of poor flying weather. They would wait for a break in the weather, perhaps tomorrow. And, uncannily, nobody as yet had seen or reported the massive German formations.

Major Heinz Bar, Colonel Hans Assi Hahn, Colonel Josef Pips Priller, Colonel Gunther Lutzow, and other JG commodores could not believe their good fortune thus far. Would the Germans indeed pull off this bold Operation Bodenplatte against some 25 Allied airbases? By 0930 hours, none of the German fliegers had yet seen British or American planes: thirty minutes—a short half hour and the pilots of Luftwaffe West would be home free.

Chapter Twelve

At 0900, January 1, 1945, Major General Sir Frances de Guingard, deputy commander of the British 21st Army Group, sat in his headquarters at Brussels, Belgium. de Guingard was going over maps and charts on his desk with several members of his staff. The British officers were considering the best and fastest route to send two British army brigades south to relieve American ground troops at the northwest peripheral of the German advance into Belgium. The Americans, of course, had stemmed the onslaught of Operation Herbstnebel and they had pushed the Germans back in many areas, thanks to the heavy Allied air assaults during the four day period of cleared skies.

"They've got the bulge pretty well contained," General de Guingard said, "but those 84th and 28th Yank Divisions are pretty tattered and exhausted. We can send the 51st Highland and the 5th Seaforth Brigades down from Brussels. The quickest way is over Highway 17."

The aide nodded.

"Our lads can relieve the Americans at Mierchamps," de Guingard continued. "Fresh British troops in that sector can make a difference." He looked at his aide. "How soon can these two brigades be on the way?"

The aide grinned. "I've already put those units on alert. They can be off within a couple of hours."

"Good," the general said, before he looked about at his staff again. "Then we're finished 'ere?"

"Yes, sir."

de Guingard nodded and then turned when he heard the sound of aircraft beyond his quonset hut headquarters. He peered out the window, straining his neck, to watch a squadron of twelve Spitfires zooming low over Brussels. No doubt, the aircraft had just left Evere Field for morning sorties against the Germans. The field lay just beyond this advanced echelon headquarters of the 21st British Army Group. General de Guingard glanced at the aircraft in surprise. The weather was quite dismal this morning, with dark, low hanging clouds. He had been told that no aircraft were likely to take off this morning. And in fact, de Guingard had heard the reports: RAF airmen had whooped it up last night, celebrating New Year's Eve into the wee hours of the morning. The general assumed that the airmen at Evere were still asleep at this hour, recuperating from their ale and liquor.

de Guingard shrugged and returned to his map table. "If we're finished 'ere, we may as well 'ave a spot of tea and crumb cakes."

"I'll get the orderly," one of the staff officers said.

Soon, General Sir Francis de Guingard and the others of his staff forgot the squadron of Spitfires that had passed over their headquarters.

RAF airmen around Brussels as well as at other

British bases had indeed celebrated well into the wee hours. 127 Wing commander Johnnie Johnson had told the pilots last night there would be no sorties this morning except for a volunteer reconn sortie. The airmen had thus indulged in their revelries with no qualms, safe in the knowledge that they could sleep this morning.

Only Lieutenant George Buerling, as expected, volunteered, despite the protests of his 414 Squadron pilots. "We've got to help those Americans in any way we can," he had told his squadron airmen again this morning, quickly forgetting the commaradarie he had enjoyed with them last night.

Now, at 0910, Buerling was leading this three diamonds of aircraft under the low hanging clouds. He peered down at the white Belgium countryside, seeking a target: German infantry, tank, or mechanized columns. The twelve Spitfires of 414 Squadron now carried the new 30mm armor piercing rockets that had proven so successful against the hardskin of German armor. But Buerling saw nothing below him. The lieutenant then looked upward and about him, but he saw no sign of German aircraft under the low, gloomy clouds. He squeezed his face, chiding himself. He was on a futile mission.

Thinking back, Buerling remembered that German aircraft had been totally absent for the past few days. He assumed now that the Luftwaffe had indeed given their last shot during the recent German offensive, and they had lost so many aircraft they could not even conduct harassment raids, much less dogfights. Still, Buerling checked with fellow pilots of 414 Squadron. "Do you see anything?"

"Damn you, George," Lieutenant Charles

Stover said. "They won't come out. Those German ground troops will stay under cover by day and move by night. As for their aircraft, they just don't have anymore in the west, just like everybody says. We're just going to waste the morning. Why don't we go home? I'd like to go back to sleep."

"We'll cruise east for another hour or so," Lieutenant Buerling said, "and if we don't see anything, we'll call it a day."

Lieutenant George Buerling and the eleven other pilots of his squadron had not guessed that somewhere to the southeast, high above the clouds, the greatest Luftwaffe armada since the Battle of Britain was droning toward Belgium, Holland, and eastern France. For that matter, neither did dozens of other Allied air commanders realize that hordes of heavily armed German planes were heading for their bases.

Beyond de Guingard's headquarters, the Evere airbase appeared quiet and deserted. 127 Wing commander Captain Johnnie Johnson had himself enjoyed a bout of fun on New Year's and he had asked only for the morning reconn effort, and only for volunteers. Most of the airmen at Evere still slept, or lounged in rec rooms, or simply read, or drank tea, or simply recuperated from last night's merrymaking. Only a handful of ground crewmen were active, tinkering with the four lines of aircraft of 127 Wing sitting in neat rows on both sides of two runways. W/C Johnson believed his men deserved a rest, especially because they had flown numerous sorties since the Germans launched Operation Herbstnebel two weeks ago.

"This afternoon will be soon enough for sorties," Johnson had told his squadron leaders. "The skies may be clear and we'd 'ave better shots at finding some of those Jerry tank and infantry columns. That reconn patrol is enough for this morning and the lads may just as well rest."

So, except for Buerling, who had taken off for reconn patrol with twelve planes, the two runways remained cold and deserted. Only a few fuel trucks growled up and down the snow covered airstrips to fill the tanks of any aircraft that needed petrol: rows of light Mosquito bombers and rows of Spitfire and Mustang fighters. Nobody concerned himself with this total exposure, nobody from Air Marshal Leigh-Mallory to the lowest RAF airman. None had even considered the idea that German planes might attack this airfield this morning.

The gun crews in their dozen anti-aircraft pits at the sprawling Evere airbase sat bored and cold. They had not fired their weapons in weeks, and they spent most of their time scrubbing the barrels to prevent corrosion or rust from lack of use. But, while they preferred to loiter about the warm pot belly stoves in their billets, these anti-aircraft crews knew that flak guns must be on the ready twenty-four hours a day. They simply accepted the boredom of the gun pits and waited for their watches to end.

"I wish I 'ad a spot of tea," one of the gunners said to a companion.

"Cheer up, Laddy," a lance corporal answered. "You've only got a four hour stint. It's 9:30 now and you'll be off at noon for a w'ole twenty hours."

Less than a hundred miles away, II Group of JG 26 droned westward—four staffels of FW 190s and ME 109s. Two squadrons carried SG spitterbombs or TSC incendiary bombs under their fusilages, along with twenty-four 4RM armor piercing rockets under the wings. The other squadrons carried two MG one thousand pound TNT bombs to rip up the runways.

Above the Ardennes, Major Anton Hackl glanced about him from the cockpit of his lead FW 190. He could see the four plane diamonds to his left, to his right, and to his rear. II Gruppe included forty-one FW 190s of 5 and 6 Staffels and thirty-eight ME 109s of 7 and 8 Staffels. The heavily armed aircraft were geared for tactical attacks and not for interception, despite the six fully loaded .50 caliber machine guns on each plane. The major hoped they met no Allied air opposition above these low hanging clouds. He and his pilots were in no condition to engage in dogfights with heavy bomb loads and extra fuel tanks. Hackl also thought of the many inexperienced fliegers in II Gruppe, and he felt uneasy.

Major Hackl now looked straight ahead where he saw the JU 88 droning at the same 4,000 meter altitude. II/JG 26 was heading for Evere and Hackl hoped the JU 88 pathfinder, also manned by inexperienced pilots, would take the gruppe to Evere and not somewhere over the Zuder Zee. Most of the pathfinder crews had learned their work through textbook theory instead of hard experience.

Hackl himself, a Luftwaffe pilot for many years, was among the aces of the German Air force. He had joined the Luftwaffe in 1934 as a youth of nineteen. He had been another of those who had served in the Condor Legion in Spain before he became a fighter pilot for JG 11 on the Western Front. He had battled French and Belgium pilots over France early in the war, and he had battled RAF Hurricane pilots later during the Battle of Britain. Hackl had also battled the hordes of four engine Allied bombers during the heavy strategic raids over Germany. And, he had fought the American Thunderbolt and Mustang pilots during the Allied push through France in the last six months.

The years of steady combat had taken a toll. Even though Hackl was only thirty years old, aging lines had cut into his round face and his hairline had already receded.

Hackl had learned his trade under two of Germany's most distinguished airmen, fighter ace Gunther Rall and the famed Walter Nowotny, who had led the first jet fighter unit. By this January 1, 1945, Hackl had scored over one hundred sixty confirmed kills to become a leading ace. He was among the few experienced pilots to participate in Operation Bodenplatte.

Now, Hackl looked again at the clouds under him and he once more scanned the skies above. Nothing. Were the predictions true? Had Allied airmen spent New Year's Eve celebrating orgies, and were they now sleeping or loitering in their billets? Especially in this foul weather? Could Hackl be so fortunate as to come out of the clouds and find a fat English airfield jammed with exposed aircraft and no RAF pilots airborne to challenge him? He hoped so, but such a consequence would be miraculous indeed.

Major Hackl picked up his radio. "Tabak commodore to 6 Staffel kapitan; 6 Staffel kapitan."

"6 Tabak, Herr Major," Oblt Adolph Glunz of 6 Staffel answered.

"Have you seen any sign of enemy aircraft?"

"None, commodore," Glunz answered.

"Stay alert and remind your staffel fliegers to

remain alert. We will need to salvo our bombs should we meet enemy aircraft."

"We will be alert, Herr Major."

Oblt Adolph Glunz was an experienced pilot, having joined JG 26 nearly two years ago as a fliegerwebel (flying sergeant). From the first he had been under the tutelage of Colonel Josef "Pips" Priller, who was leading IV Gruppe of JG 26 to Grimberghen. Priller had shown the patience of a saint to turn Glunz into an exceptional pilot. But, the patience had paid off because Glunz had knocked down over a hundred planes during the past two years, including thirty-two Flying Fortresses. The handsome, blond haired oberst leutnant had learned well from Priller who himself had knocked down twenty-one B-17s.

Oblt Adolph Glunz squinted uneasily from his 190 cockpit as he scanned the skies. He almost hoped he did see Mustangs or Spitfires, so he could salvo his bombs and wade into such enemy fighters. Glunz was accustomed to battling enemy fighter pilots, but the lanky staffel leader was not certain he could succeed on a low level strike against an enemy airfield. Despite the crash program instruction on tactical attack techniques, and despite his ground support sorties during the initial stages of Operation Herbstnebel, Adolph Glunz was not sure of himself. Would he release his spitterbombs on time at this low level height? Would he fly too low and perhaps catch fatal shrapnel and debris from an explosion of his own making? Would his plane hit a tree or a high tension line or a building at his low level schlacht? Glunz didn't know. He only knew he wanted to strike back, to gain revenge for the horrendous destruction the Allied strategic bombers had wrought to the Fatherland, for the havoc the Allied tactical aircraft had administered on the poor Wehrmacht soldiers, and even for the damage the Allied heavy bombers had caused on his own airbase at Verrelbusch.

Glunz bit his lips when he saw the obscure tip of the Schnee Eifel that rose hazily into the low, gloomy clouds. He picked up his radio. "Tabak commodore, this is Tabak 6. I believe we are flying over the Schnee Eifel."

"Good," Hackl answered. "That means the JU pathfinder is on the correct path. We can be grateful for that."

"Yes, Herr commodore."

The 79 planes of II Gruppe droned on for another half hour, still hanging above the clouds, and still seeing no sign of enemy aircraft. Major Anton Hackl squinted once more at the JU 88 pathfinder ahead of him, and with TAT (target attack time) only moments away, the major felt uneasy. Would he and the other pilots of II/JG 26 continue the long tradition of the Abbeville Boys, the Schageters? Goring himself had visited the JG 26 unit, spoken to the men in II Gruppe, and had personally urged Major Anton Hackl to make the British again fear the Abbeville Boys.

Goring and everyone else in the Luftwaffe knew that JG 26 pilots had almost wiped out the French Air Force in 1940 and had caused most of the losses among RAF pilots during the Battle of Britain. And when the Americans began sending their B-17s over Europe, the Americans had found the Abbeville Boys more aggressive than other JG interceptor pilots. Among the sixty bombers the Americans had lost on the Schweinfurt raid, the JG 26 Schlageters had knocked down more than half of the B-17s. Thus, it seemed apropos that the Luftwaffe Reichmarshal should visit the men of JG 26 before this most important Operation Bodenplatte.

Hackl looked to the right of his cockpit, the angry tiger face insignia under the cockpit canopy of his wingman's aircraft. Throughout the war, French airmen had feared the insignia, British airmen had respected the tiger, and American airmen had marveled at the tenacity of the pilots who flew the German fighter plane with the tiger head on its fuselage. What of Evere? Could the Schlageters prove their mettle again? Would they leave the British awed once more by the planes with the angry tiger face?

"Tabak commodore. Tabak commodore!"

Now the call came from the navigator of the JU 88.

"Tabak commodore," Major Hackl answered.

"You are a few minutes from TAT, Herr Major, less than fifteen miles away and straight ahead. I suggest you begin your descent, 290 meter PS. You should come out of the clouds but a kilometer or two from target. Maintain your 6.1 course; no deviation."

"You are certain?"

"Straight ahead; perhaps five minutes. I guarantee what I say, commodore," the JU 88 navigator insisted. "We are turning back. Good luck."

Anton Hackl watched the JU 88 bank left, rise about a hundred meters, and then drone eastward back to Lichtenseim.

"This is Tabak commodore," Hackl called into his radio. "All pilots. We shall descend through the clouds at 26 meter PS. Maintain speed and bearing at 6.1. We are expected to clear the clouds over Brussels in two to three minutes. Then, our targets should be one to two kilometers ahead." He paused. "Now listen carefully to these repeated instructions. 5 Staffel will attack aircraft on west runway. 7 Staffel will attack the runway itself with MG bombs. 6 Staffel will attack any aircraft on east runway, while 8 Staffel will attack the east runway with MG bombs. Be cautious. All aircraft will form in pairs and rottenfliegers will stay close to each other and remain thirty seconds behind the rotte ahead. Please check your watches: 0959. Our TAT is one hundred twenty seconds ahead."

Now, Anton Hackl pushed the stick forward and the FW 190 disappeared into the dark undercast. Hackl watched the altimeter drop and he licked his lips. He had put his total faith in the pathfinders. If they were wrong—

At 1001 hours, January 1, 1945, General Sir Francis de Guingard had just hung up the telephone, satisfied. The 51st Highland and the 5th Seaforth Brigades would be on the way this afternoon to relieve the exhausted Americans at Mierchamps. The general leaned over the table to study the maps again, tracing with a finger the route of his British ground units. By the time he finished, the sound of aircraft engines echoed from beyond his headquarters. de Guingard paid no attention, assuming the drones had come from British planes, perhaps those same Spitfires he had seen about an hour ago.

Then, suddenly, a staff member turned from the window. "My God, sir, those aircraft are dropping something over Brussels."

General de Guingard rushed to the window to catch sight of cylinders falling and disappearing behind some Brussels buildings. He was surprised when the descending objects did not explode, for he did not know the falling cylinders were discarded auxiliary gas tanks the German aircraft had carried for the long flight from Verrelbusch. The 21st Army deputy commander then craned his neck to catch a glimpse of the low flying aircraft zooming over Brussels. He frowned again, for he did not recognize the planes as British.

"Christ," a staff member cried, "they're German planes! Dozens of them! 190s and 109s!"

Major Anton Hackl came within a half kilometer of the sprawling Evere airfield and then gaped in astonishment. His wildest hopes had come to pass. Along both sides of the two runways were countless aircraft, lined up wing tip to wing tip and totally exposed: Mosquitos, Spitfires, and Mustangs. Major Hackl could not recall the last time he had seen such a fat, undefended target, at least not since the early days of the war in 1939.

"Horrido! Horrido!" the II/JG 26 commodore cried into his radio, urging his fliegers to scramble and attack. Then, Hackl gunned his engine, dropped low, and zoomed over the line of Mosquitos, his wingman tightly at his side. Both he and his wingman loosened two spitterbombs on the first pass and they watched the four bombs sail toward the line of RAF planes. Then both pilots banked away and stared back to see the balls of fire, erupting fragments, and contorting aircraft. Their bombs had hit squarely, wrecking two RAF light bombers. Before Hackl absorbed his handiwork totally, the next pair of planes also unleashed four spitterbombs that also hit parked Mosquitos and erupted new balls of whooshing fire and flying fragments. Now came a schwarm of

190s that unleashed eight TSC incendiaries that left a stretch of belching fire over the line of aircraft.

Meanwhile, the slim Oblt Adolph Glunz leaned forward in his cockpit seat like a starved wolf staring at a herd of fawn—a potentially sumptuous feast. Glunz, like Hackl, had also experienced astonishment at the long length of exposed, undefended RAF targets: the Spitfires and Mustangs along the east runway.

"Staffel, Horrido!" Oblt Glunz cried into his radio before he gestured to his wingman. Then, Glunz and his rottenflieger, in the usual rotte pattern, zoomed over the rows of fighter planes and released four spitterbombs that exploded between or atop four aircraft, ripping away fusilages and wings. Then, Adolph Glunz whooshed a half dozen rockets. Three missed, but three hit an aircraft squarely, disintegrating the plane in a convulsive jerk before the plane exploded in a ball of fire.

As Glunz banked away his 190, he saw the next rotte of 190s zoom over the same line of Spitfires, dropping their TSC incendiaries and more whoosing R4M rockets. More parked British planes blew asunder in balls of smoke and roaring fires. One Spitfire bounced violently and then spun dizzily out of the line of planes. Other pairs of 6 Staffel aircraft shattered the lines of Mustangs with the same devastating spitterbombs, incendiaries, and rockets. 5 and 6 Staffels left in their wake flying debris, hot fires, and dense oil smoke along the lengths of lined up RAF planes.

The ME 109s of 7 and 8 Staffels also carried out their work with terrible efficiency, dropping heavy one thousand pound MG bombs in a staccato of explosions on both runways. 7 and 8 Staffels left both the east and west Evere airstrips totally potholed with deep craters.

Major Anton Hackl was satisfied. Galland had done a good job of retraining these interceptor pilots into tactical attack fleigers.

Inside his headquarters, General de Guingard and his staff felt their building shudder from the exploding bombs and whooshing rockets, and they saw the columns of smoke rising over the airfield at Evere. And soon, the British officers heard the chatter or heavy machine gun fire.

"They're bombing and strafing the airfield, sir," one of the staff officers said.

"My God," the 21st Army deputy commander answered. He stood at the window, straining to look, but he did not see a single British aircraft in the sky; only the darting, zooming, racing 109s and 190s with the black crosses on their fuselages and the angry tiger face under the cockpits.

At the airfield itself, the sudden explosions and tremors prompted the few ground crews and fuel truck drivers around the planes to charge away from the runways. A few did not make it, suffering fatal hits from exploding shrapnel or fatal burns from searing fire. The murderous attacks had also jerked loitering or sleeping men from their morning lethargy. Men in the recreation room left cribbage, chess, or pool games to rush hurriedly outside and gape at the swarms of attacking planes unleashing spitterbombs, TSC incendiaries, R4M rockets, the one thousand pound MG bombs, and .50 caliber strafing fire. The airmen stared aghast at the scene of erupting smoke and fire. They cowered and then retreated with each new explosion or with each new chatter of .50 caliber strafing fire.

"Good Christ! 'It the deck!" one sergeant major cried.

His companions did not hesitate. They bolted away from the recreation hall. Other RAF personnel of 127 Wing darted out of sleeping quarters, mess halls, officers clubs, supply sheds and ammunition houses to zig-zag swiftly into the woodlands beyond the field. The 127 Wing airmen had no foxholes, for they were fully confident that no German planes could hit their airbase with this kind of massive fire power. For months, all they had known was the occasional night time harassment raids by a few planes.

For the next half hour, the II/JG 26 German aircraft unleashed their rockets or SCs, or TSCs, or MGs before the planes peppered the smashed rows of British planes with strafing fire. Again and again, the Folke-Wulf and Messerschmidt fighter-bombers banked away after a pass and then returned over their targets—like hungry tigers unable to satisfy an insatiable hunger.

Ironically, at this very moment, the only British aircraft who could have helped were far to the northeast. Lieutenant Buerling and the pilots of 414 Squadron were still out searching empty skies and empty white terrain under them.

Major Anton Hackl had made six passes, until he had expended every spitterbomb and every rocket and much of his .50 caliber ammunition. Adolph Glunz had made nine passes, expending not only his bombs and rockets, but half of his machine gun belts.

The men in the ack ack pits were now firing furiously at the zooming, low level attackers. At the low height, the swift moving planes were elusive targets, although the gunners did manage to shoot down two of the German planes and to damage three others, a small consolation for the rampant destruction to their 127 Wing airfield.

At 1040 hours, Major Anton Hackl shouted into his radio. "All fliegers! All fliegers, this is Tabak Commodore. Break off and return to base. Break off and return to base. Do not expend any more ammunition in the event we meet enemy interceptor planes."

Some of the fliegers did not hear Hackl above the din of screaming planes, shattering machine gun fire, roaring fires, and booms of anti-aircraft guns that had left noise in the fliegers' radio receiver earphones. Nearly five minutes elapsed before Hackl reformed his gruppe to lead them eastward under the low hanging clouds.

When the drone of German planes faded to the east, Wing Commander Johnnie Johnson and some of his officers ogled in disbelief at the destruction. Johnson would later count 123 of his aircraft destroyed or damaged. The wing commander licked his lips. He would catch hell when Leigh-Mallory found out what happened. The air marshal would brutally dress down the 127 Wing leader for not taking more precautions. Johnson could not guess that Leigh-Mallory would need to dress down nine other RAF base commanders, including his own at Eindhoven, who would experience the same stunning surprise as Wing Commander Johnnie Johnson.

Meanwhile, the bulk of 127 Wing airmen at Evere slowly emerged from surrounding woodlands and walked in shock toward the blazing, shattered runways. The British airmen stood mute, gaping at the widespread devastation.

Then, a grizzly sergeant major, a man with ten years in the RAF, stroked his rubbled chin and then looked at some of the others about him.

"You know w'o the bastards were, don't ya? The Abbeville Boys. They were the Abbeville Boys with those tiger 'eads on their bloody planes. The buggers; they ain't finished with us yet; not yet, they ain't."

A lance corporal stared at the conflagrations and then shook his head. "One thing for sure, Sarge: the blighters knew what they were after and they done it. They must 'a walloped every plane and totally done in the runways, but they didn't touch anything else. Bloody straight, they were."

"That's the Abbeville Boys," the sergeant nodded. "They always did know their targets."

The others believed the grizzly sergeant major, for he had known the Schlageters of JG 26 since the Battle of Britain in 1940.

To the east, Major Anton Hackl reclined in his cockpit as his lead FW 190 droned eastward. He had only lost two planes down and three damaged, and his inexperienced pilots had delightfully surprised him with their uncanny accuracy. Surely, if other geschwaders did as well as his own II/JG 26, the Allies would reel from the blow. Allies and Germans alike would forget Operation Herbstnebel. Instead, they would vividly remember Operation Bodenplatte.

Hackl treated himself to a happy grin and he then relaxed for, hopefully, a leisurely flight back to Verrelbusch. He relished his moment of triumph. But other gruppen of Operation Bodenplatte would not be so fortunate.

Chapter Thirteen

Colonel Norman Holt's worst fears during the mid-December drive into Belgium by the German ground forces had been the possibility of panzer units overrunning Asche. Holt had warned his airmen at the American airbase to man guns in the event advancing German panzer or Wehrmacht divisions attempt to swarm into the airfield. Since Christmas day, however, Allied fortunes had changed radically, thanks to the Allied air efforts. Allied ground troops had not only stopped the German ground advance, but had begun pushing the Germans back. So, on the morning of January 1, 1945 a quiet, confident calm prevailed at the 366th Group airbase.

Most of the airmen at Asche on this dreary morning were still sleeping off their libations of the previous evening. By 0800, only a few pilots or ground crews had come into the messhall, despite a quite appetizing menu of French toast, bacon, grapefruit juice, and coffee. Colonel Norman Holt was fully awake as was his deputy commander, Major George Prader, for even the New Year's Eve festivities had failed to disrupt their habit of arising early. In fact, the two men had already eaten breakfast and left the messhall and, by 0800, both men were on the airfield, squinting at the slight mist hovering below the low clouds.

"Doesn't look as though we'll go anywhere today, Norm," Prader said.

Norman Holt shrugged. "This soup will clear off soon. Anyway," the 366th Group commander grinned, "most of our guys are still sleeping it off. If we got them up now, they'd be too groggy to even find their planes."

"Yeh," Prader nodded, returning the grin.

"Let's go to the briefing room," Holt said. "I want to call General Queseda. Maybe he can tell us if he still intends to send us off this afternoon."

"There's got to be plenty of targets with those dozens of panzer divisions trying to get out of Belgium."

An hour earlier, at 0700, orderlies had awakened Lieutenant Colonel John Meyers of the 352nd Fighter Group, the 8th Air Force Unit temporarily attached to the 9th Air Force Asche airfield. Meyers had awakened with a sour taste in his mouth for he had downed his share of liquor the previous evening. Further, he had only slept about four hours. Still, he had taken a quick shower, dressed, and then enjoyed a good breakfast. He had then walked briskly through the misty, chilly morning and by 0800 he was hurrying toward the briefing quonset hut. Meyers' 487th Squadron had been slated to conduct possible ground support sorties this morning and Meyers hoped the mist would dissipate soon.

However, when Meyers reached the briefing hut, he saw neither his group commander nor other flyers from his squadron. He found only Colonel Norman Holt and Major George Prader who had arrived at the quonset hut only moments earlier and who were now pawing through some papers on the desk.

"Colonel," Meyers asked Holt, "where the hell's Colonel Mayden and the rest of our group's pilots from my squadron? We're supposed to hold a briefing at 0815 hours for a ground support mission this morning."

"The mission's been called off," Colonel Holt said. "Nobody's going out this morning, not us, not the 352nd, and not the 361st. I had a call from 9th TAC just before you came in. They say that all three groups here at Asche will be going on escort missions this afternoon, if the weather improves."

"But they got me up at 0700," Lieutenant Colonel Meyers complained. "I could have used a few more hours of sleep."

"Sorry," Colonel Holt grinned.

"Can't we get off at least my squadron?"

Holt squeezed his face. "Some of my pilots asked me the same thing. I'll call General Queseda and see if he'll release our 386th and your own 487th Squadrons."

"I'd appreciate that, Colonel," Meyers said.

When Colonel Norman Holt called General Queseda at the TAC headquarters, he learned that Elwood Queseda was still at breakfast. "Call back at 0830," an aide told Holt. Then, for the next fifteen minutes or so, Holt, Prader, and Meyers merely loitered impatiently in the briefing room. Meanwhile, pilots of both the 352nd's 487th Squadron and the 366th's 390th Squadron filtered into the briefing room. Among them was the buoyant Captain Floyd Benson.

"We're here for our briefing, Colonel," Captain Benson told Holt.

"All morning patrols have been cancelled,"

Colonel Norman Holt said.

"Goddamn it, Colonel," Captain Benson scowled. "The roads in Belgium must be clogged with German armored columns. We could have a field day. This soup will clear off in an hour or so and we can sure as hell hit at low level without getting hurt."

"I didn't even think you'd be up yet, Captain," Holt grinned.

"Well I am, even though I could have used more sleep," Benson said. "As long as we're up, I'd just as soon go out."

"I'm waiting to contact General Queseda," Holt said. "Meyers here wants to go out, too."

At 0835, Colonel Norman Holt successfully reached the 9th Air Force TAC commander, General Elwood Queseda. However, the general's first answer to the request for the morning patrols was a mild refusal. TAC intended to conduct massive bomber strikes this afternoon on German communications to thwart German withdrawals from their growing Belgium trap. The December 25–28 bomber efforts had caused numerous traffic jams and if the 9th Air Force bombers knocked out a few more bridges, rail heads, and road junctions, the Allies could permanently stall any retreat by the German forces. The Allied ground troops could then surround the trapped German panzer and Wehrmacht divisions and annihilate or capture them before the Germans retreated across the Rhine.

"But we did have plans for some patrols this morning," Holt told Queseda, "and a lot of pilots got up early. Can't we send out some of them, General?"

"All right," Queseda said, "thirty-six planes; no

more. Keep the rest on the ready for an afternoon escort mission. I'll get back to you around noon and either advise you of a cancellation or give your Asche groups their assignments."

"Yes, sir," Colonel Holt answered. The 366th commander then looked at the loitering pilots, especially at Meyers and Benson. "The general says thirty-six planes. Meyers, you can select sixteen pilots from your 487th Squadron and Captain, you can pick sixteen pilots from your own 390th Squadron."

"Yes, sir," Captain Floyd Benson grinned.

"But you'll have to wait for the fog to lift," Holt said. "Meanwhile, you and Meyers can hold a briefing with your pilots."

When Lieutenant Colonel Meyers and Captain Benson left the briefing quonset hut to round up pilots, they found the mist somewhat thinner. They could now see quite clearly the hordes of wing tip to wing tip P-47s and P-51s lined on both sides of the Asche runway—more than one hundred fifty Thunderbolts and Mustangs of the 366th, 352nd, and 361st Fighter Groups.

"We ought to get off by 1000 hours," Meyers said.

"Yeah," Captain Floyd Benson answered.

"At 0945 hours, thirty-two pilots from the 366th and 352nd Fighter groups had arrived on the field aboard jeeps and then clamored into the cockpits of their aircraft. Ground crews had started engines that still screamed in pre-flight warm-ups on this chilly New Year's morning. The mist had lifted considerably now and both Meyers and Benson anticipated no problem with taking-off or with locating targets under the low hanging clouds.

At the same 0945 hours, some miles to the east,

Colonel Erich Rudorffer looked at his watch. Then, he looked down at the dense clouds under him before he studied the ME 109s hanging to his left and right, their green heart insignias sparkling in the sunlight above the clouds. Then, Rudorffer got a call from the leader of the three plane JU 88 pathfinder flight.

"Herr Colonel, we are ready to disperse your gruppen. I suggest you notify your gruppen commodores."

Rudorffer picked up his radio and called his gruppe leaders. "Gruppen will now break for individual targets. Major Keller, you will take II Gruppe to LeCulot; Major Weise, you will take your IV Gruppe to Asche. Pilots of I Gruppe will follow me to St. Trond. Be sure to follow your pathfinder aircraft.

"Yes, Colonel," Major Robert Weise of IV Gruppe answered.

The major looked at his watch, but then he bit his lips. He did not relish the thought of hitting an airbase housing three full gruppen of American fighter planes. Weise remembered too well the maceration of JG 54 by heavy swarms of American fighter planes when the Green Hearts had tried to attack U.S. transport planes resupplying the beleagured U.S. garrison at Bastogne. JG 54 had barely escaped with half of its aircraft in the fierce, losing dogfight. If the three American gruppen at Asche got airborne before IV/JG 54 made its strike . . . the thought sent shivers up the Major's spine.

When his pathfinder JU 88 veered left, Major Robert Bazi Weise took a deep breath and then cried into his radio. "All pilots will set course for .035 degrees." Then, Weise arched his FW 190, turned, and leveled off, following his assigned JU 88 for the flight to Asche. Forty-seven other 190s followed him, maintaining tight four plane diamond formations. In moments, Weise lost sight of the other JG 54 gruppen.

A few minutes later, Major Robert Weise again looked at his watch: 0952 hours. He had come within eight minutes of target. He glanced at the hovering 190s on either side of him, and he then got a call from the pathfinder.

"Herr Major," the JU 88 pilot said, "you are within fifteen kilometers of target, fifteen kilometers. I suggest you begin your descent through the clouds. You should find about a one thousand meter ceiling, quite low, but high enough to make your low level strike. Good luck."

The JU 88 then arched sharply and banked into a 180 degree turn. Weise kept his eyes riveted to the pathfinder until the aircraft disappeared to the northeast. Then, he called into his radio. "All pilots, we will begin descent in one minute, and we should come out of the clouds at perhaps one or two kilometers from target. 1 Staffel will strike the enemy aircraft on the north side of the runway, 3 Staffel will strike aircraft on the south side of runway. 2 Staffel will strike the runway itself with heavy MG bombs." He paused. Then: "Horrido!"

At the Asche airbase, the mist had all but disappeared by 0950 hours. Captain Floyd Benson led 16 P-47s of his Fortune Hunter's 390th Squadron towards the airstrip from the north taxiway and wheeled his lead T-Bolt onto the head of the runway. He revved the engine of his P-47, loaded with six .50 caliber strafing belts and twenty-four 37MM rockets under the wings. From the west side of the runway, Lieutenant Colonel

John Meyers led sixteen P-51s of his 352nd Group's 487th Squadron over the slippery south taxiway. He would follow Benson's P-47s. Meyers watched the light from the control tower blink green before Benson and his wingman zoomed down the runway. Seven more pairs of Thunderbolts followed the first T-Bolt until all sixteen P-47s of the 390th Squadron were airborne.

Now, Lieutenant Colonel John Meyers wheeled his lead P-51 onto the runway, his 487th Squadron wingman at his side. While Meyers waited for the control tower light to blink green again, he occasionally glanced at the jammed lines of P-47 and P-51 aircraft on both sides of the main airstrip. A moment later, the light blinked green. Meyers revved his engine, rammed in the throttle and started down the runway, his wingman next to him. But then, his eyes fell on something ahead—black puffs of anti-aircraft fire above the far end of the runway. Then, Meyers faintly caught a glance of red tracers—machine gun fire rattling into parked aircraft. Even as the lieutenant colonel roared down the runway, he cried into his radio, calling the control tower.

"Marmite! Marmite! What the hell's going on?"

"I don't know," the Marmite control tower sergeant answered. "Our guys in the ack ack pits are firing like hell, and I can see tracer fire." The sergeant paused, but only for a few seconds. Then, he hissed into his mike. "Holy Christ, Colonel, we're under attack! Under attack!" A whole goddamn sky full of FWs are coming over the field."

Meyers' heart leaped. Under attack! And he in the process of taking off! The lieutenant colonel was a sitting duck. Still, Meyers increased speed in the hope of getting airborne before German planes got him. Then, as streams of strafing fire spewed on either side of him and into parked aircraft, he pulled back the stick. The P-51 responded, teetering with its heavy bomb load, but getting off the ground. Meyers immediately retracted his wheels and looked up to see an FW 190 bearing down on him. Meyers instinctively veered right and barely pulled up to two hundred feet when another FW 190 came into him from three o'clock with guns chattering. Meyers' heart thumped again as tracers tattooed his fuselage. One hit on the bombs under the fuselage and he would be blown to confetti.

The 352nd Group lieutenant colonel quickly veered left and arched his mustang away. But, another FW 190 was coming straight toward him. The American fighter pilot instinctively loosened a barrage from his own machine guns, a stream of armor piercing and incendiary shells. The fire struck the FW at almost point blank range and the German plane exploded in a ball of fire before dropping to earth with a heavy thud and then blowing apart in a fiery, secondary explosion. Meyers, meanwhile, continued on, finding a safe place to salvo his bombs. He then veered 180 degrees to return to Asche to break up the German air attack.

Others of the 487th Squadron were not as lucky as Meyers. Some would suffer the same fate as the parked aircraft on either side of the Asche runway.

Major Robert Bazi Weise had been astonished when he came out of the clouds and roared over the Asche airfield at low level to see the parked aircraft on either side of the runway. He had been even more amazed to see the P-51s taking off, assuming the Asche warning system had somehow detected his IV/JG 54 moments before Weise arrived. The major led his 1 Staffel over the parked P-47s on the south side of the runway, unleasing a half dozen R4M rockets that pierced two of the parked T-Bolts, erupting fire and smoke. He had then unleashed his spitterbombs that sailed into more parked P-47s. More explosions erupted with two of the heavy P-47s bouncing in shuddery jerks before bursting into flames.

More FW 190s followed Bazi Weise to unload the same array of rockets, spitterbombs or TSC incendiaries that tore up and twisted Thunderbolts or erupted more flames and smoke along the length of runway. Soon, the entire south side of the Asche runway became a long line of dense smoke and belching fire.

Then, some of the aircraft from 1 Staffel veered left toward the 487th Squadron's P-51s that had taxied to the runway for take-off. Meyers and his wingman had escaped the sudden attackers without harm. However, a rotte of two 190s zoomed along the runway with blazing strafing fire to catch a pair of P-51s that were tearing down the runway. The two Mustangs exploded almost simultaneously, spun crazily and then veered off the runway to smash into parked aircraft. The burning, erratic P-51s ignited more fires. Other FW 190s roared over the runway and caught two more P-51s that were wheeling on to the head of the runway for take-off.

All total, the FW 190s macerated a half dozen of the P-51s while eight others of the 487th Mustangs did get airborne and free.

And now, 2 Staffel droned over the runway in pairs to dump their heavy MG one thousand-pound bombs. A staccato of heavy explosions rocked the base like a series of small earthquakes, while the explosions chopped huge chunks out of the airstrip, until the strip resembled extended lines of deep potholes. No further aircraft get off this runway today.

Finally, IV/JG 54's 3 Staffel zoomed over the north perimeter of the Asche runway to unleash more spitterbombs, more TSC incendiaries, and hundreds of R4M rockets. Parked P-51s of the visiting 352nd and 361st Fighter Groups burst into smoke and flames. These 8th Air Force units had come to France to pulverize the Germans, but were themselves pulverized on this cloudy January 1, 1945 morning.

The rattling explosions, bursting concussions, balls of fire and smoke had utterly astonished the personnel at Asche, who never expected such a sudden Luftwaffe attack. Both Colonel Norman Holt and Major George Prader burst out of the 366th commander's trailer. They stared in disbelief at the zooming FWs before ogling at the mass of fire and smoke on both sides of the runway.

"Holy Christ!" Major George Prader gasped.

"I'll be a son of a bitch," Colonel Holt cursed. "I don't believe it. Where the hell was our radar? How could those bastards get here from Germany without detection?"

"They came in low, Norm, real low," Prader answered.

Holt shook his head. "Not all the way from Germany they didn't. Our people must be asleep." Holt now hurried back inside his trailer, even as the din of zooming German planes continued overhead and as the deafening concussions of exploding bombs and rockets continued on the airbase. The colonel picked up his phone and called the control tower. "Sergeant, did any of those planes get off? Any of them?"

"Yes, sir," the control tower sergeant answered. "All of Captain Benson's squadron and ten of the 352nd Mustangs."

"What happened to the rest?" Holt asked.

"The Krauts knocked them off before they could take off."

"Son of a bitch!" Holt cursed again. He now picked up his radio phone and called Captain Floyd Benson. "Captain, get your ass back to Asche. The base is under heavy attack by German planes."

"Under attack?" Benson cried. "You're kidding."

"I wish the hell I was," Holt answered. "Salvo your bombs and get back here. See if you can drive them off."

"Yes, sir," Benson answered.

Then the 366th Fighter Group colonel called Lieutenant Colonel John Meyers. "Colonel, we're under attack. Kraut aircraft are really working us over. Please salvo your bombs and get back here to help out."

"I know about the attack," Meyers answered. "I've already had my pilots salvo bombs and we're on the way back."

Soon, both Captain Floyd Benson with sixteen Thunderbolts and Lieutenant Colonel John Meyers with ten Mustangs were zooming back toward Asche. But they would arrive too late to stop the Luftwaffe attack. Major Robert Bazi Weise and his FW pilots of IV/JG 54 continued to pulverize the Asche airbase. The German aircraft came again and again in new passes, nearly fifty aircraft, to lay more R4M rockets, spitterbombs, and incendiaries over the base. In fact, for more than a half hour, the raid continued unabated.

And, like Pips Priller's unit at Evere, Major Weise and his pilots had also been quite selective in their targets—striking only the aircraft and airfield. The pilots of IV/JG 54 did not hit either of the quonset huts, not one of the hordes of canvas tents, nor Colonel Holt's trailer. Every bomb, every rocket, and every tracer burst had struck only its designated target. Thus, even though the field lay in near ruins, no one at the base had been killed or injured—only those caught near the planes or runways at the time of the initial Luftwaffe assault.

Finally, at 1035 hours, Major Robert Bazi Weise cried into his radio. "All fliegers, break off attack; break off attack! We have done our job here. Do not expend further machine gun ammunition in the event we meet enemy interceptors on our return to base."

A moment later, Weise banked his FW 190 and arched into a full 180 degree turn. Then, he roared over the blasted runway, dipping his wings before he zoomed away. Soon, other FW 190s followed him and also straightened out. Then, in pairs, they zoomed over the potted airstrip before disappearing to the east. However, before the aircraft could rise and disappear into the clouds, Floyd Benson and his P-47 pilots had zoomed in from the east to meet the Green Hearts head on. Almost at the same moment, Lieutenant Colonel Meyers had organized his ten P-51s and they were on the German formations from the northeast.

"Okay boys, in pairs! In pairs!" Benson cried into his radio.

"Hit them hard! In pairs!" Meyers also instructed his pilots of the 487th Squadron.

Then, a low level dog fight, barely 500 to 800 feet above the ground, erupted between the formations of German aircraft and the formation of American planes.

Perhaps the FW 190 pilots had done an excellent job in destroying the airstrip at Asche. But, despite superior numbers, many of the German flyers were too inexperienced to take on the highly trained, combat confident American fighter pilots. Also, the FW pilots had expended too much of their machine gun ammunition, despite warnings from Major Weise. And, of course, the FWs had used up all of their rockets on the airbase assault. Within moments, the German fliegers would get another lesson in aerial combat. The German IV/54 Gruppe would be ripped apart.

The American pilots waded into the formation of German planes, sending streams of tracer and rocket fire into the FW 190s like hot horizontal hailstones. .50 caliber tracers and 37mm rockets ripped into one after another of the JG 54 aircraft before the green Luftwaffe pilots could react. Like birds caught in a wall of close range shot gun pellets, the FWs dropped out of the low sky one after another. FW 190s slammed into trees or wobbled fatally before striking the ground and bursting into flames. Other FWs exploded in mid-air or they fell to earth when American gunfire ripped off wings, tails, or even engines.

"Into the clouds! Into the clouds!" a horrified Bazi Weise cried into his radio. "Follow me into the clouds!"

But the indominable Luftwaffe Commodore, Major Robert Bazi Weise, had been so concerned for his young pilots that he had failed to protect himself. Weise had barely arched upward when a stream of P-51 rocket fire tore into the fuselage and wing of his aircraft. One shell struck his fuel tank and the FW 190 burst into flames. Weise no doubt died instantly and his suddenly flaming 190 simply flipped over and fell like a burning rock before smashing into the ground only a couple of hundred feet below. A secondary explosion followed, sending both Weise and his aircraft into oblivion.

The sudden death of the gruppe commodore only heightened the panic of his young Luftwaffe followers. Most of them, paralyzed with fear, could not even manuever against the hard hitting, highly skilled American P-47 and P-51 pilots. More FWs became fodder for American machine gun and rocket fire, and more aircraft fell to earth in fragments, fire, or with trailing smoke.

Finally, a staffel leader shook some of the young pilots from their shock when he emulated over his radio the call of the slain Bazi Weise: "Into the clouds! Into the clouds!" Then, the staffel leader zoomed upward and disappeared into the overcast, with only some half dozen other IV/JG 54 pilots following him. Other rattled IV/JG 54 pilots had simply zoomed in a dozen directions, stampeding to escape the murderous American fighter pilots. Some of the fliegers would never return to Badenheisen.

The fifteen minute dogfight had all but decimated the Green Heart gruppe. The twenty-six American pilots had enjoyed an unbelievable success. Lieutenant Colonel John Meyers, with only ten P-51s, had knocked down eight German planes, including the FW 190 of Major Robert Weise. But more astonishing, Captain Floyd

Benson with sixteen P-47s had knocked down an incredible twenty-three more planes. The surprised ack-ack gunners at Asche had knocked down two planes. Thus, IV/JG 54 had lost thirty-three of their forty-eight planes, the worst loss for any Luftwaffe West unit on Operation Bodenplatte.

The Americans themselves had only lost three planes in the dogfight, one of the 366th Group's P-47s and two of the 352nd Group's P-51s, not counting the six destroyed in the process of taking-off. None of the three pilots of these planes had been lost. One pilot, in fact, had found a bicycle somewhere to come wheeling back to the American base.

Still, before the tragic aftermath, the nearly annihilated IV/JG 54 under Major Robert Bazi Weise had destroyed totally some thirty planes at the Asche base and had badly damaged some fifty more, well over half of the planes based there. Further, the FW 190s had potholed the runway so badly that aviation engineers would need at least a week to repair the airstrip and taxiways so that planes could take-off or land.

Some three of the airborne P-47s and two of the P-51s tried to alight on the battered runway, but they could not really do so. Two P-47s hit deep bomb craters and simply flipped over. Luckily, the pilots had suffered only minor injuries. Another P-47 simply hit a pothole and stopped dead, while a P-51 bellylanded in and skidded across the potholed runway to a stop. The fifth plane, another P-51, hit a crater so hard, the aircraft bounced off the damaged runway and crashed into the burning line of planes next to the runway. The aircraft burst into flames, killing the pilot.

Floyd Benson and John Meyers had warned their pilots not to attempt any more landings at Asche and both squadron leaders now called Colonel Norman Holt to determine where they could land.

"Try to land at Amsterdam," Holt said, "or you can try Orcante. They're the only bases that are not under attack."

"Okay, Colonel," Lieutenant Colonel Meyers said. He then led the remainder of his P-51s to Amsterdam.

Captain Floyd Benson, however, elected to make Orcante. He hoped that he and his remaining P-47 pilots could reach the American fighter base before they ran out of fuel.

Meanwhile, the JG 54s other two gruppen had fared better. Unfortunately for the pilots at LeCulot and St. Trond, no squadron or group leader had tried to convince 9th Air Force TAC to give them permission for early morning take-offs. All of the aircraft of the two Mustang fighter groups at St. Trond, including the 373rd Night Fighter Group, were parked idly and neatly on their runway in wing tip to wing tip fashion.

Colonel Erich Rudorffer, leading I/JG 54 caught the personnel at St. Trond off-guard to rake the planes and the field from one end to another.

Similarly, Major Alfred Keller, leading II/JG 54, also found a complacent, peaceful field at LeCulot, where two fighter groups of P-51s also sat peacefully in straight lines along the airstrip. Keller's unit battered LeCulot with devastating results as Rudorffer had smashed St. Trond. These two other gruppen of the JG 54 Green Hearts had left more than a hundred American planes destroyed or seriously damaged at St. Trond and LeCulot, and the JG 54 gruppen had gotten away without a single loss.

As Colonel Erich Rudorffer droned back to his Badenheisen base in Germany, he felt a smug satisfaction. He had certainly avenged the B-17 attacks on his own airbase a week ago. But, Rudorffer's feathery feeling of delight would change to a sober lamentation when he learned that his IV Gruppe had been almost wiped out, and that his good friend, Robert Bazi Weise, had been killed in the attack on Asche.

Chapter Fourteen

Captain Floyd Benson would find the base at Orcante a safe haven since the 354th Fighter Group airfield would not suffer an attack on this January 1, 1945 morning. Further, Benson and his pilots would find plenty of room to land their aircraft for most of the 354th aircraft were out on a mission by 1030 hours. At 0830, Colonel George Bickel had received a call from General Elwood Queseda of 9th TAC, asking Bickel if he could conduct a support mission for General George Patton's 3rd Army. Patton wanted air support to soften a stubborn panzer division in the vicinity of Wiltz, some twenty miles southeast of Bastogne. The panzer unit was stalling some of George Patton's own armored units that were still coming up from the south.

"These low clouds won't bother me," Colonel Bickel had answered Queseda.

Thus, by 0930 hours on this gloomy morning, Colonel George Bickel had airborne his entire three squadrons of serviceable planes, totaling 59 Mustangs. The P-51s had then flown north in V patterns to hit the designated German ground targets. They were expected to arrive at the support site at about 1030 hours. Every P-51 gun was fully loaded with .50 caliber strafing belts and their wings hung heavy with a dozen 37mm rockets.

A hundred miles northeast of the 354th's whining Vs, another formation of planes was droning west. Colonel Gunther Lutzow sat in the cockpit of his lead FW 190 and stared at the clouds under him as geschwader leaders sat in other lead planes of their own units. Lutzow studied the dozens of aircraft around him, for his unit was only one of several geschwaders flying in Fliegercorps South under Colonel Werner Streib. JU 88s were scattered among the formations, the lead Junker carrying Colonel Streib himself, while one JU 88 was located in front of each geschwader or gruppe leader. These hordes of German planes, over 300 of them, would soon scatter to hit several U.S. airbases in France: Chauteudon, Juvincourt, Britegny, Conflans, Melvun, Ciastres, and Frescaty, outside of Metz.

Gunther Lutzow looked at his watch: 0933. Then, he saw far ahead a square of dots veering to the right like a flock of distant birds: JG 4 heading for Chauteudon. Only a moment later, another formation of planes up ahead, nearly one hundred of them, broke away from the long airborne column of aircraft; probably the two gruppen of JG 11 heading for Juvincourt and Bretigny. The JG 11 aircraft had barely faded to the southwest when the next formation of planes, the ME 110s of NJG 9 veered sharply to the south, almost in a full 90 degree turn to head toward Conflans, the big American air transport base.

Lutzow felt a measure of guarded optimism on the probable success of Operation Bodenplatte. The huge formations had come this far without challenge from a single enemy aircraft or from a single anti-aircraft gun. The JU pathfinders had uncannily avoided radar detection, verifying the astonishing work of agents in Western Europe who had done a precise job of pinpointing the exact locations of such radar sites. Gunther Lutzow looked at his watch: 0935. He would be breaking away soon.

Only two minutes later, the JU 88 in front of Gunther Lutzow's lead 190 veered west by northwest. The babyfaced JG 3 commodore turned his aircraft after his pathfinder and the other 36 FWs followed him.

At the American base in Melvun, most of the combat crews and ground personnel of the 416th Bomb Group and the 387th Bomb Group were just getting up after the same hard night of revelries that had prevailed in other American units on New Year's Eve. These two 9th Air Force bomb groups had been quite active during the December 25–28 strikes. The 416th, an A-26 group, had spent almost five days around Bastogne during the height of the German siege against the beleaguered 101st American Division. The group's A-26s had continually struck supply convoys that brought up guns, fuel, and ammunition for the besiegers of the battered town. Only yesterday, General Hoyt Vandenberg had recommended a DUC to the group for their efforts at Bastogne.

The 387th Bomb Group, of course, was another of the 9th Air Force's famed bridge busing B-26 units. The group had been among the six B-26 groups that had lashed out at the Rhine River bridges on Christmas morning, only a week ago. This group, along with the 394th Bomb Group, had struck the important Mayen Highway Bridge. The 387th had lost three B-26s to German interceptors on that mission. Still, the air crews had left one span of the Mayen Bridge down and the second span hanging in the river.

Two days earlier, on December 23, 1944, the same 387th Pathfinder Group had conducted the first counter offensive tactical air assault in the German Ardenne offensive when its B-26s had mauled two German panzer columns closing in on Prum in the center of the bulge. The strikes had stopped cold the German units, bringing about the first reversal for Operation Herbstnebel. The group had carried out the strikes despite severely poor weather. General Vandenberg had also recommended yesterday a DUC for the 387th Pathfinders' efforts at Prum.

Now, the airmen of these two excellent American bomb groups loitered complacently at their Melvun base. The forty-two A-26s of the 416th sat quietly and still in the usual wing tip to wing tip fashion on the west side of the Melvun runway. The forty-six B-26 Marauders of the 387th Pathfinders sat similarly inactive in a long straight line on the east side of the runway. Low clouds raced across the sky, leaving a mere one thousand feet ceiling. So, like everyone else in the Allied camps, the men here did not expect a thing to happen this morning. In fact, Melvun had never suffered anything more than nuisance raids in all of its existence.

The base commander at Melvun had received the same report from 9th TAC that all other groups had received: no missions this morning, but possible air strikes this afternoon.

So, the men at Melvun simply loitered about their rec room, sat in their barracks writing letters home, played cards, read, or listened to Armed

Forces Radio, whose announcer merely commented on the lack of activity this morning. In between, the DJ played records.

Complacency at Melvun was all but total.

But, as the minutes ticked away, FW 190s droned closer. At 0950 hours, Colonel Gunther Lutzow got the same routine call from the pathfinder as had other geschwader commodores. "Your target is straight ahead, Herr Colonel, perhaps fifteen kilometers," the JU 88 navigator said. "We are leaving you now. Good luck."

"Auf Wiedersen," Lutzow answered. Then, as he watched the JU 88 arch away and move off, Lutzow felt a tenseness build inside of him and his face sobered. He still could not quite believe that he had come all the way from Wesel without detection. He squinted hard into the open skies above the clouds, looking for Allied fighter planes. Lutzow knew he was not far from Toul where two American fighter groups based their P-51s; and not far from Orcante, where another American fighter group based its Mustangs. He regretted now that no gruppen had been assigned to hit these two American fighter plane bases. Perhaps he should have spoken up during the Operation Bodenplatte briefings.

Finally, Gunther Lutzow looked at his watch: 0955. He picked up his radio. "We must now descend below the clouds to avoid the enemy's warning installation at Melvun. We will be over target in five minutes. 1 Staffel will follow me over the west side of runway. 2 Staffel will attack any aircraft on the east side of runway. The MG flights of II Gruppe will bomb the runway." He paused. Then: "Horrido, Fliegers!"

The sixty aircraft of JG 3 dropped into the dense

clouds and descended through the mist until they emerged some eight hundred feet above the ground. Like other geschwader commodores, Gunther Lutzow ogled at the sight before him: dozens of exposed aircraft, wing tip to wing tip, on both sides of the runway and not a single aircraft airborne.

Lutzow cried into his radio. "Repeat: 1 Staffel will follow me over the west side of runway. 2 Staffel will strike the enemy aircraft on the east side of the runway. MG flights will follow to bomb the runway. We will attack in pairs, in rotte pairs."

The roar of planes drew hundreds of airmen into the open from recreation rooms, the mess hall, living quarters, group and squadron orderly rooms, the operation tent, the service shops, or the ordnance tents. The Americans simply stood and ogled as the FW 190s made their runs in pairs over the lines of parked aircraft on both sides of the runway. Soon enough came the whooshing rockets, the whistling spitterbombs, the fiery TSC incendiaries, and the chattering .50 caliber machine gun fire. Only when the heat of erupting fire and the palls of thick smoke radiated from the runways did the airmen of the two bomber groups react. They scampered into ravines and gullies beyond the airfield, or they cowered under trees, or they simply flattened themselves on the cold, vibrating earth—anyplace to escape the scene of mechanical carnage.

Finally, somebody hurried into a radio shack and called TAC headquarters. "They're bombing hell out of us! Krauts! Their goddamn planes are ripping the base to pieces."

"So what else is new?" a disgusted voice at TAC headquarters answered. "They're hitting every goddamn base in France and Belgium." The TAC clerk had already received similar calls from a dozen other bases.

"Well what are you gonna do about it?" the 387th Bomb Group airman cried into his phone.

"There's not a bitchin' thing we can do about it! Nothing! They're hitting fighter bases as well as bomber bases."

"Aren't there any fighter units aloft? Any at all that can reach Melvun?"

The TAC aide paused a moment while he shuffled through some papers. "You're lucky. The 354th Fighter Group is on the way to the Wiltz area. They can't be too far north of Melvun, maybe fifty miles. I'll call them and tell them to hurry over to your base. But I don't know if they can reach you before those German planes flatten you like they're flattening every other goddamn base in Western Europe."

A moment later, the 9th TAC man called George Bickel. "Colonel, please divert your aircraft to Melvun. The base is under heavy attack by some German fighter-bombers."

"Heavy attack?" Bickel cried. "Is that a joke?"

"No joke, sir," the TAC clerk said. "The Krauts are attacking just about every Allied airbase in Europe. They've got their targets and timing pinpointed perfectly. I don't know how the hell they got here without detection, or where the hell they got so many planes, or how they managed to hit every base at precisely 1000 hours."

"Goddamn," Bickel hissed. "That's why we haven't seen as much as a German spotter plane around for the past few days. The sly bastards were holding off for a go-for-broke strike." He paused. "Okay, we'll head for Melvun. I don't know if we can get there in time, but maybe we can catch up with them to knock a few of those sons 'a bitches out of the air." Colonel Bickel now called his own airmen. "This is White Leader! White Leader! We're altering course to Melvun. A full group of German planes are attacking the bomber base. We'll have to salvo bombs, but keep your rockets."

"George," Major Jim Howard answered the 354th colonel. "Did I hear you right? A German air unit of group strength is bombing Melvun?"

"Confirmed," Bickel answered. "They hit Melvun with complete surprise."

"How the shit could they get halfway across eastern France without radar detection? That's impossible."

"TAC says that hundreds of German planes are hitting every airbase in France. The Krauts caught everybody with pants down."

"Good God!" Howard gaped.

Colonel George Bickel quickly veered his P-51 in a 130 degree turn and then zoomed south, southwest toward Melvun.

Meanwhile, the German JG 3 fighter bombers chewed up the Melvun airbases. 1 and 2 Staffels of I Gruppe under Colonel Lutzow made multiple runs over the flaming, belching A-26s and B-26s, while the II Gruppe under Major Werner Specht laid their thousand pounders on the runway and taxiways. And, as with other geschwaders and gruppen, the German fliegers of the Udet unit picked their targets carefully. Only the aircraft and runway felt the punch from the German planes. The sixty FW 190s of JG 3 made runs over Melvun for more than a half hour before Colonel Gunther Lutzow cried into his radio.

"Break off, break off! Do not expend further

machine gun ammunition in the event we meet enemy interceptors during retirement."

A moment later 1 Staffel arched away from Melvun and jelled into formation before hoisting itself into the clouds. The other FWs of JG 3 soon followed. When the last drone of aircraft ended, and when the sight of German planes disappeared, American airmen came out of their shelters and slowly ambled toward the smoking ruins that had only a short time ago been a peaceful, quiet airbase. Few of them said anything. They were too shocked. How could German aircraft fly this far from Germany to hit them with complete surprise? How could these airmen believe that other German air units were conducting similar devastating raids on other American airbases in France and Belgium on this same January 1 at this same 1000 hours? But worse, many of the Allied airmen now felt a measure of fear over these simultaneous raids. Did these morning assaults forecast a revitalization of the Luftwaffe?

Above the dense clouds east of Melvun, Colonel Gunther Lutzow felt a satisfaction. His Udet unit had smashed Melvun without damage to a single JG 3 aircraft. As he droned back toward Wesel, a twinkle came to his eye and a hope settled on his baby face. Perhaps there was still hope for the Luftwaffe.

But, Colonel Gunther Lutzow, despite his long experience, and despite his capable leadership, now made a frightful mistake, an error he should have never made. Lutzow should have known that only the precisely mapped route from Germany enabled JG 3 and other Luftwaffe units to avoid Allied radar. Similarly, only the prescribed route back to Germany would minimize the chance of meeting enemy interceptors. But, Lutzow had assumed that since no fighter planes had challenged him, especially with Toul and Orcante nearby, he was quite safe, and he elected to take a shorter route back to Germany. Thus, he led his JG 3 planes too far to north and passed too close to the Luxembourg City radar station. An operator picked up the blips of droning JG 3 aircraft and he quickly radioed the position to the airborne 354th Fighter Group. Bickel altered his course at once to three degrees and then zoomed northward above the clouds. At 1105 hours, the lead wingman of the 354th spotted the Udet aircraft.

"Bandits at eleven o'clock; eleven o'clock low," Lieutenant James Daglis cried into his radio.

Colonel Bickel straightened and squinted beyond his cockpit. Soon, he himself saw the shapes in the distance, about one thousand feet below his own formation. "Okay, boys, they're straight ahead and down. Pick your targets, but stay in pairs. In pairs! Stick with wingmen."

Unfortunately for Colonel Lutzow, most of his pilots, like those of so many other geschwaders this late in the war, had little combat experience. Few of these pilots had ever engaged American or British fighter pilots in combat. Many of them had been hastily trained, and worse, in recent weeks they had been retrained as tactical assault pilots. Thus, even their short training as interceptor pilots had been further eroded.

At 1104 hours, Colonel Gunther Lutzow's wingman spotted the P-51s in the distance and he frantically called his commodore. "Enemy fighter planes to our right, Herr Colonel; enemy fighter planes at three o'clock high."

Lutzow squinted from his cockpit and then

screwed his face. The last thing he needed was a dogfight with a horde of aggressive American fighter pilots. But, he had no choice. His FW 190s could not outrun the speedier Mustangs. He sighed and spoke into his radio. "Enemy fighter planes at eight o'clock high. Rotte pairs, do your utmost." Then, Lutzow and his wingman arched upward and then turned southward to meet the oncoming American fighter planes.

Soon, the roars and whines and screams of aircraft engines echoed across the sky above the dense clouds. Chattering machine gun fire and whooshing rockets streaked through the lofty altitudes. The battle raged back and forth in diving, climbing, zooming, turning manuevers as fighter pilots from both sides sought advantages over adversaries. However, the half hour struggle became a slaughter against the Udet fliegers. The German pilots were simply outgunned and outclassed. Further, like the JG 54 unit that attacked Asche, the JG 3 pilots had also expended their rockets and most of their machine gun belts over Melvun. In the losing fight, the JG airmen tried frantically to get eastward and out of range, but sharp shooting American pilots continually thwarted them and only half of these pilots would make it back to the Rhine.

As whooshing rockets and staccato tracers from P-51s successfully found their marks, FW 190s exploded in mid-air, Folke-Wulf pilots died in their cockpits, fuselages broken in half, engines exploded, and tails disintegrated. At the rate of nearly one a minute, FWs fell out of the sky, plummeting downward like dead birds, falling through the clouds, and then crashing to earth in smoking, flaming, or fragmentary debris.

Colonel Bickel himself caught an FW 190 in the fuselage with two rockets that exploded and cut the plane in half before the FWs two halves dropped through the clouds to earth. Major James Howard scored his fifth German kill to go with his six Japanese kills in the China-Burma-Theatre. He caught an FW with a burst of withering strafing fire that tore away the cowling of the 190 and shattered the engine to a stop. The aircraft simply glided for several hundred feet and then tumbled end over end through the clouds before crashing to earth. The pilot, however, successfully parachuted to earth.

The aggressive Lieutenant Glen Eagleston got two of the FWs himself, his 15th and 16th kills against the Luftwaffe. As one German pilot tried to arch away, Eagleston sent a pair of rockets into the FW and blew away the tail. The German plane simply spun dizzily to earth. Moments later, Eagleston scored his next kill when he tailed an FW 190 and literally blew the plane apart with heavy rocket and machine gun fire. The fragments and the dead pilot simply fell into the clouds.

And then, Gunther lost his most important subordinate—Major Werner Specht. The II/JG 3 commodore had been trying desperately to protect his wingman from a pair of P-51s that were zooming around the 190 pilot like deadly hawks after a dove. Specht, with years of experience as a fighter pilot, shot one of the P-51s out of the air and successfully drove off the other one with his clear maneuvering. But, Specht had been so intent on this chore that he failed to see the P-51 come almost on top of him and unleash several rockets that slammed into the fuselage of his FW 190. Successive explosions broke the plane apart and sent Major Werner Specht into oblivion. The serious minded ace with one hundred thirty-six kills was no more.

JG 3 pilots did, however, get in some licks of their own. Colonel Lutzow shot down his 97th plane when he caught a P-51 crossing his path and shattered the fuselage with a burst of .50 caliber fire. Other experienced pilots in JG 3, like Leutnant Franz Buel and Leutnant Alfred Surau got their 23rd and 37th kills respectively when they downed P-51s in the furious battle.

But Gunther Lutzow could not continue the uneven fight. He cried frantically into his radio. "Into the clouds below. Into the clouds!"

Whatever remained of JG 3 ducked into the thick overcast.

The eager, hungry American pilots started for the clouds after the Germans, but George Bickel called them off. "Stay the hell out of those clouds. We'll be shooting at each other in there. Let's go home."

The vicious half hour battle had brought a loss of twenty-seven JG 3 aircraft, almost half of their sixty plane complement. The 354th pilots had also damaged at least a dozen more planes. Since December 16, between second best dogfights and the B-17 raids on Wesel, JG 3 had been reduced to forty-three planes from a total of nearly one hundred.

The severe losses of the past week brought a sober, tormented look to Gunther Lutzow. His only consolation: he had performed successfully against the American bomber base at Melvun. The 387th and 416th Bomb Groups would be grounded for some time, not only until the two American air units received replacement A-26s and B-26s, but until engineers repaired the airstrip and taxiways.

Still, the 354th had not escaped unharmed. Some of the more experienced JG 3 pilots had scored well, shooting down eight P-51s and damaging another half dozen Mustangs. At least two of the pilots of the downed P-51s had parachuted to safety, however.

But, if JG 3 had suffered badly, other units from Luftwaffe West on this January 1, 1945 multiple raid fared better. As Colonel Pips Priller had succeeded well against the RAF bases around Brussels, so too did KG 7 enjoy success. Colonel Johannes Steinhoff led his sixty-five ME jet fighter-bombers to Volkel, the home of the famed 122 Wing. Five full squadrons of English Mustangs and Spitfires used this huge base and the squadrons had caused untold damage to the panzer and Wehrmacht divisions of the German 6th panzer Army during the December 25–28 strikes. Steinhoff ached for revenge against these RAF fighter units.

122 Wing at Volkel, of course, had among its complement of pilots the bon vivant flyers of 19 Squadron. At 0955 hours on January 1, 1945, Lieutenant Peter Hearne, F/O Bob Weighill, and other pilots of 19 Squadron still slept quite soundly. They had revelled the night before far into the wee hours of the morning, many of them not going to bed before three or four in the morning. And, coupled with too much drink, the airmen still slumbered like men unconscious. Most of the other pilots of 122 Wing had celebrated just as vigorously and they too slept soundly at 0955. But why not? The wing commander had told them they would not fly any missions in the morning because of poor weather forecasts. At very

most, if the weather improved, they might conduct sorties in the afternoon.

The 122 Wing airmen would ever refer to the 1000 hour air raid on January 1, 1945 as the Hangover Raid.

Squadron Leader Peter Hearne slept so soundly that he barely stirred through the KG 7 bombardment on Volkel, much less woke up. When the whooshing rockets, whistling spitterbombs, and sailing TSC bombs tore into the parked Spitfires and Mustangs with devastating explosions, Hearne did not even open his eyes. He merely rolled over on his side. Not the explosions, but the smell of oily smoke from burning planes awoke the 19 Squadron leader. The smoke had simply filtered through the thin walls of his sleeping barracks. Hearne awoke with a start, blinked his eyes and peered about the barracks, sniffing hard.

"Lord, where's that smoke coming from?" Hearne asked.

F/O Bob Weighill was already sitting erect on his own cot, for the smoke had awakened him. He looked at Hearne, puzzled. But, both men jerked with a start when a new wave of rattling explosions and new high pitched whine of aircraft echoed over the barracks.

"What the 'ell's going on?" Peter Hearne cried.

"I don't know, Peter," Weighill answered. He hopped out of bed and headed to the window. Then, he gaped in astonishment. Beyond the barracks, he saw the dense smoke and belching fire along the runway. "Good Lord! The airbase is burning up."

Hearne leaped from his cot and hurried to the window. "What's 'appening?"

Then, the barracks door flew open and an

anxious RAF sergeant burst into the quarters. "Lieutenant," he shouted to Hearne, "bloody German jets! Jets! They're knocking out every damn plane on the base."

"Jets?"

"Yes, sir," the sergeant nodded vigorously. "An 'orde of 'em; just sendin' rockets and bombs all over the field, they are. The 'ole place is nothing but smoke and fire. Can't be a single aircraft they missed."

"Isn't anybody airborne?" Weighill asked the sergeant. "Anybody?"

"No, sir," the non-com shook his head. "Nobody. The bloody Jerrys 'ave a free 'and, they 'ave; free as out-of-season partridges."

By the time Hearne, Weighill and a dozen others came outside to view the holocaust on their air-base, the zooming, streaking jets had just about finished off Volkel. The runways lay in shambles and at least half of the fighter aircraft had been destroyed or damaged.

"Can't they do something about the bloody bastards?" somebody asked.

"They got a couple of those Polish volunteer squadrons on patrol," somebody said. "The wing commander 'as called them back to intercept these Jerrys."

Airborne, Colonel Johannes Steinhoff grinned. He had enjoyed an uninterrupted good fortune. So successful, in fact, that he and his jet pilots of KG 7 had expended all bombs and rockets and most of their .50 caliber ammunition. Steinhoff could do no more damage and he called into his radio. "We have spent ourselves; we will return to base."

"Yes, Colonel," Major Theo Weissenberger answered. "It is unfortunate that we have no further means to annihilate this base completely."

The German jet unit had droned only several miles from Volkel when somebody cried into his radio. "Commodore! Enemy aircraft at three o'clock high."

Colonel Johannes Steinhoff squinted from his cockpit until he saw the approaching Spitfires, apparently the Polish squadrons. But, he sighed in disappointment. His KG 7 pilots had used up their rockets and most of their ammo belts on the Volkel raid, and he was in no position to engage the Spitfires. Steinhoff knew that his superior ME 262s could tear the Spitfires apart—but not with empty rocket tubes and near empty machine gun belts. He picked up his radio.

"We are unable to engage the enemy at this time. We will climb away and increase speed to 650 KP velocity to avoid them."

"How unfortunate, Colonel," Major Weissenberger said.

"Perhaps at another time, Theo," Steinhoff answered.

Then, Colonel Johannes Steinhoff jerked back the stick and shoved in the throttle of his ME 262. The jet plane zoomed upward at tremendous speed, climbing all the way to 40,000 feet. The other jets of KG 7 followed him and soon the sixty-two ME 262s had left the potential Polish interceptors far to the rear and far below them. The Polish wing leader knew he could never catch the KG 7 jets and, perhaps, he was more relieved than disappointed. No Allied fighter pilots relished the idea of tangling with the superior German jet.

When Steinhoff saw the Polish Spitfires fading into the distant rear, a grin creased his face again. He knew the Polish pilots had made a weak hearted gesture to intercept his KG 7, or they wouldn't be that far behind already. The KG 7 commodore was satisfied. He had accomplished his mission with awesome effectiveness, without loss or damage to a single plane, and without death or injury to a single jet pilot.

But then, as he whined back to Aschner, Steinhoff suddenly scowled. The Luftwaffe could have had 2,000 of these ME 262 superior jet fighter planes by now, with 2,000 trained pilots to fly them. They could have wrested air superiority over Europe from the Allies with so many organized jet units. Damn the Führer! It was his fault that the Luftwaffe was not in such an enviable position. Hitler had delayed the jet fighter plane organizations for more than a year with his stupid insistence on turning the ME 262 into a bomber for the totally unrealistic dream of conducting another blitz on Britain.

Chapter Fifteen

Colonel John Samuels and Major Tom Stanton of the 322nd Bomb Group had already eaten by 0800 hours on this cold, damp morning of January 1, 1945. Both men now huddled inside their coats, collars up, and haunched across the Lille airbase. Nye's Annihilators shared Lille with the 386th Bomb Group and the 368th Fighter Group, making the base one of the larger ones in the 9th Air Force. The two men squinted at the rows of B-26s on both sides of the bomber strip and at the 368th Panzer Duster Group's P-47s along the small fighter runway. Both air groups here at Lille had been quite active along with the 322nd during the December 25–28 strikes.

The 386th Bomb Group, of course, was another of the B-26 bridge busting units. They had been on the December 25 strike against the Rhine River bridges, where the 386th and the 391st Bomb Groups had knocked out the important Ahrweiler railroad bridge. The 368th Panzer Dusters was the fighter-bomber group that had mauled the famed Leutnant Colonel Jochen Peiper's panzer regiment on December 25, with Peiper only five miles from his goal on the Muese River.

Major Stanton squinted at the low hanging

clouds and then looked at Samuels. "Do we think we're going out today, Johnny?"

Colonel John Samuels pulled the collar of his coat closer around his neck and then gave Stanton the same answer that other bomb group commanders had given other subordinates. "TAF says nothing's on this morning, but we may go out this afternoon if the weather improves. Backus would like to knock out a few more bridges so Bradley's divisions can seal off any chance of escape for those German panzer and infantry divisions."

"So we do nothing this morning?" Stanton asked Samuels.

"We'll go to operations and take stock; see who and what we've got available for a possible afternoon strike."

Major Stanton nodded.

Most of the other airmen remained quite idle on this raw New Year's morning. The drab, chilly day kept most of the combat and ground crews indoors to loiter near pot belly stoves or electric heaters. Many of the base personnel still slept at 0800, some were eating breakfast, and some had filtered into the airbase rec room to play pool, read, or to play cards. Men on duty at the radio shacks, service huts, and squadron or group orderly rooms merely sat about quietly, reading, bull sessioning, or listening to Armed Forces radio. No one loaded or serviced aircraft since no field orders had yet come for any of the groups at Lille.

During the next two hours, some of the U.S. airmen tried to wheedle passes into the village of Lille, but without luck. While the three groups here had no specific FOs at the moment, they had been alerted for possible afternoon missions. Anyway, none of the cafes or bars, or even the brothels would likely be open on New Year's day, so only those men who had friends in Lille would have anything to do there.

At 0945, with the sprawling American base still quite dormant, Colonel Hans Assi Hahn was flying westward in his lead FW 190. He had already been airborne for nearly three hours since his JG 2 geschwader had drawn one of the longest flights for Operation Bodenplatte, second only to JG 1 that would hit the British bases around Ostend near the North Sea coast. As with all other geschwaders on this New Years day mission, the usual JU 88 pathfinder droned ahead of Hahn's lead JG 2 aircraft. Hahn looked to his left and right where other FW 190s of the Richthofen unit hung like huge, hovering bees in the lead four plane diamond. Hahn sighed, rubbed his round face, and even raised his goggles and leather helmet to wipe his forehead. The long flight had been tedious and monotonous.

Hahn now craned his neck to search the skies, grateful he saw nothing above or near his JG 2. The Richthofen commodore felt mildly smug. He had told his fliegers that General Peltz had planned well to avoid detection by the enemy, and he had kept his promise. Despite the long flight across Belgium and northern France, Hahn and his pilots had not seen a single enemy fighter plane; nor heard a single bark from an ack-ack gun. Hahn looked at his watch again: 0948. Twelve more minutes. He was now confident they would avoid detection before their strike on Lille with a lethal punch. The colonel leaned back in his cockpit and once more stared at the JU ahead. Any moment now, he would hear from the pathfinder pilot or navigator.

Far to the rear in 3 Staffel, Otto Kindes sat in the cockpit of his lead plane and stared at the diamonds of FW 190s ahead. Kindes was quite surprised to come this far for so long without meeting Allied opposition. Kindes had harbored serious doubts about catching the Allies napping. But now, he reluctantly admitted to himself that perhaps Assi Hahn was right: if they followed the pinpointed route of the pathfinders they could avoid enemy radar.

The handsome, blonde haired Kindes squinted to his right where his wingman, Sergeant George Kell, sat rigid in his cockpit. Even from this distance, Kindes suspected that the young feldwebel pilot was terrified, despite his outward aura of confidence. Kell had never flown this far into enemy held territory and the deep flight had no doubt frightened him.

Otto Kindes next stared to his left at the third plane in his lead diamond of 3 Staffel. Leutnant Josef Zwernemann, an experienced pilot with sixty kills so far, offered an opposite picture to young Sergeant Kell. Zwernemann fidgeted restlessly in his cockpit, apparently anxious to reach target and get this business finished. Leutnant Kindes almost grinned when he considered the contrast between Kell to his right and Zwernemann to his left.

Precisely at 0950, the JU pathfinder pilot called Colonel Hans Assi Hahn. "Herr Commodore, you are twenty kilometers from target, straight ahead. You have about a 1,500 meter ceiling under the clouds; that should be ample to make your attacks."

"Thank you, Captain," Hahn answered.

Hahn watched the JU 88 arch away to the

eastward, and then the colonel spoke into his radio. "Staffel leaders and fliegers: we are ready for descent. We should come out of the cloud banks some two to three kilometers from target area. Stay alert, fully alert, and be sure you strike only your assigned target. 1 Staffel will follow me to attack the enemy bombers. 2 Staffel will bomb the runways and taxiways, and 3 Staffel will strike the enemy fighter planes. Let us show determination and resolve to succeed in this challenge. Remember, your efforts may save thousands of your suffering Wehrmacht and panzer comrades in Belgium." He paused. Then: "Victor, Fliegers!"

Now, Colonel Hans Assi Hahn dropped into the clouds in a symmetrical fall with the other three planes of his lead diamond. Fifty-six more 190s followed, also dropping into the clouds. For several moments the aircraft fell downward and forward in the heavy mist, with Hahn keeping his eye on his altimeter: 2500, 2000, 1500. Then, he held his breath tensely. However, the tension eased as he finally came out of the clouds at 1,400 meters. And ahead, he could see the runways and shapes lining both sides of the long airstrip—the Lille airbase. The pathfinder navigator had been quite accurate.

"We are approaching our objective," Hahn cried into his radio. "Staffel leaders will select their targets."

The few loitering U.S. airmen outside and about the Lille field had no inkling of the approaching German aircraft. The first hint came when they heard the pom pom booms of 40MM anti-aircraft guns. Some of the airmen on the base squinted towards the far end of the field to see the black puffs of exploding flak only a few feet below the clouds.

"What's going on up there?" An airmen asked. "What the hell are they shooting at?"

His companion shrugged. "Who knows. Maybe they're getting in some practice. Shit, they haven't fired those ack guns since we got here."

"Yeah," the first airmen said.

The continued b-blooms of anti-aircraft fire drew other airmen out of rec halls, officers clubs, service structures, or orderly rooms. Among them were Lieutenant Ed Steinburge and Lieutenant Jim Lonely. The two B-26 pilots squinted through the slight mist that still hung above the field and Steinburge pointed to the exploding puffs of black. "Flak," he said "How come the flak?"

"Jesus, maybe we got a couple of Kraut planes on a nuisance raid."

A moment later, Colonel John Samuels and Major Tom Stanton emerged from their operations room. They too had come outdoors when they heard the ack-ack barrages. Now, they also squinted at the puffs of flak exploding in the distance like a blossoming firework display in black.

"What the hell are they shooting at?" Samuels scowled. "I don't see a goddamn thing. Radar never picked up any sign of enemy planes or we'd have had an alert. Anyway, those Krauts would never come this far west. Tom, go inside and call that ack ack battery. Find out what all the shooting is about."

"Okay, Johnny," Stanton said.

However, before Tom Stanton took three steps towards the 322nd operations room, the calm over Lille suddenly collapsed. A deafening roar of planes echoed under the low clouds. And, before

Samuels or Stanton could react to these sudden bewilderments, a sudden staccato of numbing explosions shook the earth under their feet. Then came the eruption of fire balls and then rising smoke. Finally, the chatter of machine gun fire rattled across the Lille base.

"Jesus Christ," Tom Stanton gaped. "We're under attack! Heavy attack! There must be fifty or sixty planes."

"Goddamn," Samuels hissed.

Then, the whine of sirens echoed across the base, barely audible above the sound of roaring aircraft engines, exploding bombs, rattling machine gun fire, and crackling fires. Still, the sirens had an effect on the horde of airmen who had been standing in almost entranced shock during the abrupt, initial air assault on the Lille airbase. The sirens reminded the stunned men that they were indeed under attack. The airmen scattered, running as far as they could from the runway, taxiways, and parked aircraft until they found whatever shelter they could.

But, they need not have worried about death or injury from the marauding aircraft that had suddenly descended over their airfield. Hahn and his pilots knew exactly what to do, and they carried out their destructive deeds with methodical accuracy. Once more, not a single structure had suffered damage. Only parked aircraft, B-26s and P-47s, belched fire and smoke, or turned into warped black shapes, or fractured into metal fragments, while tail wings, fusilages, engines, canopes, and cabins spewed skyward and thumped many yards away in twisted, flaming heaps. The R4M rockets, spitterbombs, TSC's and .50 caliber machine gun chatter tore into parked American aircraft for a full half hour as the FW 190s zoomed over the base again and again.

The JG 2 pilots enjoyed an unmolested feast against some one hundred fifty parked B-26s and P-47s. A grin flattened Assi Hahn's face in exuberant gratification. Leutnant Josef Zwernemann and Sergeant George Kell simply ogled at the devastation they had left under them. Even the sober, skeptical Leutnant Otto Kindes could not help smiling, while his light blue eyes twinkled in satisfaction.

As JG 2's 1 and 3 Staffels pulverized aircraft, the Richthofen's 2 Staffel laid its heavy one thousand pound bombs in neat triple rows all along both runways and taxiways, gouging away huge chunks of frozen earth and twisting the runway mats into bizarre twisted metal shapes. The aviation engineers would need several days to repair the runways as would engineers need time to make repairs to many other American airstrips in France and Belgium.

Finally, at 1035 hours, Colonel Hahn called off the attack. By 1045 hours the sixty FW 190s of JG 2 had jelled into a line of four plane diamonds and zoomed eastward and upward into the clouds. At the helpless base, only the 40MM anti-aircraft guns could respond to the astonishing, nerve-wracking raid. The ack ack guns had only peppered four of the JG 2 aircraft and they had downed only one of the German planes—that of Leutnant Josef Zwernemann.

Uncannily, two 40MM shells had caught Zwernemann's FW in the aircraft engine, blowing away the propeller. Zwernemann had tried frantically to keep his plane aloft until he could clear the burning debris of American planes. However, the

German flieger could not do so. The aircraft stalled in mid air and then smashed into a fiery line of burning P-47s. The young Zwernemann, a former wingman for the renowned Erich Hartmann on the Russian Front, an exceptional pilot with one hundred twenty-six kills, had no doubt died instantly.

Colonel Hahn, Otto Kindes, and Sergeant Kell grieved over the loss of the popular Leutnant Josef Zwernemann. Still, they considered themselves quite fortunate. The death of Zwernemann had been their only loss, a small price for the maelstrom they had left behind in Lille. Hahn's only problem now was to reach his base in Germany before swarms of Allied fighter planes from somewhere in Western Europe might intercept him and shatter his geschwader, as American fighter pilots had decimated both Erich Rudorffer's IV/JG 54 and Gunther Lutzow's JG 3.

But, Hahn did not know that most other bases in Europe had also been struck at this same hour with the same success as he had enjoyed at Lille. Further, unlike Lutzow, Hahn carefully studied his map on the way back to Germany, not altering his course a yard from the route laid out by the pathfinders. So, he would reach Rheims safely.

When the last German plane was gone, the men at Lille walked slowly toward the airfield, ogling in astonishment at the holocaust. Of the one hundred fifty B-26s and P-47s, many had been destroyed or seriously damaged.

"If somebody told me an hour ago this would happen, I would have called the man crazy," Colonel John Samuels said.

Major Tom Stanton shook his head. "How the hell did they do it? How the hell could they get way out here from east of the Rhine without detection?"

"Excellent planning," Samuels answered. "The bastards laid out a perfect route to avoid radar. Then they came in low, maybe ten or fifteen miles from target to avoid our own airbase warning system."

"Jesus, they were sly as hell," Stanton said.

"Yeah, but we'll get the bastards," Colonel Samuels said.

But, neither Samuels nor anyone else would get most of the German assailants before the Luftwaffe concluded Operation Bodenplatte.

Even JG 1 under Major Heinz Pritzl Bar had successfully eluded radar detection on the nearly three and one half hour flight to the RAF airfields at Melsbroek and Westem near the North Sea coast. German agents had pinpointed Allied warning installations with uncanny accuracy, for no unit had caught the four plane diamonds of JG 1 as they covered nearly a thousand miles from their base at Wesel to the eastern end of Belgium. Further, Bar had reached the target areas on time, precisely at 1000 hours, with the geschwader's I and II Gruppens hitting the bigger base at Melsbroek and the geschwader's III Gruppe hitting the smaller RAF base at Westem.

Once more, total surprise had brought deadly success to a Luftwaffe West unit. JG I's three gruppen left a trail of burning spitfires, typhoons, and mosquitos in their wakes; and they left runways in potholed condition, making them useless for landings and take-offs until engineers could repair them. Further, Bar too successfully led his fighter-bombers safely back across Allied controlled Belgium to join other geschwaders of

Fliegercorps Holland in northeast Holland for return to base. Bar, like Hahn, had also followed the pathfinder route carefully on his return from target.

Other units also enjoyed success: Antwerp, Duerne, Grimberghen, and Ghent in the British sector. AR 234 Aredo jets under Leutnant Walter Kowalaski, a mere twenty-five aircraft, blasted the most forward British airbase at Tillberg. Two squadrons of Spitfires had been airborne at the time, and the sixty British aircraft carried well experienced pilots who could have made short work of twenty-five conventional German aircraft. But, unfortunately for the British, the planes hitting Tillberg were the speedy, twin engine Aredo jet bombers. Leutnant Walter Kowalaski spotted the approaching Spitfires just after his twin engine jets had finished off Tillberg. The KG 51 commodore merely ordered a steep climb and increased speed. Within moments the twenty-five AR 234s had left the pursuing Spitfires in the distant rear.

And, in a final insult against the British, JG 6 struck the proud British base at Eindhoven, headquarters of the 2nd Tactical Air Force. Two exceptional RAF fighter squadrons, the 430 and 404 Squadrons, and two renowned Mosquito units, 142 and 31 Squadrons, were included in the 205 Wing here at Eindhoven. The Mosquitos had served as pathfinders for the huge formations of British Lancasters and Wellingtons that almost nightly saturated German cities with 1,000 plane raids. However, by 1030 hours, January 1, 1945, the JG 6 Horst Wesel unit, with 117 ME 110 twin engine bombers, had caused more damage at Eindhoven than any other German air unit had caused anywhere else. Not a single one of the sixty RAF pathfinder Mosquitos escaped destruction at Eindhoven. JG 6s ME 110s had also destroyed all fifty-four Spitfires of the 430 and 404 Squadrons.

Air Marshal Trafford Leigh-Mallory himself had come out of his headquarters office with his 2nd Tactical Air Force staff to view with disbelief the utter destruction at the 205 Wing airbase. He could hardly criticize other wing commanders for allowing the German Luftwaffe to catch them off-guard, for Leigh-Mallory himself had been caught napping, even though Eindhoven maintained one of the better Allied warning systems in Western Europe. Unfortunately, no Spitfire squadrons were aloft to take a toll on the ME 110s that had all but wiped out the Eindhoven airbase.

But, the geschwaders of Luftwaffe West had shown no favoritism. Besides mauling the American bases at Asche, LeCulot, St. Trond, Melvun, and Lille, geschwader and gruppen units had been equally successful at Florennes, Cambrai, Coulimiers, St. Dizier, Chateudon, Juvincourt, Bretigny, Conflans, Ciastres, and Metz-Frescaty. Major Wolfgang Schaufer of NJG 4 had carried out his boast that his night fighter pilots could succeed by day as well as by night. His NJG 4 ME 110 nightfighter aircraft had destroyed every 439th and 440th Troop Carrier Groups aircraft at Ciastres.

Only the U.S. 354th Fighter Group base at Orcantes, the fighter plane base at Toul, and the bomber base at Neirgeney had escaped a visit by Luftwaffe West. The Germans had only missed the Mosquito base at Hasselt in the case of the RAF.

By 1100 hours, signal corps communication wires were burning north and south and east and west over Allied Western Europe. At Versailles,

General Dwight Eisenhower could not believe the reports that continually filtered into him: heavy destruction at Juvincourt or Bretigny or Lille or LeCulot or some other American airbase. The reports had come into SHAEF headquarters in bunches between 1030 and 1100 hours. To the north, in Amsterdam, Sir Bernard Montgomery got the same astonishing reports of destruction at the RAF airbases in Volkel, Evere, or Tillberg or somewhere else.

General Elwood Queseda's phone at 9th Fighter Command, also in Versaille, never stopped ringing; nor did the phone of General Hoyt Vandenberg's headquarters at Chantilly, France. Queseda was simply amazed, but General Hoyt Vandenberg scowled. The 9th Air Force commander had fought the Germans too long, ever since Africa in 1942, and Vandenberg had learned to respect Luftwaffe commanders, their pilots, and German tenacity. Vandenberg had never believed that the Luftwaffe had given up and crawled into a hole.

The 9th Air Force commander was tempted to call General Eisenhower and tell him "I told you so." He also felt like calling Air Marshal Trafford Leigh-Mallory to chastise him for not supporting Vandenberg's positions during the discussions for Operation Varsity. Vandenberg knew the Germans had been producing aircraft in great numbers during 1944, despite bombing raids over Germany. He assumed logically that the Luftwaffe would use such new aircraft if the opportunity presented itself.

"I can't believe it, sir," an aide said to Vandenberg.

"They're smart, goddamn smart," Vandenberg huffed as he read another report on still another of the raids on a 9th Air Force airbase. "Those Luftwaffe generals are not stupid. Only some intelligent men could have pulled off something like this against our warning systems and air superiority."

"What do we do, General?" the aide asked.

"Do!" Vandenberg cried. "What can we do? We chalk up one for their side. All we can do now is work like hell to replace those planes and get those airstrips back in shape. Call London and tell them to ready replacement B-26s, P-47s, and P-51s. We'll bring the planes in as soon as we have the fields repaired.

"We had one piece of luck, at least," the aide said. "We didn't lose any experienced pilots."

Vandenberg nodded.

"What about the British? Won't they need replacements?"

"Screw the British," the 9th Air Force commander gestured irritably. "Leigh-Mallory can get his own replacements, and he can repair his own fields."

The aide grinned and then shook his head. "I don't understand, sir. I can't understand why they'd send their whole air force on a raid like this. They saw what happened to them during the Christmas time air fights. They were badly beaten. If they got caught this time, we could have wiped out Luftwaffe West. Hell, they know the kind of resources we have. They must know we'll be back in business within a week."

"Yeah, a week," Vandenberg nodded. "They did this for a week."

"What the hell good is a week?"

"Enough time to get their army out of Belgium without interference from the 9th and 2nd Tactical

Air Forces."

The general's aide did not answer.

At his headquarters in Ostheim, Germany, General Dietrich Peltz sat at his desk with General Galland and General Schmidt. The three Luftwaffe West leaders read each new report with excitement and enthusiasm. Lille: badly damaged; Eindhoven: completely annihilated; Evere: almost destroyed; Melvun: utter chaos. And so the reports came in: from JG 2, JG 26, JG 3, JG 6, and a host of other Luftwaffe West geschwaders and gruppen.

Peltz grinned at Galland. "Well, Adolph, what do you think now?"

The 1st Fighter Corps Commodore shook his head. "Remarkable, totally remarkable. You planned well, Dietrich. You are to be congratulated."

"We planned well," Peltz answered sharply "*We*. You and Schmidt, and Moritz and dozens of geschwader and gruppen commodores.

"What about losses?" General Schmidt asked.

"Yes, there were losses," General Peltz suddenly nodded soberly. "Some of the gruppen met heavy anti-aircraft fire and two met unexpected heavy interceptors. Thus far, the reports indicate we lost just under a hundred aircraft."

"That is not bad, considering the destruction we caused," Schmidt said.

By 1300 hours, most of the German geschwaders and gruppen had cleared Allied occupied Holland, Belgium, and France and they had come within an hour of home and safety. Excited radio garble was now streaming back and forth among geschwader, gruppen, and staffel leaders. They extolled on their victories and they boasted of their complete surprise.

But, at the height of this excitement among Luftwaffe West airmen, none could foresee the tragedy that would soon befall countless German planes and Luftwaffe fliegers before they got safely home. Within the hour, many of these returning pilots who had escaped Allied interceptor pilots and Allied anti-aircraft would suffer a bitter fate. Nearly two hundred of these elated airmen of Luftwaffe West would suffer an ironic death.

Chapter Sixteen

General Dietrich Peltz and his staff of Luftwaffe West had seemingly done a thorough job in planning Operation Bodenplatte. They had carefully determined the locations of Allied radar installations, carefully briefed all pilots, and carefully laid out routes to targets. Further, they had meticulously assigned take-off times so that all units would reach their targets at 1000 hours. Finally, they had planned to hit the Allied airbases with complete surprise, a must for success; and they had accomplished this surprise. The bulk of returning planes had met no enemy interceptors; nor had interceptors found and chased the Luftwaffe West aircraft.

Only by accident did IV/JG 54 get caught at Asche because Benson and Meyers had persuaded 9th TAC to allow them to conduct morning strikes. JG 3 had taken severe losses because Colonel Gunther Lutzow, a man who should have known better, had become overconfident on the return flight to Germany. Other than the heavy losses by these two Luftwaffe units, only a few other planes went down before Allied anti-aircraft guns.

In return for the Luftwaffe West losses, the

Allies had suffered badly. General Hoyt Vandenberg would find astonishing statistics on his desk by the end of the day. The runways of ten RAF bases would be reported out of commission and the 2nd TAF would count 133 aircraft totally destroyed and another 205 aircraft badly damaged. The 9th TAF would count fifteen bases out of commission, 203 planes destroyed and another 200 planes badly damaged.

By 1300 hours, the bulk of Luftwaffe West aircraft had pretty well left the danger zones and seemed certain to return safely to their airbases. But, while Peltz, Galland, and Schmidt had planned well, they had overlooked a very important point. Most of the aircraft from Fliegercorps Holland and Fliegercorps Belgium were flying home in the round about route across northern Holland to avoid Allied radar and the possibility of interception by RAF fighter planes. The German planes would then come directly over northwest Germany to their bases east of the Rhine River.

In and around Wilhelmshaven, in extreme northwest Germany and just east of the Dutch border, were some two dozen V 2 launch sites. The V 2 was the long range, unmanned rocket bomb that travelled at tremendous speeds and at very high altitudes to strike Allied targets in England or in Allied occupied Western Europe. This potent weapon had frustrated the Allies for months and air commanders might have paid any price to knock out these launch sites. The Germans knew this and the Flakoberst Commando of the Luftwaffe had taken every measure to protect the launch sites.

Besides a jet fighter gruppe to intercept any

potential Allied planes that might locate and attempt to knock out the sites, the flakoberst commando had also assigned one of the best anti-aircraft units in Germany to the area, Flakbateilung 851. This anti-aircraft unit possessed the best gunners and the best guns in Germany. Some of the guns were powerful 145mm that could shoot accurate anti-aircraft fire up to 60,000 feet. The 851 flak unit was even experimenting with special gases that could penetrate aircraft cowlings and smother the engines. Finally, Flakbateilung 851 used the latest electronic rangefinders and the new Wuerzburg radar complex that could detect aircraft up to fifty miles off and as low as 500 feet.

General Peltz, Colonel William Moritz, and Colonel Pips Priller all knew that Fliegercorps Holland and Belgium would take the northwest Germany route back to their bases, and that these aircraft would fly within close proximity of the V 2 launch sites around Wilhelmshaven. Luftwaffe West staff had notified the jet unit of the route of the returning aircraft, but they had failed to notify the Flakbateilung 851 commodore to expect returning Luftwaffe planes to be over their area at about 1300 hours on January 1, 1945. While Operation Bodenplatte demanded as much secrecy as possible, Flakbateilung 851 should have been the last unit to have kept in the dark.

At about 1300 hours, some four hundred planes, most of Fliegercorps Holland and Belgium crossed northern Holland into northwest Germany at an altitude of about 10,000 feet. Dense, low clouds that extended over all of Western Europe also hung over the Wilhelmshaven area. When the blips of approaching aircraft appeared on the Wuerzberg radar screen, not a single stab officer in the 851 flak regiment doubted that the blips represented enemy raiders, especially since the number of aircraft appeared to be in the hundreds. No one in 851 could recall the last time the Luftwaffe had mounted so many planes, so the aircraft must be Allied. Also, since these aircraft were coming from the north, instead of flying through the Dummer Corridor, the usual route for Allied planes attacking Germany, the 851 officers were certain these "enemy" planes were after the V 2 launch sites.

Thick clouds had served the Luftwaffe well for Operation Bodenplatte. But, the same dense cloud cover would cause havoc for these returning German formations. At 10,000 feet on a clear day, flak observers, with binoculars, might have identified the droning planes as German aircraft. But alas, the heavy clouds prevented such visual observations.

At 1315 hours, the gunners of 851, through the help of their excellent range finders and radar equipment, zeroed in on the droning formations. Moments later, a numbing tremor of heavy ack ack fire shot upwards through the clouds with devastating effect. Heavy 145mm bursts smashed into the tight diamonds of FW 190s, ME 109s, and ME 110s. Accurate hits began knocking one plane after another out of the air in burning, smoking, or fragmented pieces, and taking dozens of Luftwaffe pilots and crews to their death.

Colonel Wilheim Moritz, utterly shocked by the sudden, telling flak, ogled in dismay as the aircraft of his Fliegerkorps Holland fell and disappeared into the clouds below. "My God! My God!" he hissed. He tried desperately to contact the headquarters of Flakbateilung 851, but without success. He then tried Luftwaffe West headquarters—anybody that could stop the anti-aircraft fire. "Flieger West! Flieger West! Please come in, come in!"

But, a full five minutes passed before somebody at Luftwaffe West finally answered Colonel Moritz's desperate call.

"Yes, Colonel."

"Idiots! The flak units at Wilhelmshaven are shooting down our planes! Shooting our own aircraft out of the sky like so many ducks! I cannot reach flak headquarters. You must do something! Do something!"

"Yes, Herr Colonel," the equally distressed voice answered from General Peltz's Ostheim headquarters. The aide now frantically called Flakbateilung 851 headquarters himself, but he could not reach anyone. So, he called the 851 IC and then a subordinate stab office, where an officer finally answered the phone. "Your flak guns are shooting down our own planes. Our own aircraft!"

"My God!" the stab officer gasped. "I will act at once."

Meanwhile, as Colonel Josef Pips Priller's own Fliegercorps Belgium droned behind Mortitz's units, Priller was equally shocked to see the heavy ack-ack fire. He too stared in astonishment as he saw his own planes tumble out of the air and drop through the clouds. He jerked with each new flak explosion, some of which came dangerously close to his own aircraft. He felt panic, too, expecting one of the explosions to get him. All the elation for his success at the Brussels airbases suddenly drained out of him, replaced by a feeling of tragic helplessness.

As Priller looked about him, he could see gruppen formations simply breaking apart, their aircraft scattering or arching off in different directions to evade the murderous ack-ack fire. Priller also tried frantically to reach the Flakbateilung 851 headquarters. But, before he reached anyone, the numbing ack-ack fire stopped as suddenly as the barrages had begun. The stab officer at 851 had apparently come through. Priller slumped into his cockpit seat and simply sighed in relief.

"Thank God, thank God."

But, the heavy attack had prevailed for ten minutes and during that period the scientifically controlled fire from Flakbateilung 851 had knocked an astonishing 162 German aircraft out of the air. But worse, many of the pilots who had scattered in panic were young, inexperienced flyers who had only minimal training in navigation. Now, without their staffel or gruppe leader to direct them, they were simply lost. Thirty of them would never find their way home. They would simply run out of fuel, parachute to safety, and allow their planes to crash. Thus, a total of 192 planes and most of the pilots had failed to return to base by the evening of January 1, 1945.

Thus, ironically, what the Allies could not accomplish with their superior air forces against Operation Bodenplatte, the German flak gunners of Flakbateilung 851 had done for them.

When General Dietrich Peltz learned of the tragic losses over Wilhelmshaven, he was completely stunned. He felt tormented, blaming himself, and he offered to resign at once as oberkommando of Luftwaffe West. However, Generals Galland and Schmidt, along with men like Moritz and Priller, who had suffered through the ack-ack barrages, talked Peltz out of it.

"Herr Peltz," Colonel Moritz told him, "this burden was not yours alone. All of us, every man down to staffel leaders, were included in this operation. None of us thought of the possibility of attack by the Wilhelmshaven flak units."

"But 277 aircraft failed to return, most of them through my neglect," General Peltz lamented. "It was my responsibility. Look at the figures. We lost fifty-nine staffel leaders and a dozen gruppen leaders, men so vitally needed because of their fine records, long experience, and inspiring leadership. How can we replace these vitally needed men? It was my fault."

"Dietrich," General Adolph Galland now spoke, "these losses were heavy, true, and perhaps many of these capable leaders cannot be replaced. I was among those opposed to Operation Bodenplatte. I did not believe such a plan could succeed. Yet, the plan succeeded beyond all expectations, thanks to your faith in the operation and to your excellent direction."

"Dietrich," General Josef Beppo Schmidt now consoled the Luftwaffe West oberkommando, "think of the positive side of this effort today by our brave fliegers. They may have saved our land armies. The loss of 277 aircraft and most of their flyers is still a small price to pay for such an accomplishment."

No one would have agreed more with General Schmidt than the elated generals of Army Group B. At the Osnabruck headquarters of Field Marshall Gerd von Rundstedt, the report of the heavy devastation against twenty-five Allied airbases in Western Europe had brought an exhilaration to Field Marshal Walter Model and his Army Group

B commanders: General Sepp Dietrich, General Hasso von Manteuffel, and General Ernst Brandenberg. They drank continued rounds of cognac with each new report of damage to an Allied airbase.

The ground force commanders had not considered unusual the loss of so many aircraft or seasoned pilots. They had suffered their own heavy losses during Operation Herbstnebel, and they saw nothing unusual in losing nearly 300 planes in Operation Bodenplatte.

Even the perpetually sober Gerd von Rundstedt, oberstkommando of the German Armies of the West, had softened his solemn face. He too was quite impressed with the Luftwaffe effort. Von Rundstedt willingly accepted a glass of cognac from Walter Model to toast the success of Bodenplatte.

"Mein Field Marshal," Model said, "surely this is an occasion for a celebration, do you not agree?"

"True," von Rundstedt answered, a rare grin cracking his stoic face. "I will have two cognacs, Walter. But then, we must work swiftly to determine how we can best retire Army Group B from Belgium."

"We will work throughout the night, if necessary," Model said.

Model did work for hours during the night of January 1–2, 1945. He, von Rundstedt, and the commandos of the German Armies of the West kept subordinates hopping in directing Wehrmacht and panzer commodores into the best avenues of escape from Belgium. The German generals plotted routes to bridges still intact, to roads still passable, and to rail lines still open. The staff of Armies of the West not only led panzer and

Wehrmacht units to safety, but also sent truck convoys and trains westward to meet the tattered Germans with supplies of food, medicine, clothing, and ammunition.

However, Field Marshal Walter Model issued a directive to all Army Group B commodores: "You must leave behind anything that encumbers your withdrawal: guns, vehicles, even panzer tanks. This equipment can be replaced, but we cannot replace combat experienced troops and leaders. Simply destroy such equipment; leave nothing that might be useful to our enemies."

Throughout the first week of January 1945, retreating Germans stayed ahead of pursuing Allied units as they moved swiftly out of Belgium, behind the West Wall into Germany, and then across the Rhine. Vandenberg and Leigh-Mallory could only read the reports of German escapes with frustration, for they could not strike at the retreating Germans with the bulk of their superior air forces until Allied aviation engineers repaired airstrips and until ETO air headquarters sent replacement aircraft. Because of the cold, snowy weather, engineers needed the better part of a week to get the twenty-five airfields back in operation. By then, much of Army Group B had extricated itself from a potential Belgium trap.

True, the Germans had lost 100,000 ground troops killed or captured in the abortive Operation Herbstnebel. They had lost over 1,500 tanks, more than 15,000 motor vehicles, and several thousand artillery pieces. But, as Model pointed out, they could replace this hardware. Most fortunate for Germany, and most unfortunate for the Allies, some 200,000 experienced German infantrymen, artillerymen, and panzer combat troops had escaped. They would fight again and delay for some time the eventual conquest of Germany.

General Elwood Queseda conceded after the war: "The January 1, 1945 raids accomplished an important mission. By the 1st of January the German leaders knew their Belgium offensive had collapsed. But, thanks to their multiple air assaults on our airbases, we could offer little air interdiction for nearly a week. If we could have, we may have knocked out enough roads, bridges, and rail lines to totally trap the whole German army in Belgium. Further, our fighter-bombers could have macerated in low level attacks the German forces trying to escape Belgium. General Bradley and General Montgomery might have overrun West Germany a lot sooner."

"It was a remarkable operation," General Sir Francis de Guingard of the British 21st Army Group said later. "The German offensive had been stalled completely from stiff opposition and the terrible Allied air attacks. Our units were cutting off escape routes and it appeared the entire German Army Group B would be trapped and annihilated—like Tunisia or Stalingrad. The German air attacks on our air bases stopped our aerial assaults for several days, allowing many of the German infantry and Panzer units to get away."

In the successful January 1, 1945 air attacks on the Allied air bases, the Luftwaffe had enjoyed at least one last aerial triumph in the deteriorating German fortunes. Every Allied air commander, from General Hoyt Vandenberg down to squadron leaders, had gained a new respect for the German Air Force. They no longer saw the Luftwaffe as a dead issue, especially when more

German jet units took to the skies to challenge Allied fighters and bombers.

The Luftwaffe West commanders who had planned and executed Operation Bodenplatte ended their careers in divergent fashions. For his efforts in the January 1, 1945 operation, General Dietrich Peltz earned command of Fliegercorps Reich for the air defense of Germany. He was lost in the final battle for Berlin, and no one ever heard from him again. Some Germans believed the Russians had captured and killed him when Red troops overran the German capital during the final stages of the war. The Russians remained ever mute on the fate of the capable Luftwaffe strategist, and General Dietrich Peltz fell into that permanent category of fate unknown.

General Adolph Galland, shortly after Bodenplatte, had another row with Hitler and lost his command. A month later, Galland received permission to form a new jet fighter unit, JV 44, the Geschwader of Aces. Among the brilliant aces who joined JV 44 were many of the heroes who had participated in Operation Bodenplatte: Gunther Lutzow, Johannes Steinhoff, Peter Eder, Otto Kindes, Erich Rudorffer, and many more. All of them distinguished themselves in JV 44, whose ME 262 jet fighter pilots shot down more than 200 Allied planes during March and April of 1945. The geschwader of Aces ceased to exist in the last week of April when U.S. 1st Army troops overran JV 44s airbase at Rheims. Galland had been wounded during an air attack on Rheims and he had been taken prisoner.

General Beppo Schmidt was reassigned back to interceptor duties in Luftwaffe Reich, where he headed up the German warning systems against the Allied heavy bomber assaults. His final fate was unknown, but he was believed to have been killed during an Allied bombing raid on Berlin.

The remarkable Major Heinz Wolfgang Schnaufer, the greatest night fighter pilot in the history of aviation with one hundred twenty-one night time kills, never forgave the Allies. He never reneged on Nazi Germany, either. On the eve of his capture by American troops, the Ghost of St. Trond told his NJG 4 pilots: "We will never forget our achievements. Long live the Fatherland and the Third Reich!"

Despite Schnaufer's refusal to acknowledge any wrong doing on the part of the Führer or the Third Reich government, the Allies found no evidence of war crimes against him. They released the famed Ghost of St. Trond shortly after the war and Schnaufer returned to Frankfurt to melt into oblivion.

In fact, none of the planners or fliegers of Operation Bodenplatte who survived the war (save for Herman Goring) were ever brought up on trial for any war crimes. Many of them, likes Johannes Steinhoff, Peter Eder, and Otto Kindes wound up in the new West German Air Force. Johannes Steinhoff became commander of the new German Air Force in the 1950s.

Among the Americans, General Hoyt Vandenberg ended his career as a deputy commander of the United States Air Force. Some, like Lieutenant Glen Eagleston and Lieutenant Floyd Benson went on to fly jet fighter planes during the Korean war. Others, like Colonel George Bickel, Colonel Norman Holt, and Major James Howard remained in the U.S. Air Force until retirement.

Among the British, Air Marshal Sir Trafford

Leigh-Mallory became the air chief of the RAF by the end of World War II and remained in this position for several years before his retirement. Captain Johnnie Johnson rose to the rank of air marshal and headed the RAF air forces in the Middle East until he retired from the RAF in 1965. The loner, sober faced George Buerling, never could stop flying combat. After World War II, he worked for the new state of Israel, flying for them, until he was killed in an air crash in 1950.

Some historians have brushed off the January 1, 1945 raids by the determined Luftwaffe West as a mere novelty that had little impact on the result of the war. They called the simultaneous raids of Operation Bodenplatte (also referred to as Operation Hermann) a useless exercise in futility. But, the raids did accomplish a purpose.

In the words of Field Marshal Gerd von Rundstedt: "At that moment during the struggles of the European conflict, the war seemed utterly lost. What could we do without these experienced panzer and Wehrmacht troops if they had fallen into the hands of the enemy, such as happened in Tunisia and Stalingrad? When nearly two hundred thousand troops successfully retreated into Germany, I knew we still had the nucleus of a fighting army and perhaps we could win favorable peace terms. But, unfortunately, the Allied superiority was too overwhelming and we eventually were forced into unconditional surrender."

The raids had brought about the destruction and damage of nearly seven hundred aircraft and the destruction of twenty-five airbase runways on a single morning, in a remarkable one half hour period. And, the raids saved thousands of young German Wehrmacht and panzer soldiers who escaped Belgium and still live today. For them, Operation Bodenplatte was a significant achievement. How then can anyone call inconsequential an event that flattened twenty-five airbases, put out of action nearly seven hundred Allied planes, and saved thousands of German troops against overwhelming air and ground superiority?

Participants

Allied

9th Air Force - General Hoyt Vandenberg
2nd Tactical Air Force - Air Marshal Sir Trafford Leigh-Mallory
12th Army Group - General Omar Bradley
21st Army Group - Deputy Commander Sir Francis DeGuingard

Air Units:
- 322nd Bomb Group - Colonel John Samuels
- 352nd Fighter Group - Lieutenant Colonel John Meyers
- 354th Fighter Group - Colonel George Bickel
- 366th Fighter Group - Colonel Norman Holt
- 122 Wing - Air Commander G. R. MacJohnson
  - 19 Squadron - Lieutenant Peter Hearne
- 127 Wing - Captain Johnnie Johnson
  - 414 Squadron - Lieutenant George Buerling
- Also: 386th Bomb Group, 387th Bomb Group, 391st Bomb Group, 394th Bomb Group, 397th Bomb Group, 416th Bomb Group, 361st Fighter Group, 368th Fighter Group, 205 Wing, RAF.

German

Luftwaffe West - General Dietrich Peltz
1st Fighter Corps - General Adolph Galland
Jagdivision IX - General Josef Schmidt
1st Nachtcorps - Colonel Werner Streib
Army Group B - Field Marshal Walter Model

Air Units:

JG 1 (Oesau) - Major Heinz Bar
JG 2 (Richthofen) - Colonel Hans Hahn
JG 3 (Udet) - Colonel Gunther Lutzow
NJG 4 - Major Heinz Schnaufer
KG 7 (Nowotny) - Colonel Johannes Steinhoff
JG 26 (Schlageters) - Colonel Josef Priller
KG 51 - Oblt Walter Kowalaski
JG 54 (Green Hearts) - Colonel Erich Rudorffer

Also: JG 6 (Horst Wesel), NJG 101, JG 77

Bibliography

Arnold, General H. H., *The War Reports,* "The Air War in Europe," Philadelphia: J. B. Lippincott, 1947

Bartz, Karl, *Swastika in the Air,* London, Eng: William Kimber Publishers, 1956

Craven, Wesley and Cate, James, *The Army Air Forces in World War II, Volume III, Europe—Argument to VE Day,* Chicago; Univ. of Chicago Press, 1951

De Guingard, Frances, Sir, Major General, *Operation Victory,* New York: Charles Scribners & Son, 1947

Ellis, Major L. F., *History of World War II, Volume II, Victory in the West,* UK Military Series, London, Eng: Her Majesty's Military Office, 1968

Flower, Desmond, and Reeves, James, *A Taste of Courage,* New York, Harper & Brothers, 1960

Freeman, Roger, *Mustang at War,* Garden City, NY: Doubleday & Company, 1974

Galland, Adolph, *The First and the Last,* New York: Henry Holt & Company, 1954

Garnett, David, *War in the Air,* New York: Doubleday, 1947

Golberg, Alfred, *History of the U.S. Air Force,* New York: Van Nostrand Publishers, 1957

Jablonski, Edward, *Air War, Vol. 2,* "Wings of Fire," Garden City, N.Y.: Doubleday & Company, 1971

Jackson, Robert, *Fighter Pilots of World War II*, "George Buerling—Defender of Malta," New York: St. Martin's Press, 1976

Jacobson, H. A. and Rohwer, J. *Decisive Battles of World War II: The German View*, New York: G. P. Putnam & Sons, 1965

Killen, John, *A History of the Luftwaffe*, Garden City, NY: Doubleday & Company, 1968

Lee, Asher, *The German Air Force*, New York & London: Harper & Brothers, 1946

Manteuffel, von General Hasso, "Memoirs of the Ardennes," from *Fatal Decisions*, New York: William Sloan Associates, 1956

Manvell, Roger & Fraenkel, Heinrich, *Goring*, New York: Simon & Schuster, 1962

Maurer, Mauer, *Combat Squadrons of the Air Force in World War II*, USAF Historical Division, Department of the Air Force, Washington, DC, 1969

—— *Air Force Combat Units of World War II*, Air University, USAF Historical Division, Department of the Air Force, Washington, DC, 1960

Nowarra, Heinz, *The Messerschmitt 109*, Los Angeles: Aero Publishers, 1963

Price, Alfred, *Battle Over the Reich*, New York: Charles Scribners & Son, 1973

Rudel, Hans, *Stuka Pilot*, New York: Ballantine Books, 1958

Rust, Kenn C., *The 9th Air Force in World War II*, Fallbrook, California: Aero Publishers, 1967

Sims, Edward H., *American Aces in Great Battles of World War II*, "Surprise at Asche," New York: Harper & Brothers, 1958

Snyder, Louis L., *Masterpieces of War Reporting*, DeGuingard—"Comments on Attack on Evere," Hitler—"Speech of 12:05 AM, 1 January 1945,"

Manteuffel—"The Führer Briefing, 11 and 12 December 1944," von Luttwitz—"Surprise of the New Year," New York: Julian Messner Publishers, 1962

Tantum, William & Hoffschmidt, E. J., *The Rise and Fall of the German Air Force,* 1933 to 1945, Greenwich, England: We Company, 1969

Toland, John, *Battle, the Story of the Bulge,* New York: Random House, 1959

—— *The Last Hundred Days,* New York: Random House, 1965

Toliver, Raymond & Constable, Trevor, *Blond Knight of Germany,* New York: Doubleday & Co., 1970

—— *Fighter Aces,* New York: Macmillan & Company, 1965

—— *Fighter Aces of the USA,* Fallbrook, Calif.: Aero Publishers, 1979

—— *Horrido,* New York: Bantam Books, 1968

Verlag, Gerhard Stalling, *The Luftwaffe War Diaries,* translated by Cajus Bekker, New York: Doubleday & Company, 1966

Wood, Tony & Gunston, Bill, *Hitler's Luftwaffe,* London, England: Salamander Books Ltd, 1977

Wykes, Alan, *Hitler,* New York: Ballantine Books, 1970

Historical Record Sources

Research Division, A. F. Simpson Historical Research Center, AAF, Maxwell Field, Alabama

Unit Histories:

- 354th Fighter Group - Microfilm #B0347
- 366th Fighter Group - Microfilm #B0329
- 368th Fighter Group - Microfilm #B0328
- 322nd Bomb Group - Microfilm #B0515
- 387th Bomb Group - Microfilm #B0518
- 394th Bomb Group - Microfilm #B0447

GSA, National Archives, Modern Military Records, Suitland, Md

Mission Reports:

- #330, 1/3/45, 354th Fighter Group
- #461 & 460, 1/1/45, 366th Fighter Group
- #161, 1/10/45, 387th Bomb Group
- #6, 12/25/44, 391st Bomb Group
- 404th Fighter Group Mission Report, 1/1/45
- #157 to Zinzig, 408th Bomb Group, 1/1/45
- #160, 1/3/45, 408th Bomb Group
- #148, IX Tactical Air Command A-2 Report, 1/1/45

File Records

- #400, History of the 386th Bomb Group, 9/44 to 5/45
- #688, History of the 366th Fighter Group, 11/44 to 2/45

#694, History of the 361st Fighter Group, 5/44 to 5/45

#694, History of the 352nd Fighter Group, 5/44 to 5/45

#697, Manuscript, "Column Cover," Colonel H. Norman Holt

#1210, 9th Air Force Journals, 10/1/44 to 12/31/44

#1211, 9th Air Force Journals, 1/1/45 to 4/2/45

German Records:

#24 - Headquarters of the German Air Force High Command Generalluftzeugmeister file, Roll #12, to Jan 16, 1945 Luftgaukommando, Roll #29, 1944–1945

#25 German Air Force Records - Luftgaukommandos and Flak Flakabteilung 851-1943-1945, Roll #17 Luftguakommando IX - Roll #36, 1944–1945

PHOTOGRAPHS

Imperial War Museum, London, England

National Archives, (USAF) Washington, D.C.

Boehm Collection (through USAF A/V section), Washington, DC

2. Air Marshal Sir Trafford Leigh-Mallory, commander 2nd Tactical Air Force, Holland

3. Colonel Norman Holt, CO of 366th Fighter Group, Asche, Belgium

4. Lieutenant Colonel John Meyers, Deputy CO of 352nd Fighter Group, Asche, Belgium

5. Lieutenant Urban Drew, pilot of the 361st Fighter Group, Asche, Belgium

6. Colonel John Samuels, CO of 322nd Bomb Group, Lille, France

7. Major Tom Stanton, 449th Sq., 322nd Bomb Group, Lille, France

8. Major Jim Howard and Colonel George Bickell, 354th Fighter Group, Orcante, France

9. Lieutenant Glen Eagleston, 354th Fighter Group pilot ace

10. Pilots of 354th Fighter Group discuss interceptor results on Jan. 1, 1945

11. A/C Johnnie Johnson, CO of 127 Wing, RAF, Evere, Belgium

12. Lieutenant George Buerling, S/L of 414 Squadron, 127 Wing, RAF, Evere, Belgium

13. Lieutenant Charles Stover, 414 Squadron

14. Lieutenant Frank Hanton, 414 Squadron

15. Pilots of 19 Squadron, 122 Wing, Volkel, Holland, RAF. S/L Peter Hearne 4th from left, standing; F/O Bob Weighill, 3rd from right, standing.

16. General Deitrich Peltz, Obercommando of Luftwaffe West, Ostheim, Germany

17. General Adolph Galland, Commodore of 1st Fighter Corps, Treuembrieyzen, Germany

18. General Joseph Schmidt, Commodore of Jagdivision IX, seated center, with staff at Ostheim, Germany

19. Colonel Werner Steib (L) of 1st Nachtkorps with Herman Goring (C) discuss Operation Bodenplatte. Officer on right unidentified

20. Field Marshal Walter Model (L) with General Tamale (C) and General Hasso von Mantueffel (R) discuss Operation Herbstenbel.

21. Colonel Joseph Pips Priller, commodore of JG 26, Verrelbusch, Germany

22. Major Anton Hackl, commodore of II/JG 26

23. Major Peter Eder (R) staffel leader of JG 26. Officer left unidentified

24. Colonel Priller (L) with Leutnant Adolph Glunz, also of JG 26

25. Colonel Erich Rudorffer, commodore of JG 54, Badenheisen, Germany

26. Major Robert "Bazi" Weise, (R) commodore of IV/JG 54, talks to his young pilots.

27. Colonel Hans Assi Hahn, commodore of JG 2, Rheims, Germany

28. Oblt Otto Kindes, squadron leader in JG 2

29. Leutnant Josef Zwernemann, pilot in JG 2

30. Colonel Heinz Pritzl Bar, commodore of JG 1, Wesel, Germany

31. Major Bar looks at a four-engine bomber he downed, one of four he shot down.

32. Colonel Gunther Lutzow, commodore of KG 3, Wesel, Germany

33. Colonel Johannes Steinhoff, commodore of KG 7, the jet air unit at Aschner, Germany

34. Major Theo Weissenberger, deputy commodore of KG 7, and later commodore of KG 7

35. Major Heinz Wolfgang Schnaufer, commodore of NKG 4, Lichtensein, Germany

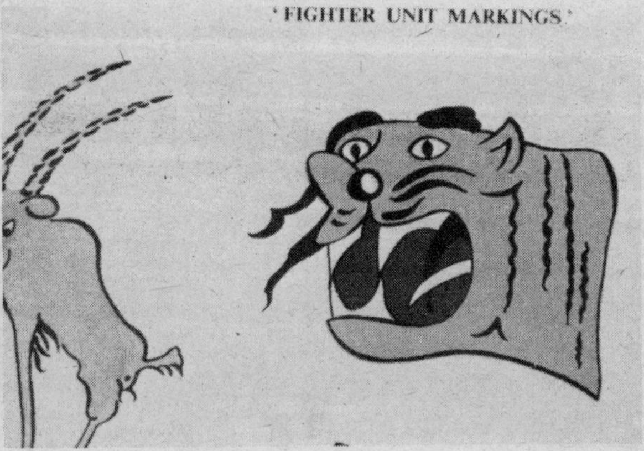

36. (R) the angry tiger insignia of the Schlageter JG 26, the Abbeville Boys

37. An aircraft of the JG 54 Green Hearts

38. German aircraft at Wesel prepare for Operation Bodenplatte

39. A rotte of FW 190s zoom over American base at Asche in Jan. 1, 1945 attack

40. Burning P-51s at Asche after attack by IV/JG 54

41. B-25 of U.S. 344th Group at Coulimiers burns after SG 4 attack on Jan. 1, 1945

42. Dense smoke rises from burning planes in RAF base at Evere after JG 26 attack

43. More destruction, at another RAF base, this one in Melsbroek

44. Mosquito of 122 Wing at Eindhoven, Holland, burns after attack by I/JG 6.

45. More B-25s of 344th Group burn up at Colimeirs after SG 4 attack on Jan. 1, 1945

46. Aftermath: a burned out P-47 of 366th Fighter Group in Asche, Belgium